Another Part of the Fifties

ANOTHER PART
OF
THE FIFTIES

PAUL A. CARTER

NEW YORK

Columbia University Press

Paul Carter, Professor of History at the University of Arizona, Tucson, is also the author of *Another Part of the Twenties* (1977), *The Creation of Tomorrow* (1977), and *Little America* (1979).

Unless otherwise noted, the photographs are reproduced by courtesy of H. Armstrong Roberts. The quotation from *The Wall Street Journal* in section III of chapter 2 is copyright ©1958 by Dow Jones & Company, Inc. All rights reserved. Used by permission.

Library of Congress Cataloging in Publication Data

Carter, Paul Allen, 1926–
Another part of the fifties.

Bibliography: p.
Includes index.
1. United States—Civilization—1945–
2. United States—Intellectual life—20th century.
3. United States—Politics and government—1953–1961.
I. Title.
E169.12.C295   1983   973.92   82–23623
ISBN 0–231–05222–7
ISBN 0–231–05223–5   (pa)

Columbia University Press
New York and Guildford, Surrey

10 9 8 7 6 5 4 3

TO CHRIS,
who was born into the tumultuous 60s,
and grew through the witless 70s,
and yet,
through faith, strength, persistence, and personality,
bloomed magnificently in the 80s.

CONTENTS

PREFACE

WHAT probably ignited the composition of this book was a remark during a graduate student's oral exam—that most dreaded of all student experiences, which nobody, no matter how articulate or well-prepared, seems able to take in stride. My fellow inquisitors and I were taking our victim through various aspects of the history of the United States, and I asked the student for comment on some of the general works which have become classics in American cultural and intellectual history: *The Course of American Democratic Thought,* by Ralph Gabriel; *American Minds,* by Stow Persons; and *The American Mind,* by Henry Steele Commager. At that point a fellow examiner exclaimed: "Why, those were the books I was asked about on *my* orals!"—twenty years before.

Two conclusions at once suggested themselves. The first was that since the fifties there had been surprisingly little forward movement in American intellectual history. Important monographs had continued to appear, such as Henry May's splendid study of the American Enlightenment; but nobody had tackled the job of re-thinking and re-doing, in the light of more recent experience, the kind of overall synoptic work undertaken by Commager (1950), Gabriel (second edition, 1956), or Persons (1958). A partial exception was Sydney Ahlstrom's monumental *A Religious History of the American People* (1973), but many professional reviewers of that work struck a lugubrious note, suggesting that no one person would ever be able to do such a book again.

Some scholars indeed have abandoned the premise that the historical study of American thought and culture is viable at all. Such scholars have been soundly spanked for their pains, most notably by Arthur Schlesinger, Jr., and (implicitly) by William Appleman Williams; I shall not re-argue the controversy here, save to note that among younger scholars in European intellectual history there has been no such failure of nerve as among the Americans. They have continued to explore the culture of the past, and continued also to believe in its relevance for their own time.

The other conclusion that followed logically from my colleague's remark was that the 1950s were an especially favorable climate in which to do American cultural and intellectual history. It was in fashion as a kind of U.S. history into which promising graduate students were choosing, or being counseled by their mentors, to go. Yet inside the ivied walls, that is not at all the way the Eisenhower era is typically described. On the contrary, academicians usually think of that period in the national life as having been more than usually *anti*-intellectual. At that point it became apparent that in the established concept of the fifties there is a great gap between image and experience, comparable to the gap in our understanding of the twenties between a sloganized "Jazz Age" and, for many people, quite a different period as lived.

Meanwhile, others among my fellow historians had been re-studying the political context within which the cultural life of the fifties occurred. In recent years the Eisenhower Administration has received a thorough going-over, and when those inquiries began, the reputation of that administration in the opinion of most U.S. historians had no direction to go but up. In the fifties, however, not only historians but most of the carriers of formal culture were pretty uniformly anti-Eisenhower. I have taken account of such attitudes, and of the more recent change in them, in my first three chapters. Generational turnover has been a blessing here. One high school student in the eighties, asking who Adlai Stevenson was, got back the parental answer

"He ran twice for president against Eisenhower," and then, after a reflective pause, "In those days voters in a national election actually had a choice between two *good* candidates"—a fact perfectly clear to ordinary blokes in the fifties, but a strange idea for many who had endured the elections culminating in that of 1980.

Beyond those three opening chapters the reader will find my own reassessment of the culture of the fifties. I have not attempted to be complete; there is no mention in these pages of, for example, Hank Williams, Patti Page, Bill Haley, Rosemary Clooney, Elvis Presley, or Kitty Wells—all of whom are authentically and importantly a part of the story. Nor does my account overlap as much as it should with the experience Susan Toth reports in her personal memoir *Blooming* (Boston: Little, Brown, 1981), a book with the ring of truth—forgotten truth, for many—about growing up in the 1950s. What these pages do chronicle is the attempt by Americans in the fifties to tell each other (and the world) who they were and where they thought they were going. There was a high seriousness in this undertaking which it is all too easy to dismiss as stuffiness, especially after the sloppy counter-moralizing of the sixties. Far from being anti-intellectual, Americans in the fifties would never have dreamed of closing down a university—as happened one one campus in 1968—on the grounds that there was, in one student demonstrator's words, "too much rational learning" going on there! Nor were the aspirations of the fifties merely a confused prelude to Camelot; they had a vitality and an integrity of their own.

Many teachers and students of history in the fifties openly or tacitly accepted Carl Becker's dictum "Every man his own historian," too culture- and psyche-bound to make any kind of judgment that might be termed "objective." I mistrust it; far too often, that kind of subjective relativism becomes a way of evading a personal judgment—rational, practical, or moral—about the real world. Nevertheless a book of this kind, dealing with years its author personally lived through, must be to a great extent subjective. The early fifties coincided with my own graduate-school years; my first teaching employment occurred during the remainder of that decade. The historian-teacher's explanatory role, trying to make sense of the past for younger people who live in a confusing present, has never been more congenial or satisfying to me than in the Eisenhower years.

I am particularly thankful that I spent the first and last parts of that decade in sharply contrasting parts of the United States—New York City and Montana. The juxtaposition of those two worlds has, I realize on re-reading the pages that follow, decisively shaped my interpretation of the fifties. Debts to many people in both places, particularly at Columbia University and at the University of Montana, are so countless that I shall not attempt to list them, lest I leave somebody out. The writer's usual disclaimer, that such other persons are absolved from any errors or misinterpretation deriving from them, would in this case be impertinent. Tennyson was existentially right when he wrote: "I am a part of all that I have met"—the exact reverse of our own era's shallow solipsism to the effect that all that I have met gets its significance from being part of me.

Closer to the present I have other intellectual debts, most of which I hope are properly acknowledged in the course of the bibliographical essay at the end. To my friends at Columbia University Press, and especially my editor, Leslie Bialler, and my designer, Laiying Chong, I owe careful, craftsmanlike, imaginative bookmaking. To Marilyn Bradian and Nikki Matz I owe cheerful, resourceful deciphering of my scribbled-over drafts as they fed this opus into a malignly intelligent, but not altogether sane, computer processor. To the University of Arizona I owe the sabbatical leave during which this book began to be written; to the University of Montana, in Missoula, I owe library and other nurture during the 1979–1980 Academic year; to my wife, who was herself of the generation of the fifties, I owe patient toleration of a view of that decade which has been quite divergent in many ways from her own.

Tucson, Arizona
April 1, 1983

Another Part of the Fifties

PART ONE
THE POLITICAL FRAMEWORK

CHAPTER ONE

"A Healthy Irreverence for Your Own Government"

I

EVERY four years except during a world war this planet pauses to celebrate the Olympic Games; and every four years, war or no war, the United States pauses to celebrate a presidential election. Both events express a humane and rational hope that the reign of violence on Earth may one day be displaced by more civilized behavior. We watch the conventions and go to the polls, say the Americans, instead of confronting each other across barricades; we march into a stadium to play games, say the Olympians, instead of marching onto battlefields to fight wars. Far too often in both cases the experienced event mockingly contradicts the ideal. Many a twentieth-century American political contest has dissolved into a host of self-important people pouring out millions of meaningless words, and many a twentieth-century Olympiad has been marked by peevish boycotts and hypocritical expulsions; even, in one dreadful instance, by murder. Yet the ideal continues to tug at people's hearts, as at the end of a presidential campaign, when the loser assures the winner that the people have worked their will, or as at the end of the Games, when the presiding officer summons "the youth of the world" to assemble in another city four years hence, to continue their competition "on the friendly fields of amateur sport."

The idealized Olympic athlete as visualized by Avery Brundage, who during the 1950s headed both the U.S. and the International Olympic Committees, would have needed not only the physique of a Greek god but the self-transcendence of a Christian saint. Free of the faintest taint of commercialism, he or she must also be "unmindful of national rivalries, jealousies and differences of all kinds." As Brundage noted, "There is no scoring of points in the games, which are contests between individuals and teams and not between nations." Avery Brundage, however, was not popular among the mass media reporters who covered such contests. To sports writers and commentators, the scoring of points *is* the game. So it had been at the notorious "Nazi Olympics" in 1936 at Berlin, and so it was evidently going to be at the 1952 Summer Games at Helsinki, the first modern Olympic contest to include the USSR.

The Russians had not been present for the first postwar Olympiad in 1948. On December 31, 1951, they announced that they would participate in the next one, but on their own terms. The sacred Olympic Torch en route from Greece to the site of the Games would not be allowed to cross Soviet or East-bloc territory. Therefore, instead of carrying the torch to the Finnish border by way of Tallinn, Estonia, which would have shortened the distance by thousands of miles, the relays of runners would have to go the long way around the North and Baltic Seas, through the Arctic wilderness in northern Sweden and Finland. Moreover, the Soviet athletes would not be living in the International Olympic Village; they would be quartered in Leningrad, and flown the two hundred miles to Helsinki and back each day.

Sadly, what Brundage termed "contests between individuals and teams" were again going to be a medals race between nations. "The summer games," the *New York Times* summed up in its pontifical manner, "thus will bring the first major test in the world of sports between the Russians, who are reputed to have some first class athletes and have claimed scores of world records, and the United States, traditionally the strongest." The pot at once began to call the kettle black. *Soviet Sport* charged that the Navy controlled the U.S. team, and that the primary purpose of the Winter Games—for which the Soviets had just missed the filing deadline—was to stimulate business. Conversely, Harry Schwartz wrote in the *New York Times* on how "Stalin Trains His Olympic Team"—one of many American caricatures of Russian Olympians, including the women, as grim, muscle-bound professionals. Regularly each side accused the other of violating the true Olympic amateur spirit, and to considerable extent each side's accusation was true.

On January 5, 1952, the International Olympic Committee, meeting in Helsinki, officially announced that a team from the Soviet Union would compete in the Summer Games of the XV Olympiad.

The next day, January 6, Senator Henry Cabot Lodge, Jr., officially announced in New York that General of the Army Dwight D. Eisenhower would be a candidate that year for the Republican presidential nomination.

That was the kind of world it was in 1952.

II

The quadrennial contests for the U.S. Presidency, like the Olympics, are run as morality plays. This did not begin in 1952, when television first allowed close-up views of the actors' frowns and smirks; acute observers of national nominating conventions such as H. L. Mencken had noted long before that much of what went on at such gatherings was pure theater. Many political scientists now argue that the national electorate has become less formally partisan than it was in the nineteenth century, and more "issue-oriented." The statistics of party affiliation—and disaffiliation—seem to bear such savants out. Nevertheless, at a national party convention it is not enough to have "issues." The reading of a party platform—whose function it is to blur and smudge those very issues—typically is a signal to go out to the refrigerator for a Coke, despite valiant efforts to jazz that reading up. To hold an audience there have to be Good Guys and Bad Guys, or at least apostles of tried-and-true values (otherwise described as heartless, repressive Scrooges) and champions of social progress (otherwise described as a blend of manic revolutionaries and self-indulgent bums).

For the GOP in 1952, a script was available from the party's own past, which with minor changes of lines and scenes could be played again. Even the family name of one of the candidates—Taft—could be re-used. In 1912, the first year in which presidential primaries made a real difference, insurgent young progressive Republicans supporting Theodore Roosevelt had risen against the party's Old Guard under William Howard Taft. Roosevelt and Taft delegates had challenged each other for the right to be seated, and the Republican national convention—firmly in the control of an incumbent president—had thrown out enough of TR's delegates and seated enough of Taft's to secure the nomination. To be sure, the progressives of 1912 were not quite the tribunes of the people that they made themselves out to be; they included a former Morgan partner, George W. Perkins, and an unspeakable buyer and destroyer of newspapers, Frank A. Munsey. Conversely, the conservatives were not quite so elitist as their opponents claimed; their government had just enacted into the Constitution that anathema for conservatism, a federal income tax. Nevertheless, the dramatic legend of that 1912 Republican convention at Chicago was one of Popular Democracy versus the Machine—and, behind the Machine, Corporate Wealth.

William Allen White, who was present, left us an engaging picture of the casual-mannered Roosevelt floor leader, Herbert Hadley, who wore "the guileless smile of lingering youth—boyish, disarming," as he did battle against permanent chairman Elihu Root, an elderly man with "gaunt thin-lined features . . . the symbol of the Taft machine." It was the same image, of fresh, idealistic young political figures tilting their lances at fusty, crusty Old Boys, that Dwight Eisenhower's supporters would carry into the 1952 Republican convention, again held in Chicago, against the grandson of the previous Taft.

Eisenhower was persuaded to run on behalf of Popular Democracy by the same forces of Corporate Wealth, especially in the modish new communications field, that had promoted the progressive insurgency of Wendell Willkie in 1940. However, the issues between Progressive Republicanism (1912) or Modern Republicanism (1940 and 1952), and the Old Guard had been crucially changed by demography. The political drama of Theodore Roosevelt versus William Howard Taft had played within a Republican Party whose voters constituted a national political majority. In the Depression and New Deal years that majority had disappeared, and the drama of Dwight Eisenhower versus Robert A. Taft played within a party that hadn't won a presidential election for twenty-four years. The clash, apart from its ideological dimensions, had become an argument about how best to break that spell.

The modernists' theory was that a minority party had to lure votes away from the opposing majority, and therefore had to embrace some of its opponents' policies. The traditionalists believed that a forthright appeal to the canons of "real" Republicanism—"a choice, not an echo"—would draw voters who, displeased with the bland sameness of both national party programs, hadn't been bothering to vote at all. (Further down the road the modernists would feel their strategy vindicated by the election of 1964; the traditionalists, by that of 1980.) Eisenhower insurgents therefore entered Republican local caucuses and state conventions, wrested control from Old Guardsmen, and chose delegates to the national convention. Their right to do so was promptly contested on the ground that many of them were instant converts from the Democratic Party rather than regular, card-carrying, dues-paying Republicans.

The regulars believed that status and influence in a party, like much else in life, ought to be earned. But this legal/professional argument, which had more substance than liberal political commentators in 1952 were willing to acknowledge, was swept aside in a tide of moralistic indignation. Eisenhower, seeing his delegates being counted out by a machine-controlled convention credentials committee just as Teddy Roosevelt's had been, gathered it up in a battle cry that hit the convention—and the media— like a ball of lightning: "Thou shalt not steal!" In the showdown of the rollcall, a delegation chairman further expressed the insurgents' Theodore Rooseveltian moral: "Lou'siana casts twenty-six [pause] hard-earned votes for Dwight D. Eisenhower."

Like millions of other veterans of World War II, Dwight Eisenhower found a civilian job after the war.

And the all-seeing TV eye, predominant at a nominating convention for the first time, made the Taft machine *look* like a
machine. Its adherents tended to be overweight, wear rumpled
business suits, and smoke cigars.

The Democratic script was a bit more complicated. A party
which in the nineteenth century had quite unselfconsciously
called itself "The Democracy" renewed that aspiration in the
twentieth by prophesying a "century of the common man."
(What America needed, Herbert Hoover grumpily retorted on
his 80th birthday in 1954, was more *un*common men; if he got
sick he didn't want to go to a common, ordinary doctor, he
wanted the best he could get.) But the Democracy had also a
tradition of patrician leadership. Alternating with its plain, or
at least plainly born, champions—its Andrew Jacksons and Al
Smiths—were its aristocrats and gentlemen, such as Thomas
Jefferson and FDR. Which candidate was better fitted in 1952,
the Democrats asked themselves, to lead the hosts of the people
against the other party's wealthy mountebanks and sour reac-
tionaries? A plain fellow who put on no airs such as the sitting
President, Harry Truman? Or an elegant, literate orator who
could summon the masses to aspire to higher things?

Estes Kefauver, who demonstrated during the spring of 1952
that one can win presidential primaries by wearing out enough
shoe leather and shaking enough hands, had already led one
charge against the Powers of Darkness as chairman of a Senate
committee investigating organized crime. (As usual, the Powers
lived to fight another day.) Kefauver also had the underdog's
moral advantage: the "regulars" in the party didn't much care
for him. "We love him," cried his nominator at the convention,
Senator Albert Gore, "for the enemies he has made." In addition
Kefauver—Phi Beta Kappa from the University of Tennessee—
was a skilled user of the Benjamin Franklin ploy, in which a
highly civilized individual plays hick, in the Senator's case by
donning a coonskin cap. Adlai Stevenson, in contrast, scion of
an Illinois political family whose native Corn Belt accent was
heavily overlaid with the tones of Choate and Princeton, wore

no cap and—in 1952—indulged in no folksy games. Many at the end of that year considered the election a shattering defeat for intellectualism in America. Nevertheless it was not the simple-seeming Kefauver but the egghead's egghead, Stevenson, who won their party's presidential nomination.

III

Between the close of Dwight Eisenhower's convention and the opening of Adlai Stevenson's, the Summer Games of the XV Olympiad began. In the meantime the Soviets had softened their stand against capitalist contamination. Their athletes would not have to commute from Leningrad after all; they and their East Bloc peers would be quartered near Helsinki, in an Olympic sub-village of their own—which the *Finns* promptly surrounded with barbed wire. Soviet newspapers, however, like those in the West, continued to comment on the Games as part of the eternal struggle between Good and Evil. "Bourgeois businessmen and their masters have turned sport into means of profit and propaganda among youth," said the Moscow *Komsomoletz,* whereas ordinary people throughout the world saw the USSR's team as "the vanguard of a mighty movement of peace partisans and a movement against a new war." The athletes themselves—comparing technical notes on sport equipment, trading souvenirs, clowning, flirting—became the force that finally broke what *Life* inelegantly termed the "Muscle Curtain." "The Americans," the *New York Times* deigned to acknowledge, "have found Russian athletes likeable and warm human beings." Why on Earth should anybody have expected otherwsie?

On July 19, 1952, President Juho Paasikivi of Finland formally opened the games of the XV Olympiad. The Muse of History could harld have chosen a more impressive stage than Finland. "The little nation that paid its debt and stood unafraid," having fought the Soviets *twice* in the course of World War II—losing both times and yet somehow not quite slipping under the Iron

Curtain—managed to pay off the last of its heavy reparations to Russia just in time to be the gracious host for a greatly enlarged Olympic games. Appropriately Finland's greatest Olympic hero, Paavo Nurmi, ran into the stadium under dripping skies and lit the Olympic flame.

Then something happened which the script did not include, but at which Clio might knowingly have smiled. In the lull following the lighting of the flame "a buxom, titian-haired young woman in flowing, pure-white robes left her seat in the lower stands at the south end and started on a run around the track," after which she headed for the reviewing stand with its microphones. All she wanted to do, it turned out, was to make a personal plea for peace in the world; however, as soon as the officials realized she was not part of the program, they stopped her and took her away. Suspicious Western observers at first supposed that this runner for humanity was a Soviet-planted "peace-partisan"; if not, they condescendingly surmised, she must be mentally deranged. Too many Americans, and many of their most vocal politicians, typically made just such appalling judgments during the Cold War years: with a few grudged exceptions such as the Quakers, anyone who talked of peace must be either a Communist or a nut.

That malicious caricature was going to be an immense political problem for the next President of the United States, if he made any moves—however tentative—toward a less warlike world.

Henry A. Wallace, formerly FDR's Vice-President and an heir to the liberal hopes of the New Deal, running as an independent candidate for President in 1948, had valiantly tried to break the spell. We *must* learn to get along with the Russians, he pleaded, or the day would inevitably come "when American soldiers will be lying in their Arctic suits in the Russian snow." But Wallace's message hadn't convinced enough of the people to make an electoral difference. In the moment of truth at the polls his party had polled fewer votes than a reactionary, anti-civil rights ticket headed by Strom Thurmond, which carried four states; Wallace got none. And in the campaigning summer of 1952, as the Korean War ground from its second into its third year, neither major party would risk picking up the gambit of peaceful coexistence with the USSR. The partisan pitch was, rather, that *our* kind of anti-Communism is more effective than *their* kind.

The Republicans, for this rhetorical purpose, had Senator Joseph R. McCarthy, who cried that the period since the advent of the New Deal administration in 1932 had been "twenty years of treason"—years during which hard-core Communists and soft-headed liberals were supposed to have prepared the way in America for Red revolution. But the Democrats could play at that game also. Harry Truman, who did not much care for his party's nominee that year but who labored for the cause like a good professional, commended Adlai Stevenson as one who had seen early "what the Communists were up to" in postwar Europe, and who deserved credit as "one of the first to warn that the Russians were becoming a threat to peace." Moreover, the Democratic President counterattacked the *Republican* candidate for having been soft on Communism. At a campaign stop on September 30, 1952, in Havre, Montana, where he smoked the pipe of peace with some of the local Indians, Mr. Truman cited a statement Eisenhower had made before a Congressional committee in 1945: "There is no one thing that guides the policy of Russia more today than to keep friendship with the United States." The current Republican nominee, Truman noted, "was then commanding general in Europe and he was in close contact with the Russians. His advice carried much weight and it therefore did a great deal of harm."

Stevenson himself gave McCarthy's "twenty years" charge a vigorous Cold War rebuttal. The Communists, the Democratic nominee declared on October 7, 1952, had begun to make headway in the U.S. only after the Republican regimes of the 1920s had bungled the national economy into collapse. Thereafter, Adlai Stevenson argued, vigorous Democrats and tough-minded liberals had averted the danger, rescuing a discouraged electorate and a discredited capitalism "from depression and from communism or fascism over the opposition of the Republican leadership." Stevenson, during his campaign, also talked a lot about "fair play" and denounced McCarthyism. Nevertheless, he reminded his fellow Americans, "Soviet secret agents and their dupes" had "burrowed like moles" into every government in the world; not even the police-efficient Nazi machine or the militant Japanese imperial regime had been immune. Citing the director of the CIA, Walter Bedell Smith, as his authority, Stevenson declared—with resolute paranoia—"We cannot let our guard drop even for a moment. The only assumption is that no place is safe."

In campaign years more recent than 1952 the Central Intelligence Agency has not ranked high in the esteem of liberal Democrats, and anti-Communism has learned at least to temper its language. It is difficult to imagine those intrepid Cold Warriors JFK or LBJ—or Jimmy Carter, whose notion of a vigorous response to Soviet misbehavior was to take the United States *out* of the Olympic Games—ever getting off an oratorical flight quite like Adlai Stevenson's, in a radio and TV "fireside speech" he delivered on September 29, 1952: "One by one the lamps of civilization go out and nameless horrors are perpetrated in darkness," the Democratic candidate declared. "All this is done by an enemy of a kind that we have never faced before. He is primitive but he is also advanced. He goes with a piece of black bread in his hand, but in his mind he carries the awful knowledge of atomic energy." This ignoble savage was "careful, cool, calculating, and he counts time, not impatiently as we do, by the clock, but ... in terms of centuries." In such alarming words it is hard to find anything with which Richard Nixon, or even Joe McCarthy, could have found fault.

IV

The summer came and passed; the Olympians, notably Bob Mathias in the decathlon and the great Emil Zatopek in the distance runs, won their medals; the United States, in aggregate point scores, edged the Soviet Union; and the two leading U.S. political parties, their respective self-inflicted convention wounds healed or at least covered with Band-Aids, squared away for the formal fall campaign.

Despite all the verbal cannonades of Joe McCarthy and his ilk, liberalism—at least in its broad, imprecise meaning of "innovativeness"—remained still so rampant in the America of 1952 that a British subject who had taught and studied in the U.S. for six years could in all seriousness write an essay on "Conservatism: The Forbidden Faith." Nevertheless, the campaign waged by Adlai Stevenson in 1952 gave conservatives cheer and comfort of a kind they had not received from Roosevelt or Truman. Americans who had listened for two decades to the New Deal/Fair Deal argument that a humane national government's social activity could bring blessings to all were startled when Stevenson, in his first campaign speech, deplored "the increasing centralization of power over our lives in Washington" and called for revitalized local government. "The states," he declared, in language uncannily foreshadowing that of Barry Goldwater and Ronald Reagan, "are the dikes which we can build more strongly against the flood water sweeping toward the District of Columbia." Then he neatly resolved the paradox of how a person can condemn presidential power while at the same time seeking it: "While I want you to sweep me down there, don't sweep any more government jurisdiction down there."

The problem for a Democratic politician who plays the conservative game—as two long-forgotten nominees, Alton Parker in 1904 and John W. Davis in 1924, both learned—is that Republicans play it much better. Confronted by a Stevenson partisan with the Democratic candidate's warnings against the "tidal drift toward the capital," one hard-bitten Young Republican from Connecticut (who had supported Robert Taft) replied: "Governor Stevenson is unusually enlightened for a Democrat, but—damn it, he *is* a Democrat." Perhaps Stevenson, in thus criticizing "the mess in Washington," was only trying to distance himself from a presidential administration he perceived as unpopular; or he may have been adding to partisan politics a note of Olympian good sportsmanship. In so doing, however, he opened himself to a devastating retort in a speech soon afterward by Eisenhower: "My subject tonight is—quote—the mess in Washington—unquote."

Later in that decade NBC anchorman Chet Huntley would remark that a conservative is one who uses the clichés of the 1920s as principles, while a liberal is one who uses the principles of the 1930s as clichés. Conceivably Stevenson, a craftsman with words, may have been trying to break away from political language which in the course of twenty years had gone stale. In one crucial area, however, the Democratic candidate retreated not only from liberal rhetoric but from liberal principle as well. There was nothing clichéd in the bold initiative Harry Truman had taken on behalf of black Americans. In 1948 he had willingly split the party over civil rights, and won the election anyway. For 1952, however, the party quietly shelved the previous campaign's hard-won platform commitment to "endorse President Truman's civil rights program," and the candidate teamed with a running-mate, John Sparkman, who hailed from Alabama, where the printed Democratic Party ballots still carried the label "White Supremacy." If coalition politics during the 1952 election contest led Dwight Eisenhower to the great shame of embracing Joseph McCarthy on the campaign trail and deleting from a speech a favorable reference to General Marshall—a McCarthy target whom Ike personally admired—the same kind of coalition politics led Adlai Stevenson to an embarrassing meeting with the Governor of unreconstructed, black-disenfranchised Mississippi, one of the states which in 1948 had cast its electoral votes not for Truman but for Thurmond. After praising the national party's 1952 nominee as "an elegant gentleman" whom Mississippi Democrats would be pleased to support, Governor Hugh White smoothly parried a reporter's question about Stevenson's position on civil rights: "We did not discuss civil rights."

For a people who had lived through the New Deal and the war it was a strange experience: Democrats vying with Republicans in being rough on Russia and on Communism; Democrats endorsing Republican states' rights views even at the cost of racial justice; Democrats charging Republicans with being big spenders, as when President Truman at another of his campaign train stops bragged of a recently achieved four-billion-dollar budget surplus and then warned of what Eisenhower might do with it: "A military man doesn't know a single thing about economy. He has been in the army forty years and all the army thinks about is how to spend money." It begins to sound as if the Henry Wallace Progressives at their 1948 national convention, singing "It's the same old merry-go-round. The elephant and the donkey go *up* and down, and *up* and down," had been right after all. In recent elections all politicians, regardless of ideology, have tended to campaign against the "System": liberals, who perceive that system as run by Big Business; conservatives, who perceive it as run by Big Government; and radicals, who perceive it as run by both.

In such a situation the radicals' logical response usually is to call for outright secession from the bourgeois two-party system, in order to realign national political life toward genuine social reconstruction. But logic, in the 1952 election, was up against certain inescapable realities of history. Even if economics is the ultimate basis for politics, as Marxism maintains, the economic motive that drove millions of depression-born and war-deprived Americans in the forties and fifties was not class solidarity but individual possession. The real dampener of any movement toward Socialism in America, rather than McCarthy or the FBI, may have been the thirty-year, fixed-payment home mortgage, which converted more than half the population into property owners; a counterrevolutionary force which did not falter until the Great Inflation of the late 1970s.

In one important respect the parallel between the 1912 and 1952 campaigns breaks down. Eugene Debs in 1912 won the highest vote proportion—6 percent—ever polled in America for Socialism. In contrast, the election of 1952 was a discouragingly low moment for the American Left. The vote of the Progressive Party, no longer linked with Vice-President Wallace's special personal appeal, dropped disastrously. The poll for the three perennial U.S. socialist parties, or rather sects, was even less impressive; the Prohibitionists fared better, as did new splinter parties on the Right, including one that called itself Christian Nationalist and nominated Douglas MacArthur. Clio perhaps will pardon the pundits of the fifties, who, lacking the gift of prophecy, failed to foresee the rise of the energetic, joyously angry New Left of the sixties. After the cloudburst of Republican votes on Election Day in 1952, reasonable observers of the political landscape could properly have concluded that radicalism in America was dead.

Could the Left find any comfort in the electoral outcome in 1952? Ingeniously a writer for *Labor Action*, the newspaper of the Independent Socialist League, concluded that it could. That avalanche of votes for Eisenhower, Hal Draper reasoned, was not an outpouring of Republican votes as such. Stevenson, drawing more votes than Truman had in 1948—and, indeed, more votes than any previous *winning* candidate, except Roosevelt—had evidently held onto "the same coalition of social forces that has been backing the Fair Deal up to now." Therefore, the landslide must have been composed not of erstwhile Democrats but of people "who had never gone to the polls before. They came crawling out of their political cellars to vote for Eisenhower," and they did not vote as Republicans. This was a "flotsam which had not before even reached the level of political consciousness enough to fluctuate between the parties," and it cast "a vote of blind frustration, of discontent against WHAT IS, without even a clear idea of what this vote was against, let alone for. . . . It was not so much against 'the mess in Washington'; it was against The Mess, period." This was no mandate for conservatism; "the people were not registering any substantial turn to the right in political feeling." Whether the forces Eisenhower had thus "pulled out of the nether reaches of the social structure" would ultimately turn Right or Left depended "on what major social force can give them a lead, can offer them a channel to express their legitimate resentment against the going concern, can offer a way out."

V

Like millions of other veterans of World War II, Dwight Eisenhower found a civilian job after the war. In 1947 he accepted an appointment as president of Columbia University. After Truman sent him to Paris in 1951 as the leader of NATO, and even after he had resigned from the Army to seek the Republican nomination, the General retained his Columbia post on leave of absence. An important post-Convention conference with Senator Taft took place at the university's official presidential residence on Morningside Heights, and later on in the campaign Eisenhower came back to Columbia to attend Sunday morning service at the university's handsome Byzantine chapel, visiting afterward at coffee time in the crypt with members of the choir— one of whom, as he shook Ike's hand, impertinently displayed a Stevenson button on his maroon choir robe. The gesture was symbolic. For Columbia people the 1952 campaign had a local and personal animus that it lacked elsewhere.

College professors never really like their presidents, but the feud between the Columbia faculty and Ike had been the stuff of which legends are made. In the national partisan contest the New York-based academicians saw a chance to get even. Not long after the 1952 fall semester began at Columbia a faculty committee for Stevenson, chaired by the distinguished American historian Allan Nevins, called a meeting in order to raise money to buy a full-page ad in the *New York Times*. Mock-seriously one participant warned of possible consequences: if the rebels' efforts were successful, the faculty would "have *him* back here on the campus in January." The chair, equal to the occasion, counter-quipped: "We have to put the interests of the country ahead of the interests of the university."

That political advertisement, when it appeared on October 16, hit the Republican standard-bearer in a vulnerable spot. Describing Eisenhower as "a soldier who has served his country well but has not mastered the arts of civilian statecraft," the professors declared that his campaign had "degenerated into nothing more than a drive to replace Democrats with Republicans—not just bad Democrats with good Republicans but any Democrat with any Republican, good, bad, or intolerable"—an obvious reference to McCarthy. It might have been desirable to rehabilitate the GOP "as an agency of nationwide constructive leadership," they conceded; but the General, "by leaning indiscriminately on its most undesirable elements, has thrown away his magnificent opportunity to do so." What was most damaging in the ad, however, was not its words but its names. The signers added up to an impressive array of Columbia faculty superstars. In sociology they included, for example, Paul Lazarsfeld, Robert Lynd, C. Wright Mills, and Daniel Bell; in history, such renowned names as Henry Steele Commager, Dumas Malone, and Richard Hofstadter; in philosophy, the winsome Irwin Edman and the dynamic John Herman Randall; and in literature, Lionel Trilling and Mark Van Doren. Across the street at related institutions Virginia Gildersleeve, of Barnard, R. Freeman Butts, of Teachers College, and those formidable prophets Reinhold Niebuhr and Paul Tillich, of Union Theological Seminary, all signed.

Such a challenge could not be allowed to go unanswered, for it implied that the great architect of United Nations and NATO cooperation could not cope with a rebellion in his own front yard. Within a week, therefore, a faculty and staff for Eisenhower committee responded in the *Times* with a counter-ad. This move somewhat blunted the insurgents' blow; the co-authors of a widely used American history college textbook, for example, Harry Carman and Harold Syrett, turned up as signers on opposite sides. And although the prominent names on the list

of Eisenhowerites ran heavily to locally powerful administrators
and deans rather than to nationally known teachers and scholars,
they had a heavy numerical edge—714 signers, as against 324
for the Stevensonians.

The opposition promptly called "foul." Four members of the
Stevenson group combed the Eisenhower list, found that only
259 of its names really belonged to Columbia's teaching staff,
and charged that the roster was padded with "dietitians, building
superintendents, stenographers and students." Despite its local
rootage, the Columbia political conflict was a microcosm of what
was happening on the nation's campuses in general—and of
the snobbism that subtly corrupted the Stevenson campaign.
Even without the irritant of Eisenhower as their immediate
employer, professors across the country overwhelmingly supported Adlai Stevenson—and the deans, janitors, office secretaries, and students supported, and helped elect, Eisenhower.

The professors' emotional involvement with Adlai is one of
the curiosities of the 1952 campaign. They did not merely work
and vote for Stevenson, as activist intellectuals variously had
for Franklin D. Roosevelt, Norman Thomas, Henry Wallace,
or Harry Truman; they identified with him. Their psychic investment in this candidate led many of them to act throughout
the campaign, David Riesman shrewdly observed a year later,
"as if *they* were up for election." Here was a person who, in
striking contrast to Truman's fast-draw confidence, Roosevelt's
lordly superiority, Wallace's idealistic fervor, or Thomas's moral
sureness, seemed to have a Hamlet-like hesitancy in making up
his mind—just as they did. He was, moreover, a platform speaker
who got off witty lines that people talked about afterwards—
the kind of impact classroom lecturers would have liked to make
upon their own students, and usually didn't.

In the heat of battle, scholar-partisans persuaded themselves
that their commitment carried no such subjective taint; that
they were supporting the Governor of Illinois simply because
he represented, in their Columbia colleagues' words, "the wisest,
steadiest, and most responsible leadership we can find." To a

very great extent this now looks like rationalization, especially considering that many of these same scholars have since then, in retrospect, turned pro-Eisenhower and, in some cases, anti-Stevenson. Besides, had they had the candor to acknowledge it, such citizens had self-interested grounds as understandable as those of labor unionists or bankers for voting together as a class. "The New Deal and World War II gave many intellectuals and academic people a pleasant feeling of being close to the seats of power, of being in on big doings," Riesman noted. Even if much of this had to be discounted as merely a part of Franklin Roosevelt's "amiable come-on," it was in stark contrast to the atmosphere of Truman's Washington.

As for the Republicans, they had been running against the "eggheads"—to use the 1952 jargon term—at least since the days of FDR's Brain Trust. Indeed, as one literate and reflective Columbian for Stevenson, Irwin Edman, ruefully admitted after the election: " 'Intellectual' has never been altogether a complimentary adjective in this country." The peril in the kind of personal and class identification with the Democratic candidate that swept Academia in 1952 was that his defeat inevitably inflicted psychological scars. "Surprised, as I hardly think they should have been, that Eisenhower swept the country," Riesman continued, "they felt they had been rejected. In their despair, they neglected the impressive fact that their man, their identity, had garnered over 27,000,000 votes [from dietitians, secretaries, and janitors?] against one of the most appealing candidates ever put up."

VI

"Crabbed age and youth cannot live together." "Don't trust anybody over thirty." Age is cold-hearted, youth is warm-blooded; age lectures and frowns, youth frolics and laughs; age hands out the Olympic medals, youth wins them; age is conservative, youth is liberal. Such is the historic folklore, however much it

"My own life has been spent with America's young people."

breaks down in political, if not in athletic, practice. For several years prior to 1952 younger voters had statistically been somewhat more likely than their elders to vote Democratic. Unaware that this statistic was about to change, Adlai Stevenson, when introducing a venerable, feisty political warrior—Alben Barkley, Truman's 74-year-old Vice-President—on August 14, 1952 at the Illinois State Fair, contrasted him with the serious-minded rising young man who had spoken at the Fair just the day before, Senator and vice-presidential candidate Richard M.

Nixon: "The Republican Party is the party which makes even its young men seem old. The Democratic Party is the party which makes even its old men seem young."

But as Dwight Eisenhower was to remark a year later, "My own life has been spent with America's young people."

No other U.S. military leader, except perhaps Omar Bradley, could have gotten away with that line. Imagine Patton or MacArthur saying it! Nor could it have been said after any other American war, particularly after America's most recent Southeast Asia war, whose ill-used veterans are bitterly aware that their youth was, to say the least, misspent. For Eisenhower in the fifties, however, the gambit worked.

The fraction of America's young people (by 1952 no longer so young) that had spent the years 1941–45 in uniform was large, and toward the end of the war there had been anxious public discussion—much like that prompted more recently by Vietnam—about the Problem of the Returning Veteran. To put the question in its most alarmist form, what would happen to America when a rapidly demobilizing army dumped ten million "trained killers" upon the civilian population? Or, to translate it into political terms, what would happen when a great mass of men, estranged from civil society for several years, became conscious of its potential social power? The sentimental popular-culture image of "G.I. Joe," whose deepest longing was for a slice of Mom's apple pie, was interrupted from time to time by nightmares from recent history, of the marching Black Shirts, the *Stahlhelm,* and the Ku Klux Klan.

What the veteran's wartime experiences actually brought into postwar politics, however, was the ex-enlisted man's desire to get the Army off his back. The crucial, myth-destroying fact was that the veteran of World War II, even though (unlike his Vietnam equivalent) he came home as the popular hero of a popular war, did not *want* to be a veteran. Typically he did not even join one of those alumni drinking clubs, the American Legion or the VFW. The title of an early postwar Broadway musical, *Call Me Mister,* well summed up his philosophy: he would take the kisses and the parades, considering them his due, and perhaps afterward a college degree on the G.I. Bill or a house on a V.A. loan, but thereafter he wanted simply to disappear. Dwight Eisenhower, who in a lifetime spent in the Army had never quite stopped being a small-town kid from Texas and Kansas, was politically well suited to preside over a generation of such men, and the women to whom they came home.

This is of course not the whole story. The rise, in reaction to the tumults of the sixties, of the "new middle" or working class cultural bigot of the Archie Bunker type, pictured as a man in his forties or fifties and thereafter as shaped by World War II, suggests that the veteran, as an invisible component in what Richard Nixon called the "silent majority," may well have contributed to the rise of political conservatism in our own time. The citizen-soldier's resentment of the arbitrary, and at times idiotic, authority of Army brass could well have been transferred to the IRS. But to make such an assertion would be to distort the "veteran's" experience, by blending it with his reactions in maturity to events that had happened long after the end of his own war. When the men of Archie Bunker's generation were young, in the 1940s, they were children of the New Deal. They had literally grown up under FDR; the only president they personally remembered, save for whatever horror stories their parents may have told them about Hoover. Entering the armed forces from all walks of life, but skewed toward the poverty end of the scale like all draftees in all wars, they were proportionately even more Democratic than the population at large, which was a major reason why the Republicans in Congress were reluctant to enact a federal absentee soldier-vote bill. No doubt many of these citizen-soldiers, if they lived long enough, would end up voting for Ronald Reagan; in a sense, therefore, the New Deal regime, both civil and military, molded men who in 1980 would help overthrow it. But in the 1950s, when they helped elect Dwight Eisenhower, the veterans were emotionally a good deal closer to Roosevelt than to Reagan—who himself had not yet worked his way out of the forest of New Deal liberalism.

Rather than being militarized by their war experiences, the G.I.s to a remarkable extent had civilized the armed forces in which they served. They had had, for example, considering the necessities of military censorship, a remarkably free and critical press, as is convincingly shown by the investigative journalism of their newspaper *Stars and Stripes,* the anti-officers'-privilege stance of their magazine *Yank,* and the sardonic, bitter, devastatingly funny drawings of their greatest cartoonist, Bill Mauldin. Budding totalitarians, of either the Right or the Left, these ex-enlistees were not; the parallels with the steely-eyed veterans of World War I, who beat people up at Nazi party rallies or marched on Rome, will not hold. Had a "man on horseback" appeared in America at the end of the forties, intent on crossing the Potomac as Caesar crossed the Rubicon, he would have faced the thankless task of rousing *these* troops to march behind him, not some imagined Black, Brown, or Silver Shirts. But these troops were not about to march anywhere.

In spite of the healthy negativism shown by the returned veterans, a number of intelligent and perceptive liberals—who really ought to have known better—persuaded themselves in the course of the 1952 election that the man on horseback was here in the person of Dwight David Eisenhower. In New York City on election night, while a large roomful of well-liquored Young Republicans gleefully applauded the telecast image of Walter Cronkite in his TV anchor debut with election returns and of choral director Fred Waring as an impromptu cheerleader outside Eisenhower headquarters ("All together now, folks, *I—like—Ike!*"), a little band of Stevenson mourners in the back coatroom solemnly told each other that Fascism had come at last; that Eisenhower would re-enact the part of old duffer/war hero Hindenburg, the last properly elected president of prewar Germany; and that rabble-rousing Joe McCarthy would be our Hitler. An observer of that celebration and wake passed along some of these terror tales, which had been circulating in the metropolis for weeks, to a radical young German exchange student with whom he had roomed at a Quaker-sponsored international student gathering in Vermont during the long summer of Olympic races and presidential nominations. His correspondent—an unruly-haired Marxist youth of a kind who would become a familiar sight on the American and European student scene in the sixties, but who stuck out like a sore thumb in 1952—had known about Fascism at first hand, as a most unhappy member of the Hitler Youth ("Five years they chased me around in a brown uniform, and I never even learned to make my own bed"). From his German experiences he had some reassuring words for those alarmed U.S. liberals: "You Americans," he wistfully wrote, "have a healthy irreverence for your own government." In a postwar era that has elsewhere been described as the rise of an "imperial presidency," this was one of the highest compliments the American people received.

CHAPTER TWO
"You Auto Buy"

I

"RONALD Reagan preached a 'New Beginning,'" *Time* noted shortly after the 1980 Republican convention, "but Americans trying to envision his Administration sometimes find their minds drifting back to the 1950s. Ike, they tell themselves. Maybe, if he won, Ronald Reagan would turn into a kind of Eisenhower." He wouldn't.

Superficially, Eisenhower's new beginning sounded at times like Reagan's. On October 31, 1952, before a roaring crowd at Soldier Field in Chicago, he pledged an end to Truman's "seven years of Fair Deal misrule" and "a change to a government of honesty, vision, and courage." But *all* challengers say such things about *all* incumbents. A few sentences later, however, the Republican candidate implied that much in the New/Fair Deals he had just finished denouncing was necessary and desirable. "The social gains achieved by the people of the United States ... are not only here to stay, but here to be improved and extended." Unlike Reagan, who earnestly promised and seriously tried to reverse the course of American political history since 1932, Eisenhower announced that his crusade would "not turn the clock back."

Turning the clock back, to an audience in 1952, would have meant turning it back to the Threadbare Thirties. "We need a government," Ike reassured them, "that will enlist all the resources of private industry and that will mobilize all the resources of Government to prevent mass unemployment from returning to America." Ronald Reagan in his 1980 campaign also talked about the danger of mass unemployment, but made emphatically clear his belief that mobilizing all the resources of government was not a proper way to prevent it. Not only did Eisenhower reject the traditional Republican domestic gospel that Reagan accepted; he also rejected traditional foreign policy concerns that some of his Republican supporters traced all the way back to Washington's Farewell Address: "Isolationism in America," Eisenhower stated flatly in the same speech, "is dead as a political issue"—killed, as will be noted later in this book, by the omnipresent Bomb.

Critics, in order to fill up dead space on paper or on the air, routinely paste the glib label "Hundred Days" onto each new U.S. Republican Administration that has just ousted a Democratic regime, and vice versa. Such critics would do well to ponder the fate of Napoleon, the first politician to learn that it is not easy to change the course of history in one hundred days. Ronald Reagan's fiscal plans took a good many more days than that to be set into motion, and Franklin Roosevelt's faster-moving Hundred Days fairly soon met sharp setbacks at the hands of the Supreme Court. As for the regime elected in 1952, "It was only the political neurotics and romantics," said Richard Rovere in a 1955 appraisal, "who looked forward, with exhilaration or with dread, to an end to what Eisenhower had called 'wickedness in government' or to the premature termination of the Century of the Common Man."

"Dwight D. Eisenhower's public performance during the First Hundred Days of his Presidency," wrote Joseph C. Harsch in May 1953, "has been so at variance with his adherents' more extravagant campaign forecasts ... that the net result almost seems to be a man whanging golf balls at the White House back fence while history flows around him." The obvious contrast was with FDR; "the memory of Franklin Roosevelt's voracious seizure and joyous exercise of Presidential power twenty years earlier," Harsch continued, "contributes to a companion illusion of a man who slipped into the White House by the back door on January 20, 1953, and hasn't yet found his way to the President's desk." Roosevelt had accustomed Americans "to think of leadership in terms of massive legislative programs trucked to Capitol Hill from the White House," and manifestly Ike was not going to work that way. And there was no reason why he necessarily should. The public had yet to appreciate "the extent to which leadership . . . might take the form of merely operating with existing laws," the writer cautioned; and within that framework the new President was already, in fact, leading: "Mr. Eisenhower is consciously and actually going in an Eisenhower direction and . . . all of us, whether we know it or not, are following him."

Eisenhower had the great advantage, for a Republican, of detachment from the political blood-feuds of the previous generation. On January 16, 1953, while working on his inauguration speech, he wrote in his diary, "I don't want to be using the inaugural address to castigate and indict the administration of the past twenty years." Some of his colleagues in Congress, however, which the Republicans in 1952 had captured by the thinnest of margins, had the emotionally difficult task of throttling down their previous militancy, as they learned to their dismay that "this administration" now meant "us." Assessing that Congress as it assembled to begin its work, the President in his memoirs discreetly noted "the unfamiliarity of Republicans with either the techniques or the need of cooperation with the Executive." None surmounted this hangup more magnificently than Robert Taft, who in the half-year of life remaining to him functioned loyally as majority leader with the same tactical skill he had shown earlier as leader of the Opposition. Yet according to Robert Donovan's firsthand account even Taft, when he learned at a legislative leaders' briefing that the first Republican budget since Hoover's was going to be out of balance, "went off like a bomb. The sedate discussion was rent by his hard, metallic voice," Donovan reported. "Fairly shouting and banging his fist on the Cabinet table, Taft declared: . . . 'You're taking us right down the same road Truman traveled. It's a repudiation of everything we promised in the campaign.' " Eisenhower titled his own memoir of this first term *Mandate for Change*, but to many of his contemporaries it could just as well have been called *More of the Same*.

Again and again in the early months of his presidency—while he still had a Republican Congress—the new President set policies and took stands that struck traditional Republicans as outright heresy. In contrast to Ronald Reagan's reformers, who proposed the abolition of at least two Cabinet posts, Eisenhower founded the first new Cabinet-rank department in forty years: the later much-maligned Department of Health, Education, and Welfare. At a Cabinet meeting on May 29, 1953, when it was suggested that federal grants for highway construction be lowered, Ike countered that they ought to be raised; thereafter in due course came the federal interstate highway program, the biggest public-works project and expenditure in the history of the world. Early in June the President went out to dedicate the new Garrison Dam in North Dakota, which would eventually impound a lake 200 miles long and 14 across; symbolic of his commitment to "a grandiose plan," as the *Christian Science Monitor* called it, for a multi-billion-dollar federal investment in "dams, irrigation for millions of parched areas of land, conservation of farm and ranch lands, construction of giant hydroelectric plants and levees, improvement of wildlife habitats, and building of long-un-dreamed-of recreational areas." And the heresies continued. Preparing for his second State of the Union message in 1954, Eisenhower proposed taking ten million more people under the shelter of Social Security and four million more under un-employment insurance—policies which surely would not have endeared his memory to David Stockman.

Conservative Republicans were understandably upset. One objector to the "New Dealers" in the government, among whom he singled out Treasury Secretary George Humphrey and the President himself, wrote an angry letter about them to the

Chairman of the Republican National Committee and under-scored his ire by sending a carbon to Mamie's mother. Other such conservatives, Eisenhower told his legislative leaders' conference on March 1, 1954, were threatening to withhold financial contributions to the Republican Party "because they thought the administration was acting too much like the New Deal." Evidently annoyed, the President said he found this criticism entirely inappropriate at a time like the present, when a business recession was descending upon the country.

II

Merely operating with existing laws might be an acceptable way to run a government—as long as nothing occurred to upset the operation. However, Richard Rovere cautioned in April 1955, "it is unsettling to think of what might happen if the Eisenhower Administration did run into economic difficulties of any gravity." Already the Administration had felt a throbbing symptom of just such difficulties, in a recession that ran from September of 1953 through the following winter. Donovan's cabinet minutes in March 1954, as unemployment reached a postwar peak of 5.8 percent, noted that "the president was in a deadly serious mood" or that "the sense of mounting urgency continued." In addition to their humanitarian concerns, the regime's leaders were in agreement that if they were going to avert a replica of the political debacle of 1932 they could allow no more 1929s. However, they had businessmen's inhibitions against the kind of action David McDonald, President of the United Steelworkers, was proposing: a massive government program of public works, slum clearance, unemployment compensation increases, and tax cuts. Except for a modest acceleration of spending projects already under way, and a little juggling of the Federal Reserve discount rate, what the Cabinet mainly did was to stall and stall, in the hope that the recession would go away. Ike, as so often happened, was politically lucky; it did.

That recession had been touched off in part by the sharp downturn in military spending as the Korean War came to an end. But the chronic ideological and strategic stress of the Cold War continued. A conservative Republican government which had misgivings against social spending might have been willing to spend for military security; at the outset of their regime the Reaganites certainly thought they were going to. Moreover, military spending can generate incidental social benefits. The defense buildup for World War II had quickly soaked up the massive, intractable pool of unemployed workers that had distressed the nation since the early 1930s; economist John Kenneth Galbraith once quipped that Adolf Hitler first solved Germany's economic problem and then proceeded to solve America's! Dwight Eisenhower, however, absolutely rejected any such solution. "You can't provide security just with a checkbook," he once told members of Congress. Inheriting a $50 billion annual defense budget from Truman, he cut it to $40 billion and held it there—with, at times, strenuous effort—for the rest of his presidency.

Some have dismissed Ike's warning against the "military-industrial complex," not spoken to the nation until the very end of his second term, as no more than a gratuitous afterthought. But Eisenhower began publicly to discuss the danger of national militarization early in his first year in the White House. He met the demand for "national security" with an insider's refreshing skepticism. "Reasonable defense posture," he declared in a public address in June 1953, "is not won by juggling magic numbers— even with an air of great authority. There is no wonderfully sure number of planes or ships or divisions—or billions of dollars—that can automatically guarantee security." Evidently the Pentagon "whiz kids" who juggled just such numbers for John Kennedy and Lyndon Johnson had their equivalents under Eisenhower, but he took them far less seriously: "The most uncompromising advocates of such magic numbers have themselves changed their calculations almost from year to year."

What really engaged Eisenhower's attention, however, was the broader social impact of the defense program. "There is no such thing as maximum security short of total mobilization," the President declared, and he spelled out exactly what that implied: "This would mean regimentation of the worker, the farmer, the businessman—allocation of materials, control of wages, and prices—drafting of every able-bodied citizen. It would mean, in short, all the grim paraphernalia of the garrison state."

Ike's vision contrasted strikingly with later Democratic and Republican administrations' insensate quest for total security; defined, absurdly, in a Pentagon acronym as the capacity for MAD—Mutual Assured Destruction—of the U.S. and the USSR if they ever went to war. Here, most dramatically, the Republican "new beginning" in 1981 parted company with the Republican "mandate for change" in 1953. Stephen Ambrose, surveying recent historical writing on the Eisenhower regime, took sharp exception to the notion that Ronald Reagan was Ike reborn. The Californian's style and rhetoric might be similar: "the quick and easy smile, low-key cabinet government on the Whig model, practical businessmen in charge, balanced budgets and lower taxes, stern opposition to communism," Ambrose conceded; "but so long as the Reagan people insist on expanded military expenditures the reality can never be the same."

Also, unlike the Reagan people, the Eisenhower people could not advise Americans in economic distress simply to wait it out until things got better. Herbert Hoover had told them that, and for him and for his party the results had been politically disastrous. Learning from that disaster, Eisenhower had said during his campaign that the country needed an administration willing to "mobilize all the resources of Government" in order to prevent the return to mass unemployment. The recession of 1954 had come and passed without really testing that campaign pledge; even so, it was promptly followed by the loss of both houses of Congress to the Democrats. The lesson seemed plain: twenty years after Hoover, every Republican politician still had to live down the reputation of Ebenezer Scrooge. The situation, for a sitting Republican president, was murky. The next economic downturn, if it did not summon forth the talents of a Roosevelt, would call at least for those of a Barnum.

Ironically, that next recession resulted in large part from Eisenhower's tactical success in disciplining the defense establishment. In late February and early March of 1957 the Pentagon top brass became aware that the Air Force was heavily overspending its budget, blaming the overruns on inflation and on the cost of developing and procuring the fantastic new weaponry demanded by modern war. The Air Force, the newest and boldest among the three armed services, had quickly learned that old axiom of the civil servant in Washington: a Congressional spending ceiling, rightly understood, is not a limit at all; it is a challenge to spend more. (Don't try to live within it; go over, and put in for a deficiency appropriation. And never, never *under*spend your budget and return money to the Treasury; you'll only be cut the next time around.) A Defense appropriation fixed at $38 billion for the fiscal year 1957 was being spent at a rate of 10.5 percent higher, and most of the excess went off into the wild blue yonder on silver wings.

The news outraged the old soldier in the White House; and behind that affable, grinning countenance lurked a passionate temper and a sulfurous Army vocabulary—both usually well under control. At first, according to Ike-watcher Marquis Childs, Eisenhower wanted to fire the Secretary of the Air Force, Donald Quarles. Backing away from so drastic a step, the President, his Treasury Secretary, and his budget director sought to dam the monetary flood. "The proudest convictions of a conservative administration were at stake"; they were not about to let the budget go out of balance, increases taxes, or—most humiliating of all—go to the penny-saving Virginia Democrat Harry Byrd, who chaired the Senate Finance Committee, and ask him for a raise in the ceiling on the national debt. Instead they lopped off programs for aircraft procurement and missile development, or deferred them. They told aircraft manufacturers—some of whom, like Boeing, were owed hundreds of millions of dollars—that they would have to wait until the end of the calendar year for their bills to be paid. "Even in the smallest matters, such as the payment of electric-power charges, the economy squad hacked and chopped and postponed."

The result demonstrated once again that in politics you're damned if you do and damned if you don't. The Democrats in Congress spiritedly resisted these defense cuts, and out of that resistance grew the issue of the "missile gap," which they skill-fully—and rather demagogically—would exploit in their next presidential campaign. In a shorter run, the effect of the drastic economizing measures quickly fell upon industries highly dependent on defense contracts. West Coast aircraft plants, in particular, laid off assembly-line workers and machinists, technicians and engineers. Together with the deliberate tight-money policies of Federal Reserve Board chairman William McChesney Martin and with a general slowing down of capital investment, the administration's military surgery helped push the country into a new recession. By the spring of 1958 more than five million Americans were out of work—comparable, with adjustment for the smaller population in 1958, to the unemployment statistics Ronald Reagan would use so effectively in 1980 against Jimmy Carter.

What should be done? Again as in the 1954 slump, notes former speechwriter Emmet John Hughes, demands came from Democrats for comprehensive, New Deal style government action, and demands came from Republicans for a substantial tax cut. Eisenhower rejected both kinds of advice, "looking over, past, and beyond all the grim warnings of possible depression to discern further ahead, the more distant and (to him) more ominous dangers of inflation." While his administration groped for a policy it looked also for some morale-encouraging battlecry, on the order of arch-cheerleader Franklin Roosevelt's "the only thing we have to fear is fear itself." A new breed of political magician was at hand to supply just such slogans, for the 1952 election had been the first one to be transformed—and, from the standpoint of rational discussion, subverted—by the minions of Madison Avenue, many of whom had afterward moved on to Washington. The slogan they invented for coping with the 1958 recession was YOU AUTO BUY.

Liberal economists had long since embraced a philosophy of "pump-priming," as the New Dealers used to call it. When the well runs dry, you pour in water until the pump works again; when the economy turns stagnant, you pour in money to stimulate it into motion. Its Republican opponents in the 1950s loosely described this philosophy as "Keynesian economics," although there is no evidence FDR had ever read Lord Keynes. They opposed it because it involved deliberately incurring a deficit, in the hope that reviving prosperity would eventually return a surpus—a hope that had been dashed in the New Deal years again and again. However, there was no necessary reason why *government* had to prime the pump, Eisenhower's ad men told each other. The consumer could be asked to do the spending instead. Don't nurse your old car along for another year; buy a new one. Don't make do with last year's wardrobe; replace it. Don't go stumbling over Grandma's atrocious second-hand furniture; get something you can live with. And so Dwight Eisenhower proclaimed that the way out of the economic doldrums was to "Buy," and in nearly every major U.S. city the copywriters unleashed a massive anti-recession psychological offensive.

Boston had its "POPS" (for "Power of Positive Selling"); Dallas was bombarded for three months with "Think Up; Think Prosperity—Have Prosperity," blazoned on six hundred billboards. Cleveland elected a "Miss Prosperity," to reign over anti-recession street rallies and parades. More grimly, the car dealers in Newark warned over local radio: "Buy now, the job you save may be your own." Elsewhere in New Jersey a tire store, echoing the same "Buy, Buy Buy" theme, added: "It's your patriotic duty." In these campaigns the advertisers reached new heights of creative vulgarity. "Eisenhower Urges Consumer Buying!" shouted a headline in Bangor, Maine, over a furniture store ad for a Big Prosperity Sale, and in even larger letters under a fake newspaper logo—actually it was the name of the store—a second headline declared "O.K., IKE . . . WE'RE BEHIND YOU 100%."

In these campaigns, the advertisers reached new heights of creative vulgarity. (Advertisement in the *Bangor Daily News,* June 17, 1958.)

A few sour notes sounded in the chorus. The State Street Council, an association of Chicago's big downtown department stores, turned down a proposed anti-recession campaign on the ground that it might only make matters worse: "Something like that might tend to produce a feeling of panic." In Detroit, a retailer confessed that "after a certain point, there's nothing you can do. You tell them to buy, but they haven't any money." "There is no use expecting a man to buy an automobile he does not have to have," columnist Walter Lipmann warned, "if he is worried about whether he may lose his job."

Many of the prospective buyers couldn't, and evidently quite a few of them wouldn't. A Cleveland housewife was skeptical that the big campaign in her town would get very far because most of her friends, now caught up on their major hard-goods purchases, had become dissatisfied with much of what they had

been sold. She challenged the store people to "get off their
rusty-dusty and sell us on good quality merchandise.... A lot of
us feel it is kind of nice now to be able to sit back for a while
and watch the salesmen squirm."

III

Eisenhower himself evidently had had second thoughts about
the whole campaign. "I personally think our people are being
just a little bit disenchanted by a few items that have been
chucked down their throats," Ike remarked early in April—
words that were not nearly so well publicized as his previous
"buy now" advice. "I think it would be a very good thing when
the manufacturers begin to give the things we want instead of
the things they think we want." The Eisenhowers themselves
hadn't been buying much lately, other than food and clothing,
intimates reported. Mamie, who was notorious for starting her
day in the White House propped up in bed reading the su-
permarket sale ads and then sending out the Secret Service
men in a van to stock up, had skipped buying a new Easter
outfit; and the President—worst heresy of all, in the tail-finny
fifties—hadn't bought and was not planning to buy a car.

But none of the negative news, not even from the White
House, daunted the forced-draft optimists. As Charles G. Mor-
timer, president of General Foods and a top industry adviser
to the Advertising Council, explained: "I do not think it is an
exaggeration to say that recession begins and ends in the minds
of men." *The only thing we have to fear . . .*

If the potential customers would not or could not buy, perhaps
their patriotic fervor could be reinforced with price cuts. A
store in Pittsburgh put up fur coats and TV sets at $5 apiece,
igniting a siege that caved in its big front window and sent five
would-be buyers to the hospital. Hotpoint, staging a two week
"OK Ike" campaign in Kansas City and Chicago, offered bait
such as no down payment with a trade-in, no payments for

three months, and a no-pay grace period of three months more if a customer were laid off from work or fired.

Most strikingly, some banks—reversing their supposed historic admonitions to save for a rainy day—were now asking their clients to spend. "Aw gwan," the Bank of St. Louis seductively called, in a Sunday *Post-Dispatch* ad; "Buy that new car." Another St. Louis bank agreed: "This is a time for healthy spending." In St. Louis 75,000 workers lacked jobs; recession is "a state of mind;" and—clear, didactic statement of what might be termed private-enterprise Keynesianism—"In times such as these, excessive saving can be as harmful as excessive spending."

The *Wall Street Journal,* that consistent voice of undiluted free enterprise, did not like private deficit financing any better than the public variety; at least, not when the public was subtly coercing the private decision. Logically, if government should not determine how a person earned his or her income, it also should not offer unwanted advice on how to spend it. "We have just bought three new Buicks, seven Plymouths, four Lincolns, and a Mack dump truck," that newspaper mockingly editorialized, under the title "Buy, Buy Baby." "We have also placed orders for six new suits, four pairs of socks, a parakeet, a twelve-story apartment and three trunkfuls of chocolate bars." They didn't need all that stuff, to pay for which they had cleaned out the savings account, hocked the life insurance, and doubled the mortgage; but they hoped those persons in and out of government who had been urging them to buy were now satisfied:

> We have always favored people buying things and other people selling them things. But we had always thought also that this was a free enterprise economy, based on the idea that it was strictly up to the consumer to buy or save or whatever, and that his patriotism was not suspect for exercising his free choice.
>
> But obviously we must have been wrong, for here are these officials of a free enterprise Administration and these free enterprise businessmen telling us otherwise. It seems that if we don't buy, the recession will become a depression and there will be a revolution or something and the Communists will take over.
>
> We certainly wouldn't want that to happen. So we have bought

the Buicks and the socks and the parakeet and all the rest and
if everyone else does, too, the economy will spin upward, upward
to new, new records.

Or so we're told. And there may be new overexpansion by
industry, and if there should be another recession—well, let's not
think carefully, only Big.

Thomas Malthus had dismally predicted that as population
grew it would press so heavily upon the means of subsistence
that its standard of living must decline. The baby boom of the
fifties, however, seemed to be having the opposite effect; the
more mouths came into the world, the more they would have
to gobble down. "Malthus was right—for a civilization without
machines," wrote Frederik Pohl in a witty science fiction satire,
The Midas Plague. In the world of an automated, high-technology
future, "the pipeline of production spewed out riches that no
king in the time of Malthus could have known. But a pipeline
has two ends. The invention and power and labor pouring in
at one end must somehow be drained out at the other." The
story's hapless hero, "drowning in the pipeline's flood, striving
manfully to eat and drink and wear out his share of the ceaseless
tide of wealth," is considered poor. Conversely, in this ironic
counter-Utopia, wealth is defined as the right to consume *less:*
as you rise in social rank, you move into a smaller house.

Pohl's imagined future was a parable about the bloated present.
In World War II, Americans had taken it for granted that the
armed forces had had to waste things in order to win the war.
Now, in the fifties, there was no war; yet the need continued
to consume things, less theatrically but no less thoroughly than
in war's fountaining explosions. If we didn't, people told each
other, we would fall right back into the economic depression
from which the war had rescued us. Waste, if you would want
not. For the austere ethic of a hard-working, scrimping-and-
saving, wrong-side-of-the-tracks family, such as that from which
Dwight Eisenhower had emerged half a century before, this
was an ironic end.

IV

From that struggling boyhood back in Kansas, Eisenhower extracted a metaphor to describe his matured attitude toward public policy. He was a "middle roader," he explained, in the spirit of his mother's work in her kitchen garden: she had saved the fruits and vegetables and gotten rid of the weeds. "Mr. Eisenhower plainly views the whole pre-Eisenhower Washington as a single kitchen garden," Joseph Harsch observed. "He doesn't distinguish between the rows planted by Mr. Truman and those planted by Senator Taft." But for the kind of Republican who regarded the whole pre-Eisenhower Washington as a greenhouse for growing Communists, that kind of pragmatic approach simply would not do. Others—high-tariff advocates who voted to extend the reciprocal trade agreements, or isolationists who endorsed foreign aid—might recant their true Republican faith, in whole or in part. But Joe McCarthy, with his gospel of "Communists in the government," went roaring through the halls in Washington as if nothing had happened.

And that was the beginning of his downfall.

As long as the government he alleged to be infested with Communists was "their"—i.e., the Democrats'—government, many Republicans were willing to believe the worst; or, more cynically, to take partisan advantage of the damage McCarthy was inflicting. On January 20, 1953, however, it had become "our" government; yet the attacks continued. The same self-preservative political instinct which had previously led Congressional Republicans covertly to abet McCarthy's activities, or at least to stay out of his way, now led some of them to the conclusion that Joe had to be slowed down or stopped.

Had the Republican machine's organizational lines held in 1952 so that Taft prevailed over Eisenhower, one can imagine a scenario in which Adlai Stevenson, having defeated Senator Taft in the general election—not at all an improbable outcome—delivers the most inspiring Presidential inauguration address of the twentieth century and then falls into four years of absolute misery. Lacking the professional military credentials to make a compromise settlement in Korea acceptable, President Stevenson watches the Korean conflict smolder on and on. The national mood of frustration escalates into punitive rage. In this poisonous atmosphere the President cannot effectively move against the Senator, because any word or deed of Stevenson's under these circumstances would be discounted by many Republicans as self-serving—much as Truman's diatribes against McCarthyism had been—or worse, interpreted as part of the ongoing Communist conspiracy. Defeated for a second term, Adlai Stevenson leaves office more discredited than any President since Hoover, only to be appreciated, like Hoover, long afterward. From *that* possible historical outcome, at least, we were spared by the election of Dwight Eisenhower.

Nevertheless Eisenhower's handling of the McCarthy problem was, and remains, one of the most hotly controverted issues of his presidency. Younger historians, put off by the war-waging administrations of the sixties and attracted to Ike's manifest good will for the world, have in recent years been revising his reputation upward; but they continue to have trouble with this question. Why didn't the President move against the Senator more forcefully, and sooner? Why, an Ike defender might retort, didn't FDR move more forcefully and sooner against Huey Long?—which does not really resolve the question, since many of the same scholars who have realized they now like Ike better have also decided they no longer like Roosevelt as much as liberal college professors used to.

For such a showdown with McCarthy, Eisenhower had resources within his own party upon which he could have drawn. On June 1, 1950—only three months after the Wisconsin Senator made his initial media splash, with the notorious speech at Wheeling, West Virginia about the 205, or 81, or 57, or however-many-it-was, Communists in the State Department—Margaret Chase Smith, of Maine, "her gray hair immaculately done, looking cool yet determined in her aquamarine silk suit," and wearing her usual fresh red rose, stood up in the green-carpeted Senate chamber to make her first major address. She got right to the point, speaking "as briefly as possible because too much harm has already been done with irresponsible words of bitterness and selfish political opportunism"—words, especially, that had been spoken in the United States Senate.

The legal immunity members of Congress properly and constitutionally enjoy, modeled on the hard-won right of members of Parliament against arrest by the Crown, had become extended to the Congressional committees' investigative hearings—even when, as was often the case with McCarthy, the investigator's committee consisted solely of himself. The result was that a senator or representative, on the floor or in a television-lighted committee room, could "impute to any American, who is not a Senator, any conduct or motive unworthy or unbecoming an American—and without that non-Senator American having any legal redress." It seemed strange to Senator Smith "that we can verbally attack anyone else without restraint and with full protection, and yet we hold ourselves above the same type of criticism here on the Senate floor."

Senator Smith could not have been accused of wishy-washy liberalism. She later introduced a bill to outlaw the Communist Party, and her proposed solution to the Korean War, should the negotiations break down, was to "drop the atomic bomb on these barbarians." Nor was she sparing of the Truman administration, which, she declared, had "provided us with sufficient campaign issues without the necessity of resorting to political smears." The country would suffer as long as the Democrats governed it, and they richly deserved defeat in 1952. Then, stunningly, she soared above partisanship. "To displace the Democratic Administration with a Republican regime embracing a philosophy that lacks political integrity or intellectual honesty would prove equally disastrous," the Senator from Maine warned. "The nation sorely needs a Republican victory. But I don't want to see the Republican Party ride to victory on the Four Horsemen of Calumny—Fear, Ignorance, Bigotry and Smear."

Afterward a "Declaration of Conscience," signed by Senator

"It is strange that we can verbally attack anyone else without restraint and with full protection and yet we hold ourselves above the same type of criticism here on the Senate floor."—Margaret Chase Smith (R., Maine), June 1, 1950. *Drawing by Fitzpatrick, in the* St. Louis Post-Dispatch.

Smith and half a dozen of her Republican colleagues, was read into the *Congressional Record.* (McCarthy, with his usual ill grace, promptly dubbed them "Snow White and the Six Dwarfs.") Significantly, however, her northern New England Senatorial colleague Ralph Flanders, of Vermont, did not sign this Declaration. He bided his time until 1954, when he introduced the motion which led in due course to McCarthy's censure. "To have introduced it earlier would have been to lose the opportunity," Flanders wrote afterward. "It could only be carried through to a successful conclusion at that particular time."

Such appears to have been Eisenhower's view of the matter: give McCarthy enough rope, wait patiently for the right moment, and eventually he will hang himself. And so McCarthy did— *eventually*. But waiting for that eventuality seemed, to many, a gamble as risky as any Eisenhower had taken since D-Day. "Whether McCarthy expects to become President I would not know," wrote Elmer Davis early in 1954, "but it looks that way," and it looked to Davis also as if opportunistic Republicans were willing to let the Senator use the Congressional elections of 1954 to promote that candidacy. "About McCarthy the ordinary citizen cannot do much if anything," Davis continued, *"unless he gets the Presidential nomination in 1956,* and we won't know that for two years." For an experienced political reporter as level-headed as Elmer Davis to treat a Republican nomination for McCarthy as a serious possibility was alarming, to say the least, and as 1954 began 50 percent of Americans polled by the Institute of Public Opinion said they looked favorably upon Joe McCarthy.

Sometimes it is claimed that the mass media, which in a sense had made McCarthy, also destroyed him. In the celebrated— and intensely watched—Army-McCarthy hearings in the spring of 1954, novelist John Steinbeck pointed out, the Senator behaved exactly like the Bad Guy in a TV Western: "He had a stubble of a beard . . . he leered, he sneered, he had a nasty laugh. He bullied and shouted. He looked evil," and, as Steinbeck's then eight-year-old son patiently explained, in those televised hearings McCarthy obviously had to be the Bad Guy. The Senate, however, had its own traditionalist reasons for taking offense. The ultra-respectable committee chaired by Arthur Watkins of Utah which took up the Flanders censure resolution allowed no television antics at its deliberations; and it was not liberal Democrats from the North but their conservative Southern colleagues like Byrd of Virginia and George of Georgia who saw to it that the members present from their party in the Senate voted unanimously to censure Joe McCarthy.

The Senate's Republicans in that showdown vote, however, split exactly in half, 22–22. Except for Majority Whip Leverett Saltonstall, *all* of the Republican Senate leaders—William Knowland, Everett Dirksen, Styles Bridges, and Eugene Millikin— voted for McCarthy! Eisenhower's program of reforming and rejuvenating the Republican Party evidently had a long way to go.

V

In the late summer of 1955 not very much was going on. The recession of 1954 was over; that of 1957 was yet to come. It was not a political campaign year. Nobody was rioting. Congress was not in session. Eisenhower was just back from a summit conference with the leaders of France, Britain, and the Soviet Union; substantively it had been inconclusive, but it had been a great triumph for him personally. Twice after his return from Geneva he held Cabinet meetings, at one of which he reminisced of old days in the Army when he and other officers going to testify before Congressional committees had been given streetcar tokens in lieu of travel expenses—a hint to Defense Secretary Charles Wilson that he ought to get on with his budget cuts. Then the President flew out to the Colorado Rockies to enjoy four days of fishing.

On September 23, Ike got up at dawn in his mountain retreat, fixed his own breakfast of hot cakes, fried mush, pork sausage, and beef bacon, and headed for Denver. After a couple of hours of routine work he went out to the Cherry Hill Country Club and played eighteen holes of golf; munched down a hamburger with large slices of raw onions; and then played *another* nine holes. On the eighth hole he thought he had heartburn. He returned to his wife's mother's house, oil-painted for awhile, dined lightly, and was in bed by ten. Shortly after 2:30 the next morning Mamie heard him tossing about in bed, and at 3:11 his personal physician diagnosed a coronary.

"Subconsciously," Eisenhower would write in *Mandate for Change*, "every healthy man thinks of serious illness as something that happens occasionally—but always to other people." Late on the 24th, after an uncomfortable night under sedation, he woke up in an oxygen tent and realized that now it was his turn. Yet, as so often before in his career, Ike was lucky, and the Eisenhower luck on this occasion was the nation's as well. If the U.S. presidency *had* to be interrupted in the fifties, fortune picked the right moment. Suppose the President had fallen ill a few months earlier, when China and the United States seemed at the verge of war; or a year later, when the world was in upheaval over Hungary and the Suez? Eisenhower himself came to believe that had a situation arisen after the heart attack such as occurred three summers later in Lebanon, "the concentration, the weighing of the pros and cons, and the final determination would have represented a burden, during the first week of my illness, which the doctors would have found unacceptable for a new cardiac patient to bear." As it was, they didn't let him know very clearly what was going on. "These doctors are a secretive lot," he groused, "and a patient at times has to form some of his own conclusions as to their beliefs."

Secretive or not, the medical profession learned a good deal from the inevitably intensive study of a patient who was President. The public also learned a good deal; especially, it unlearned the old folk wisdom that expects and dooms people with heart disease to remain flat on their backs. Heart specialist and medical researcher Paul Dudley White, Chairman of the Department of Cardiology at Harvard Medical School—and incidentally a Republican to the core—used the publicity surrounding his famous patient to educate Americans into a more affirmative philosophy, namely, that light exercise should be undertaken within a few days and increased until the patient is normally active. Indeed, Dr. White's judgment, and the second full term through which that patient served, has had a subtle but profound effect upon Americans' attitude toward aging and the aged.

This new insight was obscured for another decade by the youth image of Camelot and by the kind of insurgency that mistrusted anybody over thirty, but it would return. In this very indirect sense, Eisenhower's presidency *did* foreshadow Reagan's; after watching eight years of Ike in the White House, Americans did not find a 69-year-old nominee in 1980 nearly so "old" as they might have thought a person of that age in, say, 1950.

Dr. White's gospel was welcome news to the other members of the national administration. They were maintaining a posture of continuity; Richard Nixon regularly presided over Cabinet meetings. He ran them, we have been told, "with the efficiency of a Broadway producer," but at best these were ceremonial shadow-shows. Under the Constitution as it stood in 1955 a vice-president had no authority whatever in such a situation; literally, *none*. One member of the Eisenhower cabinet, John Foster Dulles, had a family recollection of a similar crisis; his uncle Robert Lansing, Secretary of State during Woodrow Wilson's crippling stroke in 1919, had attempted to make the Cabinet a fully decision-making body. However, that had not been constitutionally possible, and Lansing had been fired. There was a painful gap in the American governing process, only partly remedied since the fifties by the Twenty-Fifth Amendment. All that Ike's official family could do was to mark time, hope nothing critical erupted internationally, and assume Paul Dudley White was right.

As it turned out, he was. But nobody could know that for certain as 1955 drew to an end. Would there—*should* there—be a second term? Partisan hopes and fears mingled with disinterested concern for the public weal. Many who liked Ike had the most profound mistrust of Richard Milhous Nixon, a feeling given a sharp wrench by the realization that only the beat of a damaged heart now separated the younger man from the White House. The decision could not be put off forever. The New Hampshire presidential primary, traditionally the formal opening of the campaign year, was rapidly approaching. The medical tests went on; Dr. White announced that if Ike ran again *he* would vote for him; and on January 29 the President told reporters that if the Republican National Convention wanted him again "my answer would be positive; that is, affirmative." With that statement the candidate was off and running.

So was Richard Nixon.

Eisenhower's relationship with Nixon during the first term had been one of official cordiality but not of personal intimacy. Significantly, in the cabinet members' huddle with the President (and with his younger brother, Milton) on January 13 to discuss the pros and cons of a second term, the Vice-President had not been present. In spite of Nixon's wide appeal within the party organization there were serious practical political difficulties with his candidacy. Polls showed Adlai Stevenson to be more popular. Among liberals and moderates Nixon already had a deserved reputation for over-eagerness, and even some right-wing Republicans found him not to their taste. Senator William Knowland of California, for example, who had become Republican floor leader upon Taft's death—and who, in 1964, would be an active advocate for Barry Goldwater—declared during Ike's convalescence that he did "not consider a Pepsodent smile, a ready quip, and an actor's perfection with lines, nor an ability to avoid issues, a qualification for high office." (Apparently since that time California's political perceptions have somewhat changed.)

Nixon's infinite political resourcefulness was challenged to its utmost. As late as March 7, Eisenhower unhelpfully told his news conference that he had asked the Vice-President "to chart his own course and tell me what he would like to do." A graceful minuet followed—its steps may be traced in the President's and the Vice-President's respective meetings with the press—on the order of, well, of course if the President doesn't want me . . . No, of course, Dick, that's not what I meant . . . until Nixon on April 26 made what *Time* called "the most predictable announcement of the year," and the ticket was complete.

The Democrats again picked Adlai Stevenson, who, hoping to capitalize on his party's contrast with "machine" Republicans' manifest relish for Nixon, refrained from picking a running mate in the usual fashion and threw the vice-presidential nomination onto the convention floor. That experiment in rank-and-file participation brought a quickly improvised, exciting drive on behalf of John Fitzgerald Kennedy before yielding another retread: Stevenson's leading antagonist in both the 1952 and 1956 primaries, Estes Kefauver. It made a brief stir in an otherwise lackluster campaign summer, which didn't even have the Olympics for piquant contrast; the Games were in Melbourne that year, and had to be moved into late November to allow for the inverted seasons of the Southern Hemisphere. This time the Russians won, a fact which may have been more important than whether Ike or Adlai won the U.S. election.

The Republican campaign in 1956 "resembled in many ways that which Franklin Roosevelt waged when he first ran for re-election in 1936," Marquis Childs thoughtfully wrote:

> In the same way, Eisenhower moved across the country as the popular pledge that all was well, the image of a cheerful father, a kindly pastor, a modestly confident hero. He touched on issues only tangentially . . . As Roosevelt had done twenty years before, Eisenhower deliberately refrained from mentioning the name of his opponent, referring to the opposition with scorn and sometimes with half-humorous mockery. There were, to be sure, references to dangers ahead and trials still to be met. But they were made to sound as hardly more than a further challenge to one who had already achieved so much.
>
> How much all of this was the work of the skilled public-relations and advertising experts available in such numbers to the Republicans and how much it was due to the intuitive sense of Eisenhower, now the experienced campaigner, it is impossible to say . . .
>
> With a long sustained rhythm, sometimes with cheerleaders, sometimes with massed bands, the crowds chanted "We like Ike." That was what they had come out for in the soft Indian-summer weather—to cheer, to shout and laugh, to sing and wave banners for the triumphal return of Ike and Mamie and what they stood for; peace and prosperity.

VI

Statistically Eisenhower's second-term campaign in 1956 resembled Roosevelt's in 1936, with one very important exception. Ike duplicated FDR's feat of improving on the first performance; he opened his already wide popular-vote margin over Stevenson by more than two million and increased the electoral-vote margin as well. Roosevelt, however, had also been able to strengthen his grip on Congress; his own party's already impressive majority in the House of Representatives increased, becoming 328 to 107, while its Senate lineup reached an incredible 77 to 19. In contrast, the slender 1952 Republican Congressional victory had been followed in both 1954 and 1956 by similarly narrow Democratic triumphs. Behind that image of the cheerful father, during the second campaign, was a worried Eisenhower. He knew he would be the first president to whom the two-term limitation of the Twenty-Second Amendment would apply, and he believed that the size of his majority would be "the most important weapon I will have for the next four years—especially with the Republicans." Now, as it turned out, *he* had his desired majority—but *they* did not. FDR's charm had irradiated the Democratic Party as well, to the eventual benefit of Harry Truman; but somehow it had not proved possible to translate "We like Ike" into "We love the GOP."

In 1958 the Republicans had one more chance, before Ike's final term ended, to recoup their Congressional losses; and if economics were the sole determinant of politics they ought to have won. By September the 1957–58 recession was under control; housing starts, industrial production, and employment turned sharply upward. (The "you auto buy" campaign, incidentally, turned out to have been sheer froth. The sale of durable goods stayed flat during this recovery, and automobile production actually went down.) On October 14, 1958, risking comparisons with Hoover, Eisenhower declared: "All the evidence is that we are on the road to a new peak of prosperity."

The voters' reply, three weeks later, was a Democratic landslide.

Losing no Senate seats of their own, the Democrats took thirteen away from the Republicans, breaking their previous record set in the depression election of 1932. They lost one House seat, while wresting forty-six from the GOP. Their Senate majority was the largest since FDR's third-term election of 1940; their House majority was the best since Alf Landon's landslide defeat in 1936. Vermont sent its first Democrat to Congress in 106 years. In Connecticut, Maryland, and Delaware, no Republican congressmen were left; in the supposedly safe farm belt "only a few scattered districts remained as lone Republican oases." Republican causes, not simply Republican candidates, were rejected; for example, voters in five states defeated right-to-work laws.

"There is no use pretending that this was just Republican ill-luck," the *Wall Street Journal* grumbled on November 6. "For the past two years the Republican Party has done nothing to deserve victory and almost everything to deserve defeat. All the advantages that should have accrued from a popular President were carelessly thrown away." On the other hand, the election results were no credit to the Democratic party, either: "The Democrats did not really win the election. The Republicans committed political suicide." The fault, "when you come right down to it, must rest on President Eisenhower. It was he who had the sense of direction and lost it." From its own deep-seated conservative premises, the *Journal* came to exactly the same conclusion about Eisenhower as those liberal political scientists and historians who were blaming him, in effect, for not being Roosevelt: "There have been times when it almost seemed the highest officials, including the President, were ashamed of politics or thought that politics was beneath them."

Second-guessing, however, is always cheap and easy. When it came to the question of what Eisenhower as a politician *ought* to have done with his sense of direction, the guessers fell back on outworn arguments. Liberals, all unaware of the illiberal purposes for which vigorous political leadership would one day be used, seemed to want him to have been an "imperial president." Conservatives apparently also wished him to have been more forceful, in order to crush the Communists, reverse the country's social-democratic momentum, and put Americans back on the virtuous path of private enterprise. In its post-mortem discussion of the 1958 election the Republican Party fell at once into its old progressives-versus-regulars quarrels of 1912 and 1940 and 1952. "Modern Republicans" took comfort from the election of Nelson Rockefeller as Governor of New York and the defeat of Senator John W. Bricker in Ohio; conservatives were heartened by the re-election in Arizona of first-term Senator Barry Goldwater, who at once emerged as the articulate voice of their wing of the party.

"People are tax conscious," said Goldwater in a post-election statement, "and they are cost conscious." Writing in the *Wall Street Journal* for November 28, 1956 on "Conservatism's Future," Joseph E. Evans hopefully prophesied: "If the Republicans could capitalize on these presumptive attitudes, they might get somewhere." The events of the sixties—the years of the New Frontier and the Great Society—seemed to prove that prophet wrong; they certainly checked the political ambitions of Barry Goldwater. But the fear of Depression moved further into the mists of memory, and the fear of inflation loomed out of the future's fog, and in 1980 it would seem Goldwater was having the last word.

All that history to come, however, still lay below the horizon when Eisenhower entered his last two presidential years. Those powerful Democratic majorities in Congress ran up against a vigorously veto-wielding president, and their seasoned leaders soon adjusted to political reality. The State Department found it had less leverage on foreign policy without John Foster Dulles (who died in 1959), and the Pentagon was reminded again and again that "defense policy . . . is made by budget planners, and the budget planners are told by the President what to plan." As the decade of the fifties closed, the *New Yorker*'s Washington correspondent reported on January 30, 1960, Eisenhower "has become master in his own house from top to bottom."

He expressed this mastery, however, in his own characteristic way. "Mr. Eisenhower has used Presidental powers," Richard Rovere continued, "not in pursuit of active and ambitious policies but to prevent such policies from being forced upon him by others." In his early White House years the "others" had been members of his own party's right wing, clamoring for a reversion to the good old days; "this clamor was stilled mainly by allowing the proponents of change to talk themselves hoarse. The policies they wished to replace had become such firmly established features of the existing order that . . . the Right was unable to summon the external force to disturb them." Now it was the Democrats' turn to feel the same hard, restraining hand. During the Eisenhower presidency, Robert Griffith has pointed out, "federal transfer payments, the surest index to social welfare policy, remained unchanged as a percentage of the federal budget;" if there was to be no less a commitment to people's basic social needs than under the previous Democratic regime, there was also to be no more.

If they came to power in the next presidential election, Democrats vowed, they would show once again that they, not the Republicans, were the party of action. The next occupant of the White House, said Florida's Governor Leroy Collins in his installation address as Permanent Chairman of the 1960 Democratic National Convention, "must know good, not because he can sense it, but because he has done it." The Democrats' paralyzing problem was that none of their contenders, however well-intentioned—not Adlai Stevenson, not John Kennedy, not even Hubert Humphrey—could really claim to have done as much as Dwight David Eisenhower; they could only promise that, if elected, they would do more. Meanwhile, unfinished business piled high on the presidential desk, and some of it would not wait much longer. Civil rights, the liberation of women, and the claims of youth would all be high on the sixties' agenda.

"The next President," Rovere summed up his assessment at the beginning of the 1960 campaign, "will have to be an innovator whether it suits his temper or not." That sounds like typical intellectual-liberal criticism of Eisenhower, until one reflects that the innovator, in an election as close as 1960 turned out to be, could just as well have been Richard Nixon.

CHAPTER THREE
Cracked Mirror to the World

I

EISENHOWER was no phrasemaker. In his two inaugural addresses he drove no money changers out of the temple, and he passed no torches to new generations. The liberal-arts professors who sat around in their offices with their brown bag lunches lost no opportunity to make fun of the grammar and sentence structure of his press conferences. Nonetheless, from time to time the President and his speechwriters—among whom Ike always had the last say—found words that spoke clearly and plainly to America and the world.

In a speech delivered on June 20, 1953, for example, at Minneapolis—in what had been the heartland of Midwestern isolationism—Eisenhower noted that "we all hear a good deal of unhappy murmuring about the United Nations." Within vivid memory for his hearers were the Security Council filibusters of Soviet delegate Yakov Malik, wrangling over procedural motions while thousands of men blew each other up in the hills of Korea; even as Eisenhower spoke, that agonizing three-year war was still grinding toward its inconclusive close. "None of us is above irritation and frustration over the seemingly vain and tedious processes of political discourse in times of great crisis," the President admitted. "But none of us can rightly forget that neither the world—nor the United Nations—is or can be made in a single image of one nation's will or idea." To be sure, Soviet

Thousands of men blew each other up in the hills of Korea while the UN was wrangling over procedural motions.

and Western conceptions of the international organization's role differed starkly. However, even if the UN were to conform to the West's view of its purpose, "it would still be bound to show infinite variety of opinion, sharp clashes of debate, slow movement to decision"—and in this it was "a reflection of the state of the world itself."

"An image of perfect symmetry," Eisenhower summed up, "would be a distorted image—the false creation of some nation's or some bloc's power politics. And perhaps the greatest worth of the United Nations is precisely this: it holds up a mirror in which the world can see its true self. And what should we want to see in such a mirror but the whole truth?"

That reflecting surface did not show quite the whole truth. The UN at its founding in 1945 had been limited in membership to the winners of the Second World War. Neutrals in that war, such as Ireland and Portugal, and former Axis countries remained

outside. At the time Eisenhower made his speech, admission of
ex-enemies into the world organization was still being vetoed
and counter-vetoed; the Americans objected to Hungary, Bul-
garia, and Rumania as United Nations members, while the Soviets
took exception to Finland, Italy, and Japan. Thus, from the
beginning, the UN mirror to the world was cracked.

One deep crevasse in particular ran across Germany, where
two separate nations had come forth from the ashes of the
Third Reich. As they emerged, they evolved, with frightening
rapidity, into national cultures as different from each other as
those of older German-speaking states, such as Austria-Hungary
and Prussia, whose distinctive traits had taken centuries to develop. Another rift twisted and slashed its way above and below
the Thirty-Eighth Parallel on the Korean Peninsula where,
starting just five days after Eisenhower's moderately toned Minneapolis address, tens of thousands of troops began to attack
and counterattack along a 25-mile front. After an additional
month and a half of furious battle, concluding on the last day
with a final, spiteful artillery duel like the ones that punctured
the closing hours of World War I, the war in Korea at last
ended. The chasm between North and South remained, however,
politically and diplomatically unbridgeable; and at one end the
Korean fissure blended into the widest, deepest, and most dis-
torting of all the cracks in the mirror to the world. A quarter
of the planet's population was not visible in that mirror at all;
four years after the downfall of Chiang Kai-shek on the Chinese
mainland his delegate still clung to China's seat at the United
Nations.

With a skill and tenacity that pleased the Taiwan-based regime's
American admirers and greatly annoyed its opponents, Dr.
Tingfu Tsiang maintained high visibility for Nationalist China
at the UN. He worked on the floor and in the lounges to get
Taiwan elected to international agencies, notably ECOSOC
(Economic and Social Council), at the UN General Assembly
session of 1954. On occasion he even exercised China's Charter-
granted power of veto independently of the United States; for

example against Mongolia as a proposed UN member, insisting on behalf of the Nationalist government—and in agreement with the mainland regime—that Mongolia was properly part of China. At times Tsiang seemed a spokesman not for a defeated refugee regime but rather for a World War II–style government in exile. Like the Dutch or the Norwegians, who with their royal families in 1945 had been triumphantly reinstalled on the continent whence they had fled, Dr. Tsiang's sulky but dignified demeanor implied that one day the exiles on Taiwan would also return and rule at home.

Electronic communications of a kind developed for the Nuremberg war-crimes trials and perfected at the United Nations furthered this carefully fostered impression that Nationalist China, as a permanent Great Power entitled to sit with its peers on the Security Council, was alive and well. Since China had also been given by charter one of the five official languages of the United Nations, literally millions of words originally spoken in Russian, English, Spanish, or French had to be put into Chinese by the simultaneous translators, whose extraordinarily skillful feats of split-level thinking—listening to a speaker's present words in one language while speaking in another the ones just uttered—were and are one of the UN's premier tourist attractions.

Who was listening to that great torrent of words? Not the ushered young visitor in a school group, idly switching his or her earphone controls; the perfunctory foreign-language education then generally available in the U.S. might have given some slight competence in Spanish or conceivably in French, but probably none in Russian and almost certainly no Chinese. Not the mainlanders in the People's Republic, against whose admission to those halls and headphones the U.S. stood unyielding as Atlas, all unaware of the radical about-face the American government would perform in only twenty years. Not even the Taiwanese, whose spokesman was fully aware that he could not speak to the American public—whose continuing awareness was vital to his island community's survival—in an unknown tongue. Therefore, when Dr. Tsiang replied to Russian or other East-bloc references to his government as "the Kuomintang clique" or "the Chiang Kai-shek clique," he used English: if such insults continued to be hurled his delegation would be "forced to retaliate in kind, or to pay no attention to such trash," Tsiang typically told the General Assembly on October 6, 1954. "This Assembly is a dignified body which handles the important affairs of the world. It is not a street corner where street urchins quarrel."

Street urchins' quarreling was, in fact, far less in vogue at the UN in the fifties than it had been at the peak of the Cold War. Andrei Vyshinsky, the notorious prosecutor of Stalin's disgraced former comrades in the purges of 1937, was now head of the Soviet delegation at the United Nations, where his ruddy face, shock of white hair, and stocky frame in a bright blue suit had made him something of a box office draw. But the old Stalinist battler had lost a good deal of his bite. British diplomat Anthony Nutting, seasoned in Oxford Union civility, found Mr. Vyshinsky at the United Nations "an agreeable and friendly colleague and a stimulating adversary in debate." Similarly, Vyshinsky's perennial opponent Henry Cabot Lodge—named by Eisenhower to the UN job after a Senatorial election drubbing by John F. Kennedy—avoided both the stiff, moralistic Cold War postures that had typified the late 1940s at the United Nations and the icy patrician ways of the proper Boston grandfather (and opponent of the UN's predecessor, the League of Nations) after whom Lodge was named. Instead he assumed the relaxed, down-home manner of one of Hollywood's mature male Western motion picture stars. To one "gratuitous and wildly inaccurate" charge made by the USSR, Lodge, with an unmistakable Gary Cooper drawl, "doubted whether Mr. Vyshinsky believed his own accusations." To anyone familiar with Western movie lore this quiet statement would have had an ominous undertone, sounding as it did like the classic confrontation of Trampas and the Virginian: "When you say that, smile!" But it was a good deal more restrained than the language of a U.S. delegate to the UN in the Truman era who once, in a similar situation, had shouted before the cameras: "That is a *lie*. A *big* lie." The quiet

Westerner, who would retire from gunplay if he could but who will face down the bad man if he must—the hero of Western films of the fifties such as *Shane* and *High Noon*—was a perfect metaphor for the way Americans in that decade thought about their foreign policy.

II

Even in the calmer atmosphere of the post-Korea United Nations, Henry Lodge and Andrei Vyshinsky had their moments. On September 4, 1954, at 6:18 P.M. local time—the only point agreed upon by both sides—a U.S. Navy Neptune aircraft [over the high seas? In violation of Soviet airspace?] [was attacked without warning by? opened fire upon?] two USSR MIGs of the kind with which U.S. pilots had not long since been dueling in the Korean skies. The Security Council took up the matter on Friday, September 10, and Lodge and Vyshinsky went after each other like courtroom lawyers in a damage suit in dispute over what really happened in an automobile collision. Lodge fortified his case by bringing up similar episodes in the Baltic, over Hungary, and in the Sea of Japan; Vyshinsky rebutted them, and in turn accused U.S. fighter planes of shooting down an Ilyushin—12 passenger aircraft inside the People's Republic of China.

More fundamentally, in response to Lodge's contention that the purpose of the Neptune's flight was "to check weather conditions," Vyshinsky retorted that weather conditions were seemingly "checked . . . by aircraft loaded with machine-guns and carrying all kinds of other military equipment such as radar." What patrol duties did these planes have, 10,000 kilometers from the American coast? "Why do United States aircraft have to go off and patrol something or other in the region of Vladivostok? Why?"

Later that day after lunch the French delegate, Henri Hoppenot, after praising Vyshinsky's forensic brilliance, came skeptically down on Lodge's side: "While I am no more an airman than Mr. Lodge or Mr. Vyshinsky himself, all the airmen I have been able to consult agree that it is almost inconceivable that a bomber deliberately expose itself to the risk of a reply [riposte] bound to be fatal." But M. Hoppenot also commented upon the admirably mild temperature of the exchange, by comparison with U.S.–Soviet collisions in previous years: "I was glad to note that our colleague endeavored, so far as the fire of his ever youthful temperament allowed him, to adopt as moderate a tone as Mr. Lodge. I hope that in the weeks to come the exchange of views between our two eminent colleagues will continue thus to combine firmness as regards substance with this relaxed moderation [cette modération détendue] as regards form." Such was the hope also of the General Assembly's President for the year, Eelco Van Kleffens of the Netherlands. At a meeting on October 19 of the General Committee, which set the Assembly's agenda (corresponding roughly to the Rules Committee in the U.S. House of Representatives) and which had known some of the UN's most frustrating procedural quarrels, Van Kleffens referred to "the welcome improvement which had been noticeable in the tone of the General Assembly debates." Although recognizing that the forceful presentation of a country's point of view could involve its representative in strong language "and, at times, passion," and that excess and even "bitterness" were "human," the Assembly President nevertheless urged the members, "in the interest of maintaining this improvement in the general atmosphere, to exercise self-restraint."

A month later, on November 22, Van Kleffens had to inform the Assembly that Vyshinsky was dead of a sudden heart attack. Had the fiery Soviet delegate's milder manner in recent weeks been only a response to a changing signal from Moscow, or did it contain a personal testament? "To this session," Syrian delegate Ahmed Shukairi declared, "Mr. Vyshinsky has brought conciliation, as it were with an inner sense of farewell." To Pierre Mendès-France, who headed the most vigorous and effective of the Fourth French Republic's many postwar governments,

Vyshinsky's death called to mind a time of happier relations between the USSR and the West: "Only last evening, attending a social function with him, I saw him animated by the same youthful and at times caustic spirit, the same alertness, the same indomitable energy and the same ardent devotion to the service of his country with which he had so impressed me during our first meetings at Algiers in 1944, when the heroism of the Soviet armies, the allied armies and the Free French Forces, standing shoulder to shoulder . . . from Stalingrad's ruins to Africa's shores, heralded the liberation of Europe and the world," the French premier reminisced. "Of all the words he spoke in these precincts I wish to recall only those which were devoted to peace."

Mendès-France was followed by Lodge, who paid a handsome tribute to his fallen adversary: "Mr. Vyshinsky had all the skills of the great debater, boldness, humour, change of pace . . . We who vigorously disagreed with him so often respected his talent. The sympathy of the United States delegation goes out to his widow, to his daughter and to the Soviet delegation." Even in an age of subversion and terrorism, of spy and counter-spy, chivalry was not dead. Or perhaps Lodge, as he listened to other colleagues, notably India's persuasive, dynamic, and highly irritating V.K. Krishna Menon, was aware that the issues before the world forum were subtly mutating away from a simple case of "East" versus "West." At the same 1954 Assembly session a memorable verbal passage-at-arms took place between two small member states, both countable at that time as "West bloc" countries, which foreshadowed a drastically changed United Nations in a different kind of world.

The world organization expected nations which held underdeveloped lands in political custody to give periodic account of their stewardship. If a power held control over a territory in the form of a UN trusteeship—an inheritance from the old League of Nations "mandate" system—the trustee nation was expected not only to furnish statistics on the health and welfare of the territory's inhabitants but also to report formally on their progress toward self-government. Belgium had accepted a United Nations trusteeship for Ruanda-Urundi, which it had initially received as German spoils after the First World War. However, the Belgians refused any such arrangement for the much larger prize of the Congo; as Belgium's representative Pierre Ryckmans told the Fourth (Trusteeship) Committee of the General Assembly on November 2, 1954, "Belgian policy in the Congo was determined by Belgium alone."

Delegate Ryckmans skillfully countered the charge of colonialism that had been made by several Latin American members of the UN. The American states' colonial relationship with Spain had not at all been the same as the Congo's toward Belgium today, he explained. "Their revolutions had been the work of the colonists from the metropolitan country who, while claiming the right to govern themselves, had claimed at the same time the right to take up the role played by the metropolitan country with regard to the indigenous peoples"—some of whom, in remote parts of South America, still continued in the old undeveloped and "colonial" state. By that measure, the Belgians' policy toward their own indigenous peoples in Africa did not look so bad. Ryckmans spelled it out in statistics of health, education, farming, and local manufacture: 1949 had seen the production of only 100,000 Congolese bicycles, for example, as against a 1953 figure of half a million. To the obvious argument that absentee capital investment in the colony exploited the native population, the delegate replied that such investment was not "repatriated [to the mother country] in the form of simple capital;" it was permanently incorporated into the Congo's economy, in which "basic equipment such as railways, roads, bridges and electric power served the black as well as the white population." Political progress was a function of economic progress, and by that standard Belgium "claimed to have done sound and honest work in the Congo."

The case was plausible, but specious, as delegate Enrique Rodriguez Fabregat of Uruguay proceeded to show in a speech that boomed with rational indignation. The Latin Americans needed no outside interpreter of their own struggle for liberation, whose "leaders, whether white, black or Indian, had all been inspired by the desire to abolish slavery." Nor could the condition of the inhabitants of a non-self-governing territory such as the Congo be fairly compared with that of "less privileged groups in sovereign Member States," who at least enjoyed the basic civic rights of those states' other citizens. Progress in nonpolitical areas, however impressive, was somewhat beside the point; if for example one aim of education was "to enable the individual to manage his own affairs and participate in the life of his community," it made little sense "to teach a child to read and then . . . to deprive him of his fundamental rights." Colonist and native could never really function as equals, and the administering powers would have to "modify their conception of the indigenous peoples as inferior beings in constant need of their administration and advice." The Uruguayan granted the Belgian delegate's point that the roads and bridges, the railways and power stations in the Congo were neither black nor white; "but your dividends, sir!" Rodriguez shouted. "Your dividends— those are pure white."

III

History was not going to stop moving just because the Great Powers told it to. By the end of that decade the Congo would be drenched in blood, and the UN's greatest Secretary-General, Dag Hammarskjøld, while struggling to save the former Belgian colony from civil war, was destined to lose his life. Still later, while exploding populations in the Sahel, in Bangladesh, and in Latin America plumbed new depths of misery, the further disintegration of old European colonial empires would bring in a host of new UN members from the politically awakening Third World. By the 1970s they would outnumber, and at times outvote, the heirs of Vyshinsky and Lodge. But in the mid-fifties that future, or any future, was upstaged by the urgencies of the present. Should a global nuclear war happen, there might be nobody around afterward to deal with problems like those of the Congo. Nuclear weapons in 1954 were still deployed in a bi-polarized world; front and center at the United Nations, despite the polite behavior of American and Soviet sparring partners, was the Cold War. Lodge's boss, Secretary of State John Foster Dulles, continued to blur the outlines of the emerging new planetary society by verbally dividing the existing world into "they" and "we"—"the Communists" and "the free world." The halls of the United Nations were the only place where "we" and "they" met regularly on terms approaching civility, and mainland China's continuing absence from those halls was not merely an inconvenience. In 1954 it brought on a first-class military crisis.

The Eisenhower Administration had backed away from one Cold War clash earlier that year by *not* throwing American troops, planes, and/or atomic bombs into Vietnam, as its military counselors advised and as Richard Nixon publicly suggested; the only time, in the course of six consecutive American presidencies, that the U.S. stepped backward from, rather than more deeply into, Southeast Asia. (For that act of abstinence Ike has won praise from the American Left; "at crucial moments," Marxist historian William Appleman Williams has written, Eisenhower "could and did speak two very important words: 'Enough' and 'No.'") The Administration had contained another Cold War quarrel, arising from its own CIA-backed overthrow of a militant leftist regime in Guatemala, by shunting international discussion of the Guatemala question from the Security Council of the United Nations to a Charter-sanctioned regional body, the Organization of American States, where the Western Hemisphere solidarity born of World War II could still be translated into pro-U.S. votes. But it could not similarly finesse the situation in the Formosa Strait. There, Nationalist and Communist Chinese—in the Washington jargon of the day "Chinats" and "Chicoms"—contested an irreconcilable claim of sovereignty, resembling that of the Unionists and Confederates over control of Fort Sumter in the fatal days before the Civil War—or of the Americans and Japanese over the control of the Pacific just before Pearl Harbor. "Mr. President," cried William Langer, an independent-minded Republican maverick from North Dakota, as a full-dress Senate debate on China got underway, "I have not heard a single argument on this floor that was not voiced before we got into World War II."

When Chiang Kai-shek and his regime had fled from the mainland to Formosa in 1949, his soldiers had retained toeholds on a fringe of offshore islands. Some of those troops were still there, and two garrisons in particular Chiang had strengthened in token of his vow to reconquer the mainland: the bare, rocky Matsu group just ten miles out from the port of Foochow, and the larger, more habitable Quemoys which sat within easy gun range of the city of Amoy. Given that it was a scant year since Americans had been in battle against Chinese, the situation was preposterously dangerous: what would the United States do, people kept asking Dwight Eisenhower, "if Red China or the Soviet Union were encouraging a hostile army stationed on Staten Island?"

On September 3, 1954, shore batteries on the landward side of Amoy Harbor opened fire on Quemoy. One shrewd retired U.S. brigadier general, Thomas R. Phillips, afterward maintained that the Nationalists, hoping to draw the Americans more deeply into their quarrel, deliberately mousetrapped the Communists into opening fire: Chiang's men formed up two landing craft as a dock for ships unloading military supplies in a very conspicuous T pattern within easy target range from the other shore. The tactic, if that is what it was, succeeded; and the hopeful temperate atmosphere of the UN's Ninth General Assembly was punctuated throughout its fall session by distant echoes of artillery fire off the China coast.

On December 2 the Nationalists won a diplomatic triumph in the form of a formal Mutual Defense Treaty with the United States. It said nothing about Quemoy and Matsu, and with good reason. Japan had seized Taiwan (Formosa) from China in 1894 and held it for half a century. The peace treaty that ended World War II in the Pacific took away all of the Japanese Empire's overseas possessions—but, in effect, let Japan decide to which of the Chinas it would return Taiwan. Japan, which at that time had diplomatic relations with Nationalist China, duly "returned" the island to Chiang Kai-shek. For the United States to enter into a treaty with his regime thus had some show of legitimacy; it was, after all, still formally a member of the United Nations. But Quemoy, from which a strong swimmer could easily have made it across to the land, and the Matsus were by any definition part of *mainland* China. If the United States defended the offshore islands in the course of its defense of Formosa it would be taking active part in a Chinese civil war. American policy toward the offshore islands, therefore, as expressed in the new treaty, was deliberately ambiguous.

The mainland regime challenged that ambiguity on January 18, 1955. Four thousand amphibious soldiers swarmed ashore on Yikiang [Ichiang], 200 miles north of Taiwan, and over-whelmed the Nationalist garrison. Radio Peking promptly an-nounced that the fall of Yikiang showed a "determined will to fight for the liberation of Taiwan."

On the following Monday, January 24, Eisenhower asked Congress for authority to use American forces to defend the island of Formosa and the nearby Pescadores against armed attack, and for that purpose also to secure and protect "such related positions and territories of that area now in friendly hands . . . as he judges to be required or appropriate." That *could* have meant Matsu and Quemoy; he wouldn't say. Congress had changed hands in the elections of 1954, but its new Texan leaders—Senate Majority Leader Lyndon Johnson and Speaker of the House "Mr. Sam" Rayburn—could be counted on to deliver most of their Democratic troops to the Republican administration in this kind of a showdown. Mike Mansfield, however, the Democrats' Senate whip, who was destined to follow Johnson as majority floor leader, had some disquieting questions. He criticized the way the resolution was presented, "at the beginning of a new week, after a series of hurried conferences, leaks, and rumors."

> The situation in the vicinity of Formosa is not one which lends itself to improvisation. . . . If there is an impending crisis, why did not the President come in person to present the facts to Congress? Why was the Senate not advised sooner? Crises in foreign relations are not like typhoons in the Formosa Straits. They do not arise overnight.

IV

Sometimes, however, the rush of events forces people to improvise. Such seemed to be the mood of the House of Representatives, which in true Rayburn-disciplined fashion whooped the Formosa Resolution through by a vote of 409 to 3. The Senate, however, as usual took time to think, or at least to stall. After rejecting an amendment proposed by Hubert Humphrey to exclude Quemoy and Matsu from being considered part of the defense of Formosa, the Foreign Relations Committee sent the proposal on to the floor, where William Langer, Estes Kefauver, and Herbert Lehman all offered amendments similar to Humphrey's. Lehman's drew the most votes—thirteen, from Senators who ranged from stalwart liberals like Humphrey and Wayne Morse to the veteran Virginia conservative Harry Flood Byrd.

Senator Mansfield, who voted in favor of the Lehman amendment, did not oppose the measure as a whole. "I shall vote for the joint resolution," he announced, "because circumstances leave us no other choice." But on the day the vote was taken he spoke sharp words of warning, which have the true ring of prophecy when one thinks of later foreign policy actions by Kennedy, Johnson and Nixon:

> I do not regard the term "authorize," as used in the joint resolution, as conferring additional powers on the President or as detracting from his constitutional powers. I most emphatically do not regard

it as assigning to the President the power of Congress to declare war.

Mansfield interpreted the resolution as a gamble, to prevent war by striking a bargain: "It may well be that we will not let Chiang try to go back to the mainland in exchange for Communist China's agreeing not to attack Formosa." But the gamble could fail; there might be re-ignition of the Korean conflict, or full-scale war between the U.S. and China—with the possibility that Russia, under a 1950 Soviet-Chinese treaty of alliance, could come roaring in. "I do not know which, if any, of these contingencies may develop," the Montana Senator summed up, but "let us not wake up tomorrow and confront ourselves with the question 'How did this happen? Who is responsible?' "

Ultimately, as he well knew, any decision as to what would happen along the China coast was up to Eisenhower (and, of course, Chairman Mao), regardless of what Congress did. Nonetheless Mansfield saw the Formosa Resolution as an assertion that due process really mattered, even in the nuclear age; that authority must be linked with accountability:

> Responsibility for what happens in the Formosa Strait from here on . . . rests with the President. Responsibility must be lodged where, under the Constitution, power lies. The two are inseparable, and any dilution of the bond between them is an invitation to irresponsibility and the destruction of the Republic.

But so might a Roman Senator have spoken, in a military emergency that justified a formal grant of the *imperium*; yet Roman concern for lawful and proper constitutional procedure had not, in the end, forestalled the coming of the Caesars. Underneath the American Senators' at times eloquent rhetoric, the decision came down to no empirical analysis of issues, nor any rational calculation of policy, but simply to a judgment about character. The question Americans have had to ask themselves, with increasing dismay and helplessness, of every president since the second Roosevelt has been: Dare we trust him not to go to war? Senate Foreign Relations Chairman Walter George, who ably led the floor debate on the Formosa Resolution to an eventual vote of 85 to 3, reassuringly told his colleagues: "I believe that President Eisenhower is a prudent man." But the personal worthiness of leaders, prudent or otherwise, had not originally been what the Constitution was all about. Enlightened statesmen, Madison had warned in Federalist Ten, would not always be at the helm.

The scene shifted, from the national to the international stage. On January 31, two days after Eisenhower signed the Formosa Resolution, the Security Council of the United Nations voted to ask the People's Republic of China to join the UN debate over the hostilities in the Formosa Strait. Arkady Sobolev, Vyshinsky's rather prosaic replacement, abstained, and Dr. Tsiang voted "No." "I am opposed to the proposal to invite the Communists in my country to participate in the debate," the Nationalist explained; such a course would be "morally wrong and politically foolish." Evidently the Communists in his, or their, country agreed; back came a snippy cablegram from Chou En-lai, informing the Council that the People's Republic would attend such a meeting only to discuss a Soviet resolution condemning U.S. actions in the Formosa Strait as aggression (which the Council, before issuing its own invitation, had defeated 10-1), and only after "the representative of the Chiang Kai-shek clique has been driven out." It was the Red Queen's Race, as described to Alice; in the land on the other side of the looking-glass it took all the running you could do to stay in the same place!

Dwight Eisenhower's next move, in which Chiang Kai-Shek perforce concurred, was to shorten Formosa's military defensive lines. On the Tachen Islands, which were 15 miles off the Asian shore, 200 miles north of Taiwan, and only 7.5 miles from recently fallen Yikiang, a full division of Chiang's troops and several guerrilla outfits shared the rocky crags with civilian fishing villages having names like Halfway to Heaven. Their situation was precarious at best, and on February 5 the Seventh Fleet received orders to take them off. The Tachen evacuation proved highly successful. Fifteen thousand civilians and all the regular troops in the islands were moved to Taiwan, while the guerrillas— —some of whom the year before, using a "weird mixture of fifth-century junk and sampan transport combined with twentieth-century firepower," had scored a notable victory over a crack mainland unit that had fought in Korea—settled down in Quemoy. Meanwhile, men from the remote frontiers of China were streaming toward the southeast coast, while ships and planes from all over the planet moved toward the Formosa Strait.

The situation everywhere had become unbearably tense. In Europe, the promisingly effective government of Pierre Mendès-France fell, in the same capricious way as had all its postwar French predecessors; and so, more joltingly, did that of Premier Malenkov of the Soviet Union. Georgi Zhukov, a much-decorated war hero, became the USSR's new defense minister, in just the kind of cabinet reorganization which in the past had often signaled that a nation was about to go to war; compare Japan's in the fall of 1941. A still more threatening signal came from Foreign Minister Vyacheslav Molotov, the one surviving top-level Old Bolshevik from the bad days under Stalin, who in a major foreign policy address on February 8 bluntly denied the idea—beginning to take root in the Soviet Union as well as in the west—that nuclear war endangered not merely capitalism or socialism, but humanity as a whole. "What will perish will not be world civilization," Molotov declared, "but it will be that rotten social system with its imperialist basis soaked in blood." The news of that dreadful speech hit the American papers on the 9th, together with news that an American plane assisting in the Tachen evacuation had been shot down.

The Senate the same day finally, and anticlimatically, approved the formal Mutual Defense Treaty with Nationalist China, 64–6, after rejecting by 60 votes to 10 another anti-Quemoy amendment from its great gadfly, Senator Wayne Morse; and Dwight Eisenhower went before his regular weekly press conference to field questions on the Soviet cabinet upheaval and on the shooting down of that AD Skyraider twenty miles southwest of the Tachens. Eisenhower studiously avoided any bellicose note of "Remember the *Maine!*" "In one case," he said quietly, "I believe one of our planes got a little lost, wandered in a bad area and got hit, but the crew was saved"—reducing it almost, on both sides, to the level of a kids' prank. His response to the news from Russia was even more pacific; it prompted him to reminisce of old times in postwar Berlin where he and Marshal Zhukov had become good friends. Zhukov, he recalled, had presented Ike on his birthday with an "enormous bear rug." It is necessary to think and feel one's way back into the mood of the fifties to realize how remarkable a statement this was. Can one imagine Adlai Stevenson, had he been president, being permitted by the McCarthy-inflamed Right to indulge in fond recollection of a top Soviet leader as an old and true friend? Harry Truman had gotten into considerable trouble merely for remarking "I like old Joe." It was at times like these that what Eisenhower said was not nearly so important as who he was.

V

Nevertheless, for some Americans—others, of course, ignoring world affairs, preferred to watch TV game shows—the tension continued, as winter turned into a cruelly lovely spring. Through an open window in a crumbling old vine-covered college building hundreds of miles from the Pentagon and the UN, late one fresh leaf and flower scented April evening, came a thunderous explosion. Two casually conversing students put down their mugs of "choffee"—powdered chocolate mixed with instant coffee, a potent pre-exam energizer—and sat bolt upright. After an aching silence, one of them voiced what both had felt: "I thought New York had gone up."

Across the land people waited, holding their collective breath—and, gradually, they began to exhale. The crisis was not solved; it receded, like a fever. Russia unexpectedly signed a State Treaty for Austria, and after a decade of military occupation the American, British, French, and Soviet soldiers all marched away. Late in April, Chou En-lai came in triumph to Bandung, Indonesia, to a conference of all the Asian and African nations—the first such gathering in history—and talked of peace with the U.S. By the end of May in the Formosa Strait the shooting had stopped; yet Chiang Kai-shek's troops remained in place on Quemoy and Matsu. Rejecting all the experts' advice as to what ought to be done, from liquidating Chiang to joining him in a holy war of liberation, the Eisenhower Administration's own plan—awkward, illogical, incomplete, ethically questionable, and legally dubious—had worked. It rattled the Bomb and scared hell out of the world; but when the showdown came, the gunfighter's hands remained away from his holsters and he didn't draw.

The French have a devastating political proverb: "Nothing is as permanent as the provisional." Few could have foreseen in 1955 that the policy Americans had thus improvised toward Taiwan would outlive all of the three major protagonists—Dwight Eisenhower, Mao Tse-tung, and Chiang Kai-shek. In 1958, three years after the first ominous confrontation, the fever flared again, with renewed shellings of the offshore islands; and when it subsided Chiang's troops were still camped there. They were still there in 1960, when Quemoy and Matsu figured in the televised presidential campaign debate between Richard Nixon and John Kennedy. They were still there in 1972, after Nixon had visited mainland China and after the Nationalists had lost their seat at the UN. Even after Jimmy Carter finally abrogated Ike's Mutual Defense Treaty with Taiwan, relegating that realm to an unrecognized diplomatic limbo, Nationalist troops still sat on Quemoy!

Episodes like this had happened in China before. The last time a native Chinese dynasty had fallen—the Ming, in the seventeenth century—adherents of the defeated regime had held out for another generation on the island of Taiwan. History may not repeat itself, but it has a way of playing variations on the same tunes; perhaps Chiang Ching-kuo, son of Chiang Kai-shek, who succeeded his father in Taipei in 1975 as President of the Republic of China, was fated to play out the role of those last Ming loyalists three hundred years ago.

Time passed, at the UN as in the Formosa Strait. Some of the cracks in the mirror to the world began to be mended. In the fall of 1955 the superpowers stopped reflexively vetoing each other's nominees for admission to the United Nations, and fifteen countries came in as a package deal. That action erased the World War II basis for membership (the package even included the sole remaining Fascist power, Spain), and gave the world organization a powerful push toward universality. Sporadic nuisance use of the veto continued from time to time, but a day was soon coming when almost the only countries not in the UN would be the ones that were physically divided: the two Germanies, the two Koreas, the larger of the two Chinas, and the two Vietnams. Meanwhile, with each new Assembly session, the UN seemed to be acting less like an ideological boxing arena and more like Congress.

Universality, however, did not mean members' immunity from each other's aggressions—as Hungary would learn, to its sorrow, within a year of its admission. Nor did it spare the organization's Western members from those "sharp clashes of debate" into which the U.S. President in his Minneapolis address had said they were bound to fall. One such clash in particular, occurring just before Eisenhower's first term ended, wrenched the North American and West European nations' most basic mutual ties. No verbal battles between nations the size of Belgium and Uruguay were going to shake the planet, but a quarrel which could lead Britain and France to use their UN Security Council vetoes against the U.S. was quite another story.

On July 26, 1956, Gamal Abdel Nasser, leader of Egypt, nationalized "the world's foremost public utility," the Suez Canal. The once mighty British Empire of late had suffered many humiliations, and to the Tory government then in power in London this was the last straw. Prime Minister Anthony Eden promptly cabled President Eisenhower that he proposed, if necessary, to "bring Nasser to his senses" by force. As in Britain's greater days, gunboats flying the Union Jack were again going to awe the natives—in this case the "Gyppos," as militant Britons and even some Canadians were calling the people of the Nile.

Ike was on the spot. The leaders of the United Kingdom were his old comrades-in-arms; several members of the British cabinet he counted among his personal friends. At the same time he and Dulles considered Nasser's action, however high-handed, to have been well within the legal rights of a sovereign nation; and from his own experience with the Panama Canal, as a young officer stationed there thirty years earlier, Eisenhower doubted Eden's argument that the technical operation and management of traffic through Suez was too complicated to be left to mere Egyptians. On July 31, therefore, replying to Eden, he strongly opposed using military force against Nasser. "I can scarcely describe the depth of the regret I feel in the need to take a view so diametrically opposed to that held by the British," he afterward wrote. "Yet I felt that in taking our own position we were standing firmly on principle and on the realities of the twentieth century." How quaint and old-fashioned that notion now sounds, that one could stand on principle and on reality at the same time!

The British—and their French allies, who perceived Egypt's revolutionary nationalist leader as a potential new Mussolini who must be squelched at the outset—went ahead with their plans, not troubling to inform the Americans of what they were doing. Just as the presidential campaign rerun between Eisenhower and Stevenson went into its home stretch, the world and its cracked but at times serviceable mirror, the United Nations, fell into not one but *three* interrelated crises. "The Presidency," Eisenhower later wryly observed, "seldom affords the luxury of dealing with one problem at a time."

VI

On October 21, Poland's Communist Party won an important round in its never-ending tug of war with Moscow: facing down no less weighty a visitor than Nikita Krushchev himself, it ousted a Red Army field marshal as that country's Minister of Defense. In Budapest, encouraged by the Polish defiance, students and other demonstrators paraded, petitioned, and tore down a statue of Stalin that stood in a public square. Next day (the 24th), Soviet tanks rolled into the city, to be faced unexpectedly by furious Hungarians armed with Molotov cocktails. The United Nations Security Council had barely begun to deal with that upheaval when Israel, on October 29, resumed its UN-interrupted war with Egypt, driving 75 miles into Sinai toward the Canal. That evening, touching down in Washington after a typically strenuous day of political campaigning, Eisenhower huddled with his advisors and told them: "We plan to get to the United Nations the first thing in the morning—when the doors open, before the U.S.S.R. gets there."

The first thing Henry Lodge did at the United Nations the next morning, accordingly, was to introduce a resolution calling for a cease-fire between Egypt and Israel. Debate on his proposal was just getting into high gear when news arrived that Britain and France had issued an ultimatum: unless the fighting stopped within twelve hours, they would militarily occupy key positions near the Suez Canal. Smoothly, UK delegate Sir Pierson Dixon suggested that "in the interest of security and peace" nothing would be gained by further consideration of the U.S. resolution. However, if the British and French had assumed that the United States in a crunch must perforce stand with its longtime allies, they were mistaken. With an ultimatum due to expire at 11:30 P.M. New York time—four hours away—Soviet delegate Sobolev announced that he was prepared to vote in favor of the U.S. resolution. On the show of hands, Lodge and Sobolev voted together; the count was 7-2, and the motion lost because Britain and France both used their power of veto. A Soviet substitute resolution also lost, for the same reason; and in the debate preceding that second vote Sobolev actually accepted an amendment offered by the Kuomintang's Dr. Tsiang!

In the course of the Korean War the UN had devised a formula for getting around such a Security Coucil deadlock. On October 31, using that machinery, the General Assembly took up Lodge's resolution and passed it 64-5, with only Britain, France, Israel, Australia, and New Zealand voting "no." Dag Hammarskjøld immediately began recruiting a United Nations Emergency Force to keep the peace. But the two Western European powers went ahead with their plan anyhow, dropping first bombs and then paratroops along the canal. As former Prime Minister Winston Churchill tried to explain, "Not for the first time we have acted independently for the common good."

Britain's venerable war leader was strongly seconded in this country by Eleanor Roosevelt and Adlai Stevenson. Both had had a personal hand in shaping the United Nations in its earliest years, but now in the heat of a presidential campaign both argued that in this moment of truth the United States ought to be standing with its traditional Western European allies. Dulles and Eisenhower emphatically disagreed. Aggression, they maintained, regardless of who committed it, or against whom, was still aggression. "There can be no peace without law," Eisenhower declared. "And there can be no law if we were to invoke one code of international conduct for those who oppose us and another for our friends."

On November 5, 1956—Election Day in the U.S.—the Western European invaders of Egypt, although by that time physically in possession of the entire Suez Canal, abandoned their quest and agreed to a cease-fire. Quite aside from the American stand against the invasion, the great danger existed that a Soviet threat to use rocket weapons was not a brinkman's bluff. As the British reluctantly withdrew from their last imperialist venture, leaving the field to the blue-helmeted troops of the UN, Eisenhower sought to mend his own torn international fences. "To invade Egypt merely because that country had chosen to nationalize a company," he wrote to Churchill on November 27, "would raise a storm of resentment that, within the Arab states, would result in a long and dreary guerrilla warfare." Sensible words, these; a kind of good sense we can now wish had been shown by more recent presidents who were considered more worldly-wise than Ike.

Many academic intellectuals in the fifties strongly disagreed with Eisenhower's Suez decision; Hans Morgenthau, for example, called it "The Decline and Fall of American Foreign Policy." For politically conscious professors and journalists this was a strange retreat from their former emphatic stand for the United Nations; not long since they had faulted isolationist Republicans for showing narrow-minded hostility to the UN. Some conservatives, however, also criticized the President, for bearing down on Britain and France while Russia, unchecked, worked its bloody will in Hungary. Still, Eisenhower had his defenders. "Our policy on Suez," wrote a citizen in Berkeley, California, "has been made by a kindly sixty-six-year-old amateur golfer whose evident ignorance of the complexities of international relations has made it possible for him to see without the sophistication of *Realpolitik* the clear moral issues involved. . . . Men of good will who hope to see the jungle civilized one day should support him." This effort to civilize the jungle by strengthening the material and moral credibility of the United Nations as a maker of international policy was a high moment for America in the world—by dismal contrast to the situation a quarter-century later in 1981, when the American government could not even bring itself to endorse an overwhelming UN consensus for the prevention of polluted baby food, and in 1982, when Lodge's successor as chief of the US delegation, Jeane Kirkpatrick, would charge—all too truly—that what went on in the UN Security Council and General Assembly had become "a very dismal show" in which conflicts were worsened rather than resolved.

Nor did Eisenhower and most of his opponents foresee certain moral and material issues that lay a few more years down history's road, such as those arising from the energy anxieties of the seventies. An occasional amateur prophet, however, foretold them. John J. Kupka, an engineer in New Jersey, taking exception to a statement by Mike Mansfield that the Eisenhower Administration's actions in the Suez "bordered on appeasement of Egyptian arrogance," wrote to Mansfield on October 16, 1956 that the real basis of the Suez Canal dispute was oil. Dulles and Eisenhower, he argued, were looking realistically toward a time when America would need the good will of indigenous peoples "who alone will have the power of say-so regarding the disposition of their oil." Meanwhile, intelligent legislators ought to be attacking the problem of U.S. domestic fuel consumption. Dieselization of the railroads, Kupka declared, "should be stopped right now!" Americans should shift to coal and, where feasible, atomic energy. The engineer's language was even less elegant than Eisenhower's but his meaning was crashingly clear:

> The per capita oil consumption of each American is today over 2½ gals per day. The average Asiatic does not consume more than One Two Hundredth part of a gallon of oil per day. Dear Senator, how long do you think it will be, before the Asiatic minds will wake up to the fact, that they are being robbed of the greatest treasure, their oil, for a mere mess of pottage. . . .
> So please, dear Senator Mansfield, do not attack our beloved Ike on the score of his policy in the Middle East. You would do much better, if you were to attack our oil companies instead.

Attacking the oil companies was not then an American political pastime. The fifties were notoriously an era of big, gorgeous, gas-guzzling V-8 engines. And Ike's oil policy was more shady than the letter-writer perhaps realized. It included American support in Iran, which had attempted to nationalize Anglo-Iranian Oil, for a counterrevolutionary coup in 1953 on behalf of the Shah. However, the challenge of the deposed leader, Dr. Mossadegh, to big Western oil was evidence that Asiatic (and other Third World) minds were indeed waking up to the loss of their treasure. In 1960 the major petroleum producing states founded OPEC, and that mess of pottage began to be translated

into petrodollars—a few of which even found their way into
the pockets of the people making do with less than 1/200 gallon
per day.

More recently, and especially since the 1973–4 "energy recession," OPEC's annual price-setting conferences have become as
fraught with drama as any regular session of the Security Council
or General Assembly of the United Nations. To the prospect
of the "long and dreary guerrilla warfare" in the Middle East of
which Eisenhower warned Churchill has been added the world-
wide prospect of petrochemical shortages, ruinously expensive
petroleum-based agricultural chemicals, and ecologically disastrous oil spills. Science fiction writer Fritz Leiber suggested
in one of his stories that our planet's oil supply is collectively
alive, with a malign will of its own: "Created from the lush
vegetation and animal fats of the Carboniferous and adjoining
periods, holding in itself the black essence of all life that had
ever been, . . . oil had waited for hundreds of millions of years,
dreaming its black dreams, . . . until a being evolved on the
surface with whom it could live symbiotically and through whom
it could realize and expend itself." The metaphor is eerily close
to reality. Today, at times, international order and disorder
seem reflected not so much in a cracked political-diplomatic
mirror beside the East River as in a dark, iridescent pool of oil.

PART TWO
THE INTELLECTUAL LIFE

CHAPTER FOUR
"I Wandered Lonely as a Crowd"

I

IN political life if you are not visibly in motion you're dead. Adlai Stevenson, as he roamed through the wilderness that stretched between the 1952 and 1956 presidential campaigns, visited thirty countries on the hither side of the Iron Curtain and turned his reflections upon that experience into the Godkin Lectures he gave at Harvard—an echo, muted by the Cold War, of the similar globe-trotting experience that had generated Wendell Willkie's great book *One World*. Standing under the dark wooden arches of Harvard's musty Victorian Gothic Memorial Chapel in February 1954, Stevenson reintroduced himself to the liberal arts intelligentsia, from which in 1952 he had drawn his most ardent support, with "those classic words that never occurred to Horace: 'Via ovicipitum dura est,' or, for the benefit of the engineers among you: 'The way of the egghead is hard.'" Then he launched into the first of three lectures on "A Troubled World."

In the course of his personal odyssey during the fifties through that troubled world Adlai visited many other academic halls, ivied or otherwise. One such trip in June of 1955 took him to Smith College, where he delivered the commencement address. It was not, as it had been before in American history and would be again, a time for advising, in the same way one would advise young men, the graduates of a woman's college to go out and

change the world or fulfill their personal potential. Down the
road a few miles the house mothers at Smith's sister and rival
Mount Holyoke were instructing their charges in an ideology
of "Gracious Living"; behind its high green-painted fence in
roaring New York, Barnard College more sophisticatedly called
it "Modern Living." Both slogans had heavy overtones of con-
sumerism or, more bluntly, housewifery. Stevenson, articulating
the political morality of his day, in his address at Smith merely
gave this derivative role a liberal arts, "Humanities" veneer.

"You may be hitched to one of these creatures we call 'Western
man,'" he told the "Smith girls"—as they were still called even
among themselves; nobody was yet insisting they be referred
to, and treated, as women—"and I think part of your job is to
keep him Western, to keep him truly purposeful, to keep him
whole." No notion here that part of their job might be to keep

"I think part of your job is to keep him Western, to keep him truly purposeful,
to keep him whole."—Adlai Stevenson.

themselves "Western"—whatever that might mean—as well as "purposeful and whole"; their destined role in the world was to give purpose and wholeness to their men. Was that really *all* there was to life for the college-educated woman, Margaret Mead was to ask just seven years later—"Are we going to accept the popular thesis that every adult woman who isn't conspicuously occupied with married life every minute . . . has something wrong with her? Are we going to perpetuate the distrust of every woman who genuinely wishes to devote herself to work?"

But Mead would say that in 1962, after considerable national consciousness-raising had begun. Adlai Stevenson in 1955, admitting in his typical self-deprecating fashion that he personally had "had very little experience as a wife or mother," was lyrical in praise of the role: "This assignment for you, as wives and mothers, has great advantages," he lectured. "In the first place, it is home work—you can do it in the living room with a baby in your lap, or in the kitchen with a can opener in your hands. If you're really clever maybe you can even practice your saving arts on that unsuspecting man while he's watching television." In the near future, Smith alumnae such as Gloria Steinem and Betty Friedan would respond, fully and adeptly, to Adlai's inane remarks.

A few of those unsuspecting men in the Class of 1955 on twenty U.S. university campuses were interviewed that same year in a study commissioned by *Time* Magazine. What did they want in the women they would marry, who if they were lucky would keep them Western, truly purposeful, and whole? His hypothetical wife-to-be, one Princeton senior replied, would be "vivacious and easy with people. And she will belong to everything in sight too—especially the League of Women Voters." "She shouldn't be submissive," a Harvard man responded, "she can be independent on little things, but the big decisions will have to go my way." She shouldn't be a "career girl," but neither should she be "a stay-at-home wife"; what these men seemed to be after, commented sociologist David Riesman, who studied

these interviews, was "a presentable date." Another Princetonian
spelled it out in dreary, preppy detail:

> Yes, I can describe my wife. She will be the Grace Kelly, camel's
> hair coat type. Feet on the ground, and not an empty shell or
> fake. Although an Ivy League type, she will also be centered in
> the home, a housewife. Perhaps at forty-five, with the children
> grown up, she will go in for hospital work and so on.

"If they're *that* good," Riesman cautioned, "they may not want
these boys; after all, Grace Kelly has had a career and married
a prince." Subsequent divorce statistics have evidently borne
him out.

Stevenson's speech, and Riesman's findings, amply corrobo-
rated what Simone de Beauvoir had said in *The Second Sex* concerning the plight of woman: "The truth is that for man she is
an amusement, a pleasure, company, an inessential boon; he is
for her the meaning, the justification of her existence." *The
Second Sex,* published in France in 1949, had come out in America,
with an excellent translation, early in 1953. Word of it passed
from woman student to woman student, on many of those same
campuses where the men looked forward to home-centered,
feet-on-the-ground wives in camel's hair coats, and where some
of the women had begun to have misgivings about "that nice
little pattern that everyone wants to fit into; the cheery little
marriage and the husband working to get ahead on his job, the
wife being a clubwoman and helping her husband to advance,"
as one senior woman at Wisconsin put it. Simone de Beauvoir
gave to many such women what Betty Friedan would give many
more of them in *The Feminine Mystique* (1963): the saving sense
that *someone else knows.*

This was not, however, the effect *The Second Sex* had in the
fifties within the literary media which presumed to dictate what
was intellectually *à la mode.* With the distinguished exception of
Brendan Gill (in *The New Yorker*), even the critics who liked and
admired Beauvoir's work felt obliged to apologize for it. The
book was "not a petulant defense of her sex," Clyde Kluckhohn

wrote in the *New York Times;* its purpose was "to explain women, not to convert or reform," Ashley Montagu commented in the *Herald Tribune.* Yet even Montagu, who praised the book highly, hedged by saying he didn't think Beauvoir understood *American* women very well. So also Margaret Mead, who accused Beauvoir of the typical French intellectual's "bland identification of France as 'the modern world,' so that the past was a prelude to French civilization, and the present and future are seen uncritically in French terms."

Those were the minor caveats and exceptions. Many critics were far more hostile, and unfortunately some of the most cutting comments came from women. Miriam Allen de Ford in the *San Francisco Chronicle* termed *The Second Sex* "disappointing and unsatisfactory . . . a mountain which labors mightily and produces a very small and shopworn mouse"; while Phyllis McGinley, as she bustled around in her media role as the happy and fulfilled housewife-poet, called the book "curiously old-fashioned"—a "sublimation of feminist arguments we all advanced at seventeen" and have, presumably, since outgrown.

Among the male critics of *The Second Sex,* Karl Menninger played the typical psychiatrist's gambit, whereby a social grievance is transmuted into personal neurosis: "What Mademoiselle de Beauvoir assumes to be the natural meanness of males in the depreciation and exploitation of women proves upon examination . . . to be the avenging on the contemporary woman of resentments inculcated by an earlier woman." In other words, if a man treats a woman badly he is not ultimately to blame, nor is his sexist male-bonded culture; it's all Mom's fault. Americans already knew about Mom—that devouring, man-shriveling matriarch—from James Thurber's stories and cartoons depicting her menacing unloveliness, and from Philip Wylie's vivid account of her misdeeds in *Generation of Vipers* (1942). Wylie, by his own admission "the leading critic of females" in America, considered *The Second Sex* "one of the few great books of the era," which no one could leave unread "and still be considered intellectually up-to-date"; according to Wylie, Beauvoir had stated the problem correctly, but her solution was all wrong.

The popular hortatory literature of the fifties variously portrayed "the American woman" as a spoiled princess; as an emotional cripple *(Modern Woman: the Lost Sex);* as Mom; or supposedly more favorably, as SuperMom. One male writer in 1954 contrasted her with the legendary and largely mythical frivolous flapper of the Jazz Age: "Miss America of the 'twenties was the honey-pot of the merry Oldsmobile," Lovell Thompson wrote. "Taller, broader, leaner, darker, older, Miss America of the 'fifties, strapping and strapless, is the girl in the steel station wagon with safety belts"; she "is beautifully built for a stern purpose." No wonder Adlai Stevenson, blissfully unaware of the numbing reality of that station-wagon-driver's situation, could tell a graduating class of young women that the final goal of the splendid education Smith was giving them was to Serve Man!

II

What did it mean for a man to be Western, truly purposeful, and whole? Westernness, for Adlai Stevenson and his liberal Democratic intellectual allies—as well as for their Republican adversaries, albeit in a somewhat different, more consciously economic way—had something to do with individuality. Ike, as campaigner and as President, often proclaimed the unique worth of every person as a basic American value, shared—one hoped— with America's variously acquired allies (the "free world"). Stevenson, as campaigner and as lecturer, translated that axiom into terms of freshman "Western Civ."

"Since Western rationalism and Eastern spiritualism met in Athens," Adlai told the Smith students, "collectivism in various forms has collided with individualism time and again." The American generation which fought World War II had collided with collectivism in its most blatant forms: the Nazi mystagogue, submerging the rational individual psyche in the blood-wisdom of the *Volk,* or the *kamikaze,* transcending the self in an ecstatic act of death for the Emperor. Now a new generation—the warrior-Americans' younger brothers and sisters—faced the collectivist menace in a more insidious form. The challenge overseas, as Stevenson had seen it on his round-the-world tour, was the rivalry for allegiance of the uncommitted Third World between Revolution in its "Western," individualistic mode, as proclaimed by Thomas Jefferson, and revolution in its "Eastern," collectivist form, as heralded by Karl Marx. The threat at home, however, did not come from Marx's followers—they were, comparatively, few and powerless—but from an organized corporate system which didn't want any revolution at all.

That system, existing in an intricate and complex modern technical world, in order to function efficiently required people to concentrate and specialize their lives. To specialize is to limit; and to limit is to cripple. "I think one of the biggest jobs for many of you," Stevenson told those Smith seniors, "will be to frustrate the crushing and corruptive effects of specialization, to integrate ends and means, to develop that balanced tension of mind and spirit which can be properly called 'integrity.'" How that integrity was to be developed if half the human species did not share in the development he did not make clear. Nevertheless, the task he assigned to the young women of the Class of 1955 was "important work worthy of you, whoever you are, or your education, whatever it is, because we will defeat totalitarian, authoritarian ideas only by better ideas; we will frustrate the evils of vocational specialization only by the virtues of intellectual generalities." The twentieth-century collision between individualism and collectivism, "this crisis we are forever talking about, will be won not on the battlefield but in the head and heart."

Stevenson's outlook was widely shared in the fifties among academic intellectuals. At then all-male Wesleyan University, whose graduates were expected to go out and *do* some of the world's work which their wives (not a few of whom no doubt came from Smith) were expected merely to support, the school's eloquent president Victor Butterfield told the students on one occasion that if they amorally pursued their specialties by narrow professional or crass money-making standards, without reference to general questions of value, they would be only a generation of "able fascists." Phrases like Adlai's "balanced tension of mind and spirit" occurred so often in commencement addresses, remarks at alumni luncheons, and college chapel talks that they became clichés.

Much in this polemic remains attractive. The youth generation destined to slump into despond and cynicism after the brief rebelliousness of the sixties would get similarly bad marks for narrow vocationalism or for an even more narrow "narcissism," as Christopher Lasch has called it; and Stevenson's attack on corruptive, soul-distorting specialization had prophetic overtones of Herbert Marcuse's far more radical attack on "one-dimensional man." There *was* a generalist, "liberal arts" renaissance after the Second World War, signaled by a now all-but-forgotten book by Fred Millett, *The Rebirth of Liberal Education* (1945). In the fifties it was riding high and much that it accomplished was good. Nevertheless, the ideals Adlai Stevenson held up for young people at that time have disquieting implications.

There is in the first place the simple question of elitism. While the Ivy graduates were busy frustrating the evils of vocational specialization by the virtues of intellectual generalities, who would be doing the intricate work which of its nature *had* to be specialized—or the more general all-purpose work which was merely necessary and dull? Did those who failed to develop that "balanced tension of mind and spirit which can properly be called 'integrity'" therefore lack integrity? And could such a balance be developed only through formal education? "There is no more merit in having read a thousand books," said Somerset Maugham—transcending his own British culture's elitism—"than in having ploughed a thousand fields. There is no more merit in being able to attach a correct description to a picture than in being able to find out what is wrong with a stalled motorcar."

The generalist concept of vocation also runs into a diametrically opposed vision which can be pursued with equal integrity. "Whatsoever thy hand findeth to do, do it with thy might," said the Preacher (Eccles. 9:10). The champion athlete, subordinating personal life to training; the virtuoso musician, living in and for the music; the absent-minded scientist, leaving food untouched at the laboratory door—these, too, are as much lopsided vocational specialists as the executive who brings paperwork home from the office or the politician who is constantly on the phone, and Western Civilization would be poorer without them. Most such men do end up "hitched," to use Stevenson's inelegant term, and what are *their* women supposed to do to keep them Western? An unliberated wife in that situation is almost bound to find it maddeningly "no-win": her choice is to distract or to stay out of the way. Quite likely, in the suburban culture that came to fruition in the fifties, her role would become one not so much of bringing Western values into her man's life as of substituting for him as a consumer of those values. This is the classic Victorian-bourgeois stereotype, of the tired, tin-eared businessman dragged to the opera or symphony by his wife.

Moreover, the sequence of Stevenson's argument, pairing the defeat of totalitarian, authoritarian ideas with the frustration of vocational-specialist evils, suggests that the integration of ends and means, mind and spirit was subordinate to another purpose. He may not have intended it this way, but when he said that the individualist/collectivist crisis of the twentieth century would be won not on the battlefield but in the head and heart he seemed also to be saying that the head and heart had become a battlefield. Those young women whom he told to keep their future spouses Western, truly purposeful, and whole would thus, as they did their jobs with baby in lap or can opener in hand, hearten and energize those husbands to carry on in the Cold War. And of course that was what Western Civiliztion had expected women to do for their men in all its wars. Kay Summersby in the fifties had not yet told her full story—she, and others who knew it, remained discreetly silent during Eisenhower's political years—but when she did, in *Past Forgetting* (1976), she described (and subtly justified) her relationship with Ike in the dangerous times around D-Day as one of having helped him to keep whole while he fought his war.

For some husbands, that part of Stevenson's message which cautioned against specialization may have been wide of the mark. The men in the Class of 1955 whom David Riesman studied seemed relatively free from narrowly focused vocationalism; "The career they want is to find the good life." Many of them self-consciously contrasted that goal with their own fathers' nose-to-the-grindstone workaholism and lone-wolf cantankerousness. For these young men Western wholeness was *not* conceived in individualistic terms; they would serve their time in the armed forces (not making much fuss about it), marry, move to the suburbs—successively different suburbs, as they moved up the advancement ladder—and settle in for the long haul in a professional office or large corporation which would thereafter finance the Good Life.

The boundaries of that life, however, seemed to be the backyard barbecue and the small social group. The Princeton youth whose vivacious wife was going to be active in the League of Women Voters announced that he was going to "belong to all the associations you can think of—Elks, V.F.W.'s, Boy Scouts and Boys' Clubs, Y.M.C.A., American Legion, etc."—but all of them conceived as extensions of private life rather than as vehicles for public action. A Michigan student said he would like "to work with the youth of the community, especially in athletics," but he made it plain that his community activities would definitely not include politics: "I hate to say anything against politicians, but they just waste too much time . . . I want to live my own life, not a public life." This was in startling contrast to the Western political tradition which Stevenson praised. The Athenians and their allies who had routed the collectivist Persian hordes, thereby launching the whole notion of a Western "free world," had insisted that public life *is* the good life; man in contrast to other species, said Aristotle, is a political animal. In contrast, most of Riesman's collegians asked about the political future found the topic boring. They seemed deliberately to limit themselves to the same private universe to which society had long since consigned their women, although they at least were able to get out to the office.

The nonpolitical sphere afforded ample opportunity for purpose and wholeness, of course, as it always has. But the iron law of "togetherness" (a term *McCall's* coined in the fifties), which set a moral requirement that family members do things together or else not do them at all, if consistently applied would shut off *both* partners in a marriage from further individual development, Western or otherwise. "It is safer," Margaret Mead observed in 1960 of such marriages, "to read what both agree with (or not to read at all and simply look at TV together), attend the same clubs, listen to the same jokes—never for a minute relaxing their possession of each other, just as when they were teen-agers." Caught up in the baby boom, they would not have had surplus energy for anything else anyhow. The U.S. population was expanding at a rate comparable to India's, and among young Americans of that generation approval of that explosion seemed absolute and unquestionable. "I'd like six kids," one of Riesman's young men remarked. "I don't know why I say that—it just seems like a minimum production goal."

III

"A world populated by the men who appear in these interviews, and by the girls they almost without exception have in mind," David Riesman concluded, "would be a decent world; nobody in it would blow up or blow it up." If his own generation—the Class of 1931, which had experienced so much active history— managed "to live the next fifteen years in such a world, we may count our bland blessings," although some among them might not regret that they had lived for their own first fifteen post-graduate years "in a world of passion and turmoil." A major philosophical problem for *any* generation, however, is that it considers its own time to be the culmination of human history and imagines that its present is the future's blueprint. But that is rarely the way it happens. Fifteen years past 1955 would land them all, young and old, in 1970—the year of the U.S. invasion of Cambodia and the shootings at Kent State and Jackson State universities; hardly a time free from passion and turmoil. In 1970, scholars of Riesman's stature would not be describing a decent world in which nobody would blow up. They would talk instead of "counterculture," and of youths they judged to be permanently and irrevocably "radicalized." In 1955, all unaware of this different future, they were talking about "conformity"— and some of them were much more worried about it than Riesman was.

Team spirit; Groupthink; Togetherness; "Love that System!" William H. Whyte summed them all up in his cutting study of *The Organization Man* (1956). Others wrote, sometimes quite entertainingly, about secondary symptoms of the new conformism; about the endless acres of look-alike split-level tract housing, with their forests of television antennae tuned to the same program. The author of *The Organization Man*, however, was after bigger philosophical game. He argued that the Protestant Ethic of full individual moral responsibility for one's actions— and, he should have added, the Renaissance ideal of self-realization—had become subverted by a Social Ethic, which Whyte defined as "that contemporary body of thought which makes morally legitimate the pressures of society against the individual." Its catechism could be construed thus:

> Man exists as a unit of society. Of himself he is isolated, meaningless; only as he collaborates with others does he become worthwhile, for by sublimating himself in the group, he helps produce a whole that is greater than the sum of its parts. There should be, then, no conflict between man and society. What we think are conflicts are misunderstandings, breakdowns in communication. By applying the methods of science to human relations we can eliminate these obstacles to consensus and create an equilibrium in which

society's needs and the needs of the individual are one and the same.

So much for Emerson's bold, self-reliant cry "Whoso would be a man, must be a nonconformist." Whoso would be a woman, the dominant voices of the fifties insisted, must conform totally; and now it appeared that whoso would be a man, if he does not wish to be considered neurotic, must do likewise. From the coffee-(or martini-) fueled conference rooms in government, business, or grant-giving foundations, with their "brainstorming" sessions that produced many slogans but few ideas, to the "progressive" schoolrooms where kids learned little reading and less math but a great deal (such schools claimed) about good citizenship and getting along with other people, the Organization sought to legislate the ornery, free-standing individual out of existence.

Whyte did not say much about McCarthyism, or other overt forms of ideological coercion. To the organization minion, "the real issue is far more subtle. For it is not the evils of organization that puzzle him, *but its very beneficence.* He is imprisoned in brotherhood"—and, in the relatively affluent fifties his imprisonment often paid him well. Yet he must not submit. "He must *fight* the organization," the author led off the book's closing paragraph. He must remain vigilantly aware of what he is fighting, "for the demands for his surrender are constant and powerful, and the more he has come to like the life of organization the more difficult does he find it to resist these demands, or even to recognize them." What the old-fashioned tyrant "wanted primarily from you was your sweat. The new man wants your soul."

It was, in fact, in organized society's own ultimate interest that you fight it. "If every member simply wants to do what the group wants to do," Whyte tartly observed, "then the group is not going to do anything." The same society that believed in "security" also believed in "progress." But progress, except in a grossly quantitative way (more and more of the same old garbage), requires innovation; and who is going to innovate except the nonconformist?

How, then, does an individual fight the system? "Not self-destructively," Whyte cautioned; "he may tell the boss to go to hell, but he is going to have another boss." And not egocentrically: "The defects of individual self-regard are no more to be venerated than the defects of co-operation." What he must learn to do is use the Organization against itself. He must learn, for example, to cheat on personality tests, so that he will slip through the Organization's screening nets, seeming to accept its values while actually retaining his individuality. (In a helpful Appendix, Whyte explained in concrete detail how to do this; for example, when asked word-association questions or for "comments about the world," the writer advised, "give the most conventional, run-of-the-mill, pedestrian answer possible.") Thus, the Organization Man as he rises within the system obtains leverage upon it; "and with wisdom and foresight he can turn the future away from the dehumanized collective that so haunts our thoughts"—the kind of collective that was depicted in George Orwell's *1984*.

Nothing more clearly illustrates the difference between the temper of the fifties and that of the decade which was to follow than this anticlimactic conclusion to *The Organization Man*. As a diagnostic analysis, the book was brilliant; thirty years later its pages on the homely details of life in an Organizational suburb, for example, can still be read with profit. The advice it offered, however—*evade, don't confront*—would be indignantly rejected by social critics in the sixties, for whom confrontation was the very essence of social progress. To translate Whyte's issues into their rhetoric, the truly autonomous individual did not "work within the system"; he collided with it head-on. The 1960s alternative to the Organization was the Movement: *We shall overcome.*

IV

Prophets, poets, and science fiction writers imagine the future. On occasion they accurately predict it; if they are eloquent they sometimes help to bring it about. But they cannot *know* it. The word "Movement," to Americans living through the Eisenhower era, did not connote what it would in their near future: the pure tones of Joan Baez and the murmuring voices of outdoor throngs as they sang "We shall overcome," or the irreverent cries of peace marchers as they chanted "Hell, no, we won't go." It conjured up, instead, a horrid memory of hoarse shouts of "Sieg Heil!"—from the throats of young people who in another time had also declared that they should overcome; and that, yes, they would go, wherever and whenever their leader told them to. *Movement,* for people in the fifties who remembered a previous epoch of industrial chaos and international lawlessness, was a term even more sinister in import than *Organization.*

The argument that some movements are "good" and others "bad" had been heard in America before, and it would be heard again. But that idea had been oversold in the thirties by articulate, desperate intellectuals who insisted that your only choice was between Communism (defined as the Stalinist variety) and Fascism; if you were not for the one you had to be for the other. Somehow the Western democracies had come through depression and war without becoming either, a circumstance making it easy afterward to contend with a certain smugness that *all* ideological movements were "bad"—and that, fundamentally, all of them were alike. "There is a certain uniformity in all types of dedication, of faith, of pursuit of power, of unity and of self-sacrifice," wrote Eric Hoffer, the longshoreman-philosopher, in 1951:

> All mass movements generate in their adherents a readiness to die and a proclivity for united action; all of them, irrespective of the doctrine they preach and the program they project, breed fanaticism, enthusiasm, fervent hope, hatred and intolerance; . . . all of them demand blind faith and single-hearted allegiance . . . Though there are obvious differences between the fanatical Christian, the fanatical Mohammedan, the fanatical nationalist, the fanatical Communist and the fanatical Nazi, it is yet true that the fanaticism which animates them may be viewed and treated as one.

Eric Hoffer, like William Whyte, had long since vowed that

he did not want his soul absorbed into the Organization, but his personal method of escape was considerably less bourgeois than the kinds of dodges Whyte recommended. Hoffer at the age of eighteen had decided he would be a day laborer all his life. Washing dishes, following the crops, and finally working on the waterfront as a longshoreman, this self-made intellectual did not allow the System to buy him; it could only rent him, day by day. "I work, and am probably the world's most independent man because of it," he once said, and "some of my best stuff"—referring to his writing—"has come to me on company time."

In his later years Hoffer lived like an urban Thoreau, alone on a hill in San Francisco's Chinatown, with no television, no telephone, no radio; he usually dressed in "a rough-woven pea jacket, bright wool shirt, rumpled trousers, a nondescript cap, and heavy shoes." Unimproved and unspoiled by formal education, he read, voraciously—Montaigne, Brooks Adams, Epictetus, Tocqueville, Goethe, Renan, Heine, Machiavelli, Trotsky, Hitler; and he wrote, "laboriously in longhand, clutching a pencil in a fist the size of a small ham." An editor at *Harper's* "discovered" him, and in 1951 some of his philosophical musings, which Hoffer molded into highly disciplined prose that had echoes of Pascal and La Rochefoucauld, became a book titled *The True Believer.*

Pigeonholing critics didn't know quite what to make of Eric Hoffer. He had "pursued his postulates with a logic so cold and relentless," Eugene Burdick wrote in 1957, "that he emerges with conclusions that, in some subtle way, seem an outrage to the manners of scholarship and academic discourse." (Eric Sevareid once confessed that he had avoided reading Hoffer's books because Dwight Eisenhower had publicly praised one of them!) When Hoffer appeared, cloth cap in hand, to give a lecture at Berkeley in 1964, a student snobbishly asked: "What do your colleagues as longshoremen think of you writing books?", apparently expecting that such lowbrow characters would be suspicious of this egghead in their midst. With a winning grin, the old man roared: "Oh, they're not surprised; they're convinced that a longshoreman can do *anything*." He liked to write, he explained in an interview, "like a longshoreman packs a ship— with no space left over."

In the case of his first book, *The True Believer*, surely some of the psychic discomfort it provoked came from its author's relentless relativism: "The book passes no judgments, and expresses no preferences." The concluding chapter seemed to hedge that claim by discussing "Good and Bad Mass Movements." However, Hoffer's "good" movements turned out to be those whose active phases in history were mercifully short. Moreover, all the supposed basic and irreconcilable differences among ideologies were, at bottom, irrelevant. "When people are ripe for a mass movement," Hoffer wrote, "they are usually ripe for *any* effective movement, and not solely for one with a particular doctrine or program . . . The hammer and sickle and the swastika are in a class with the cross."

Activist Catholics were outraged by his inference that they and the Nazis belonged in the same species; humanitarian reformers were put off by his assertion that the person who sought to be his brother's keeper would end by becoming his jail-keeper. "We shy from the idea that our impulse to mold and save and change, which we consider to be our noblest passions, may really spring from a dry rot of rage against others," Burdick commented. "It is unnerving to think that the glint in the eye of a liberal reformer might harden into the glaring certitude of a Lenin or Hitler . . . And yet we have the light gnawing sensation that something about this is true."

Conformity to the Party, or to Holy Church, or to the Fatherland was obviously a more serious business than conformity to an Organization, which merely asked that you fit in and be one of the gang. A corporation president in the fifties might get so carried away by his vision of the company in a community that he could say, as President James F. Leftwich actually did, that "we live Woolworth"; but it would never have occurred to such an official to urge that his kind be ready to *die* for Woolworth.

And the recruitment of True Believers into a mass movement was quite a different matter from the way recruits were inducted into an Organization. The early Christian martyr, the hot young Communist, or the budding Nazi would no doubt have flunked most of those personnel testers' multiple-choice questions. They were not tactful, cooperative team players; nor were they, as individuals, well-rounded and in harmony with themselves. Quite the contrary. The prospective True Believer was a misfit whose private self and life were "irremediably spoiled."

In a sequel, *The Passionate State of Mind* (1955), Hoffer further explored the psyche of this kind of misfit. The potential True Believer was a kind of political or religious Don Juan: "There is in most passions a shrinking away from ourselves. The passionate pursuer has all the earmarks of a fugitive . . . Passions usually have their roots in that which is blemished, crippled, incomplete and insecure within us." And the Church, or the Party, or the holy Nation stood ready to gratify that passion. "Faith in a holy cause," Hoffer wrote in *The True Believer*, "is to a considerable extent a substitute for the lost faith in ourselves."

Nowhere in this analysis—much of it quite convincing—is there any acknowledgment that the adherents' struggle in a holy cause might be a means for *gaining* faith in themselves. When Rosa Parks on December 1, 1955, refused to move to the back of a Jim Crow city bus, thereby igniting the famous Montgomery, Alabama bus boycott, she asserted just such faith. In the course of the strike a black minister who worked for one of the car pools that had been organized to make the boycott effective stopped to give a ride to an old woman who had obviously been walking a long way. "Sister," he said, "aren't you getting tired?" To which she replied, "My soul has been tired for a long time. Now my feet are tired, and my soul is resting." It would be demeaning, to say the least, to dismiss such lines as the mere ideological colloquy of two True Believers.

"The Negro people of Montgomery," commented Martin Luther King Jr. after it was all over and they had won, "came to see that it was ultimately more honorable to walk the streets in

"The Negro people of Montgomery came to see that it was ultimately more honorable to walk the streets in dignity than to ride the buses in humiliation."— Dr. Martin Luther King.
Photo by Dan Weiner (1956). Used by permission of Sandra Weiner.

dignity than to ride the buses in humiliation." Neither William Whyte's prescription, of surviving in the organization world by protective camouflage, nor Eric Hoffer's, of skeptically observing from the sidelines while the competing fanaticisms fought it out with each other, could match that degree of dignity and honor. Group nonviolent resistance as employed in Montgomery "does not immediately change the heart of the oppressor," Dr. King conceded. "It first does something to the hearts and souls of those committed to it. It gives them new self-respect." And even if it did not ultimately change the oppressor's heart—a matter concerning which King and other black leaders later came bitterly to disagree—that gift of self-respect was beyond price. Perhaps there does lurk, in concepts such as "the black community" or the feminists' "sisterhood," a danger of evolving into a mass movement of the kind Hoffer described—but some of the dehumanizing forces in modern society cannot be faced alone.

V

"However much we guard ourselves against it, we cannot overcome the tendency to shape ourselves in the image other people have of us," Eric Hoffer wrote in 1955. "The people we meet are the playwrights and stage managers of our lives; they cast us in a role, and we play it whether we will or not." Here he was describing the condition not only of the True Believer, actual or potential, but of Everyman. The personnel directors' utopia of *The Organization Man,* in which everybody adjusts to the expectations of everybody else, was not a program for the future but a description of present reality—and this mutual stage-managing and role-playing game did not even require the retaining walls of an Organization. Carry the process one psychological step further, as Hoffer suggested—so that the adjustment became automatic rather than willed—and we are dealing with the "other-directed" character type as described by David Riesman, Nathan Glazer, and Reuel Denney in their classic study of the changing American character, *The Lonely Crowd* (1950).

As early as 1947 Riesman noticed, when conducting some interviews with Chicago teen-agers on their tastes in popular music, that when he had occasion to interview an entire group "its individual members looked around to see what the others thought before committing themselves." That, said Riesman and his associates, was what Americans in the age of Eisenhower were becoming. Other pitfalls besides the pressure of specialization, the seduction of organizational conformity, and the self-transcending attraction of the mass movement lay in the path of any person who wanted to be Western, truly purposeful, and whole.

Social philosophers, like the natural scientists whose method they emulate, build models and construct ideal types. Making due allowances for the artificiality into which any abstraction can entrap the inquirer, such a construction can be a tool of great analytical and interpretive power. The physicist who for certain purposes treats gas molecules metaphorically as billiard balls does not leap into madness by believing they *are* billiard balls, but is able to learn a great deal about the behavior of gases by thinking of them as if they were. So with social theory, which in the fifties, after decades of the table-compiling, graph-drawing, and jargon-inventing which had almost caused sociology in the U.S. to displace economics as the "dismal science," enjoyed a grand renaissance. A previous generation had gotten its understanding from its fiction—its Hemingway heroes and Fitzgerald flappers; the generation of the fifties found it instead in this new imaginative sociology. "Does any novel speak as distinctively of and for the past decade," wrote Robert Langbaum in 1955, "as, say, *The Lonely Crowd?*" Alongside the ideal-typical Bourgeois and Proletarian of Karl Marx, or the ideal-typical Bureaucrat, Entrepreneur, and Charismatic Leader of Max Weber, American thinkers were now setting forth the Organization Man; the True Believer; and that trinity of character types, Tradition-directed, Inner-directed, and Other-directed, whose evolution and interaction Riesman and his colleagues found helpfully explanatory of modern America and, by inference, of modern Western civilization.

Tradition-directed society—the unchanging, or slowly changing, folk culture that had preceded the rise of capitalism and all the other disruptions of modernity—had inducted its members into a system of values and a pattern of behavior it judged to be eternal. Taking their cues from the elders of the tribe, reinforced by an often elaborate structure of do's and don'ts (classically, the Hawaiian *kapu*), a young member of such a society learns what it is needful to know in order to transmit those values intact and uncorrupted to the next generation. The tribal elders "expect of him not so much that he be a certain type of person [as] that he behave in the approved way."

In contrast, "the society that emerged with the Renaissance and Reformation and that is only now vanishing" expects very much that one be a certain type of person. It cannot ask one simply to behave in the approved way, because it also believes in "progress," a criterion by which all previously approved ways are by definition out of date. Rather than imposing patterns of etiquette and taboo, it implants attitudes in childhood which will guide a person throughout life. This is "inner-direction;" its sanction for behavior, rather than the *shame* imposed by tradition-directed society, is an inescapable feeling of *guilt*. Inner-directed man is the classic bourgeois man, condemned by Marxists for his acquisitiveness and by aristocrats for his bad taste. He is also the generalized Oedipal "man" posited in Freudian theory, with his true self held in check by an inner voice of conscience; but he is not, as he was for Freud, the universal human type who emerged in prehistory out of a Primal Horde and who has continued to suffer neurotically throughout all subsequent history. In Riesman's hypothesis he becomes merely transitional, in evolution between tradition-direction and other-direction.

The emergent "other-directed" society—whose "hegemony," Riesman wrote, "unless present trends are reversed . . . lies not far off"—is a society of people whose "contemporaries are the source of direction for the individual." Like the tradition-directed, they take their behavioral cues from other people, rather than from the inner-directed person's nagging, parentally planted superego. Unlike the tradition-directed, they cannot take these signs from the fixed codes of tribal elders, for such codes and elders no longer exist. They must take them—a complex, ever-changing barrage of signals—from their own generational peers. To use Riesman's striking metaphor, the inner-directed psyche was kept on course by a psychological gyroscope; the other-directed by something more like radar.

Neither the guilt-ridden, self-centered, insensitive inner-directed type, nor the anxiously conforming other-directed person, with no sure sense of self at all, could be considered entirely attractive. Riesman and his co-writers posited a fourth model, the *autonomous* person, who would be emotionally open with and aware of others but not anxiously conformist to them. (The final chapter of their study was titled "Autonomy and Utopia.") However, that was not the way readers received the book in the fifties. Although Riesman warned that the inner-directed person seemed to be "far more independent than he really is: he is no less a conformist to others than the other-directed person, but the voices to which he listens are more distant," readers of *The Lonely Crowd* typically confused *inner-directedness* with *independence of mind*.

"The authors of *The Lonely Crowd* are not conservatives harking back to a rugged individualism that was once a radical Emersonian ideal," Riesman insisted, in a new preface he wrote for the book in 1961 after it had been in circulation for a decade. There was indeed a lot of *bogus* Emersonian individualism— sometimes it called itself "Nietzschean"—among educated youth in the fifties; "Little gestures of personal assertion—or a solipsistic lack of concern for others—have often masqueraded as autonomy." Riesman rebuked this pseudo-autonomy for being merely the latest example of an old American tendency for individuality to degenerate into eccentricity and egocentrism; and he pointed out the humane alternative:"No lover of toughness and invulnerability should forget the gains made possible by the considerateness, sensitivity, and tolerance that are among the positive qualities of other-direction."

Readers, however, take from any book what they see in it rather than what its authors might want them to find. "The great majority of readers in the last ten years," Riesman ruefully admitted, saw the choice as simply between "the well-heeled organization man (other-directed) and . . . the well-shod cowboy (inner-directed)," with no possibility of acting a part in history which would be more constructive and satisfying than either: "Everybody from the free enterpriser to the socialist has come out against conformity." And, to a great extent, this modish anticonformity was itself only a species of conformism. The group of Smith College students in the fifties who ranked themselves (for a sociologist's questionnaire) as being more "inner-directed" than their parents, their friends, or "the 'average' Smith girl," without a word of protest against Adlai Stevenson's advice to immolate their independent souls on the altars of their future husbands' wholeness, were only kidding themselves.

VI

At the end of the fifties it seemed far less likely than it had at the beginning that "the hegemony of other-direction lies not far off." The authors of *The Lonely Crowd* had been tripped up by the truth in an older but still vital sociological idea, namely culture-lag. "The institutions that inner-directed men set going now appear to run, as it were, under their own inertia," Riesman wrote in his 1961 reprise. In fact, a people who were becoming other-directed might be *less* able to grab hold of the machinery and change it than their inner-directed predecessors would have been: "They are often somewhat disaffected, but they lack the conviction that things could be done any other way—and therefore cannot see, save in a peripheral way, what is wrong with how things are." In the whole lot of those interviews with members of the Class of 1955 there had been "very little stirring of the discontent which could presage new needs, new wants, let alone an image of a social pattern organized to supply them." Indeed, Riesman generalized in an essay for the necessarily future-conscious *Bulletin of the Atomic Scientists* in 1958, "serious discussion of the future is just what is missing in the United States . . . we live now, think later."

Contrasted with the penny-pinching ethic of earlier middle-class generations who had foregone living, and instead had done without and denied themselves in order at the end to lavish it all on a gold-plated wheelchair, this was liberation. But the future would not stay away forever. The horn of plenty was not inexhaustible; the racial and sexual revolutions were on their way; the smog, and the clouds of radioactive particles, yearly grew thicker and dirtier; year by year those nice, empathetic young people in the suburbs from the Class of 1955 added more babies to the sum total, with hardly a thought of how many people the planet could accommodate in the comfortable fashion to which Americans of their economic class had become accustomed. If we did not *think* now, prudent counsel suggested, we might not *live* later. As the homespun philosopher Harry Golden put it early in 1960, "The civilization that perpetuates itself is the one that lives for *tomorrow*. If we beat the game by playing for the present, it will be the first time anyone has done so."

But why live for tomorrow if today's experience is "a giddy success story"? The going mass-media portrait of America, James Wechsler observed in 1960, was one in which "the poor . . . are virtually no longer with us; the rich have learned to accommodate themselves to the realities of the welfare state; the middle class is serenely clipping its coupons and the workman is driving his Chrysler." Darker areas in the portrait, "the harassment of Negro school children in Little Rock," or "the discovery of an unexpectedly high level of fallout in St. Louis's milk," were being dismissed as "the random disturbances of democracy." *Time*, in its characteristic mood of American self-celebration, declared in August of 1959 that the United States was a country "in which fear and fretting were made ridiculous by the facts of national life."

Coincidentally, however, *Newsweek's* issue of the same date reported that the favorite reading among a substantial majority of American college students was *Mad* magazine—whose grinning nonhero, Alfred E. Neuman, as he piped "What, me worry?", made it comically and painfully clear that there was plenty to worry about. Weightier thinkers than Alfred agreed. Albert Schweitzer, for one, told Adlai Stevenson as the fifties waned that he considered their times the most dangerous in all human history; theretofore nature had controlled man, but now man had learned to control nature's elemental forces—before learning to control himself.

Stevenson on his continuing pilgrimage had come to Dr. Schweitzer's jungle hospital in equatorial Africa after a summer's visit to the USSR, from which the wandering candidate took away "an overwhelming impression of thrust and purpose in most aspects of Soviet life . . . They, not we, are firing the shots that are heard round the world—and also the satellites that orbit above it." Americans, in contrast, seemed to Stevenson to have lately reinterpreted their traditional pursuit of happiness as no more than a frantic chase after consumer pleasures and mass distractions. In the world of the Cold War this would not be enough: "Outer tyranny with purpose may well triumph over the inner, purposeless tyranny of a confused and aimless way of life." It did not require the stark contrast of Soviet Russia or of emerging post-colonial Africa to prompt such judgments. At the end of 1959 John Steinbeck came back from eight insulated months in England to find in his home country "a creeping, all-pervading nerve gas of immorality." Deeply troubled, the novelist wrote to his fellow homecomer Adlai Stevenson that he did not think the U.S. could survive on such a basis: "If I wanted to destroy a nation I would give it too much, and I would have it on its knees, miserable, greedy and sick."

Steinbeck's letter was published (inadvertently, he afterward declared) in the *Long Island Newsday,* and it generated the kind of heart-searching in which Americans have engaged—or indulged, for self-censure can be a sentimental parlor game if it does not become connected with action—ever since the times of the Puritans. "We're breeding a new type of human being," declared Charles Siepmann, head of the New York chapter of the American Civil Liberties Union—"a guy with a full belly, an empty mind and a hollow heart. I see them walking around, and I don't like them one bit." They were not—at least, not yet—True Believers, nor even Organization Men, and certainly not whole, purposeful Westerners. "If Steinbeck and all the other critics are to be credited, this moral miasma which afflicts us is well-nigh universal," commented Thurston Davis, editor of the Jesuit weekly *America*. "It's the itch for the fast buck, for the irresponsible pleasure, for the short cut to power or payola or prideful status. It's the clever dodge, the inside track, the deal, the gimmick, the angle, the guy you know who'll 'fix' it . . . the omnipresent yen to push somebody else out of the way and become the fellow who's got everything." However, Father Davis also had some harsh words for the current form moral protest in America was taking:

> Can we honestly say our fear is the trepidation of God-fearing men—fear for ourselves and our souls and our fate, for the harvest of our sins and our wretched confusions? Or is it nothing but a camouflaged lust to cling on to the very possessions we protest are our undoing? There is reason to suspect that it may be the latter, that what we are really worried about is that the whole kit and caboodle of our American way of life—missiles and credit cards, Cadillacs and pop-up toasters, our freedoms, fun, filters and foolishness—is about to go down the drain. If so, then we do have reason to be concerned for ourselves and our future.

Historian Arthur Schlesinger, Sr. was more hopeful. "The very fact . . . that acute observers are sharply questioning current standards suggests to me that the condition is not as hopeless as they think." Recovery after a period of letdown had recurred throughout American history, and Schlesinger thought the symptoms of another such recovery were already on the horizon. These might be merely "tokens of a false dawn, but if the cyclical movement of history means anything, I suggest that they signify that the era of what Steinbeck calls 'cynical immorality' is already on the way out." Like father, like son; Arthur Schlesinger, Jr., in that same winter of critical discontent, was touring American campuses with a lecture in which he described the rallying of the thirties after the alleged downswing of the "Roaring Twenties" as a hopeful precedent and prophecy for the United States in the very near future, perhaps in the next presidential election. What America needed at the end of the fifties politically, the younger Schlesinger argued, was another New Deal; and the Democrats' nominee in 1960, similarly conscious of historical cycles and parallels, would duly name his cause the New Frontier.

But the great merit in books of the fifties like *The Lonely Crowd* and *The Organization Man,* in spite of their tendency to forecast the next fifteen years as a time in which (to use Riesman's words) "we may count our bland blessings," was that they opened the question of basic structural change in American life. They did not assume the continuance of the kind of sociopolitical rhythm the Schlesingers believed in, which neatly sorts out history into symmetrical, thirty-year cycles. (How much Marxism, had it not been the great intellectual "no-no" of the decade, could have contributed to such a discussion!) If the new sociology's vision of this permanently transformed society should prove true, pro-phesied Paul Goodman—the most trenchant of all the social critics of the fifties—the young people coming of age within it would confront a crisis far more profound than the one fore-shadowed in Stevenson's portrait of a "nation glued to the tel-evision screen" or in Steinbeck's charge of greedy infantilism ("Only a baby cannot refuse a second dish of ice cream when he is full").

They were going to find, as bureaucratic routine and me-chanical automation transformed formerly productive activities into paper-shuffling and button-pushing, that as time passed in America there would be, as Goodman put it in 1969, "fewer jobs that are necessary or unquestionably useful; that require energy and draw on some of one's best capacities; and that can be done keeping one's honor and dignity." To face the fact, as one entered the job market, that "during my productive years I will spend eight hours a day doing what is no good"—if indeed one had, thanks to robotization, any job at all—was to realize the full horror of *Growing Up Absurd.* Yet even Paul Goodman's book with that denunciatory title did not cut all the way to the bone. "It's hard to grow up when there isn't enough *man's* work,"

Goodman complained. Did he mean that women (only ex officio, as wives and mothers) already had jobs that were necessary and unquestionably useful? Or did he mean that the work of women need not be taken seriously ? Social understanding in America at the end of the fifties still had a long, long way to go.

It still does.

CHAPTER FIVE
Under God, by Act of Congress

I

MIDDLING-AND-OLDER Americans who were in grade
school before 1954 still remember that once upon a time
they started all their winter weekdays by pledging allegiance to
the flag, and to a Republic which that pledge defined in a surging
cadenced line as "One nation, indivisible, with liberty and justice
for all." Some of them, called upon as adults to repeat those
words in a public gathering, stumble; the beat they remember—
"one *na*-tion in di-*vis*-ible"—is interrupted with a thump: "Under
God." In the fifties the old flag pledge, which since its inception
in 1892 (for the four hundredth anniversary of the voyage of
Columbus) had served the Republic through two world wars,
a depression, and eleven presidencies, had had to have this
reinforcement patched onto it in order to serve the needs of
the Cold War.

On February 7, 1954, the Reverend George M. Docherty,
after recounting how his own children used to describe "with
strange solemnity the ritual of the salute to the Flag," warned
his congregation at the New York Avenue Presbyterian Church
in Washington, D.C. that in his imagination he could hear "little
Muscovites repeat a similar pledge to their hammer-and-sickle
flag," for the USSR also claimed to be a republic with justice
and liberty. To distinguish our school children from theirs,
therefore, the American liturgy ought to be amended. In its

original form, without "Under God," the Pledge of Allegiance ignored "a definitive factor in the American way of life."

That way of life, Docherty explained in his soft Scottish burr, meant more than "going to the ballgame, and eating popcorn and drinking Cola-cola, and rooting for the Senators—one of the bravest things I've been called upon to do" (the long defunct Washington baseball team in the fifties regularly ended the season in or near the cellar); it was also "a freedom that respects the rights of minorities but is defined by a fundamental belief in God." Docherty was aware that some Americans had constitutional scruples about the separation of church and state, and that others, "honest atheists," might object. The First Amendment, however, meant only that there should be no established church; "it is not, and never was meant to be, a separation of religion and life." As for the atheists, the pastor pronounced, "an atheistic American is a contradiction in terms."

New York Avenue Presbyterian Church is only about five minutes' walk from the White House, and the Eisenhowers were in Docherty's congregation that morning. Later that same Sunday the chief executive went on national radio with three prominent clergymen, Protestant, Catholic and Jewish, to do some preaching of his own. "Whatever our individual church, whatever our personal creed," the President declared, "in our fundamental faith we are all one. Together we thank the Power that has made and preserved us a nation." Other memories echoed back from elementary classrooms besides the flag pledge: "We remember from school days the tiny ship of destiny called the Mayflower," Ike went on. "On that ship self-government on our continent was first conceived by the Pilgrim Fathers. Their immortal compact began with the words, in the name of God, amen."

Three days later Senator Homer Ferguson of Michigan introduced a motion to amend the pledge of allegiance, thereby breathing new life into a similar proposal that had been offered the year before in the House by Louis Rabaut, also of Michigan. Spurred by letter-writing campaigns from churches, veterans'

organizations, service clubs, radio stations, and the Hearst newspapers, Congress passed the resolution and sent it to Eisenhower
for signature in time for Flag Day, June 14. On that date, on
the steps of the U.S. Capitol, led by Ferguson and Rabaut, a
crowd for the first time chanted the newly revised Flag Pledge,
with the words "under God" added after "one nation." CBS
carried the ceremony live on its morning news show.

In the judgment of two historians of the change, Ferenc Szasz
and Gerard Kaye, "Adding 'under God' was not considered
much of an amendment." Such language was consistent with
the diffuse religiosity that had accompanied the republic since
its foundation. The phrase itself came from the Gettysburg
Address, long hallowed in the canon of American political scrip-
tures; thus, its incorporation into the flag pledge by an Act of
Congress "was simply a form of democratic exegesis." The United
States Supreme Court, however, in recent years had been ruling
quite otherwise on such matters. The "wall of separation between
church and state," as Thomas Jefferson had described it, "must
be kept high and impregnable," Justice Hugo Black declared
in a landmark opinion (*Everson* v. *Board of Education*, 330 U.S.
1, 1947). "We could not approve the slightest breach." Evangelical
piety might be all very well in campaign speeches, but it had
no force as law.

Specifically, the Court had ruled that the flag salute and pledge
could not be enforced upon school children whose parents believed that no line can be drawn between venerating a flag and
worshiping an idol. The sect of Jehovah's Witnesses, who affirmed
that a flag so used is a "graven image" within the meaning of
Exodus 20:4,5, had legally tested this claim upon the conscience
by the state, and won. "Any spark of love for country which
may be generated in a child," wrote Justice Frank Murphy (con-
curring in *West Virginia State Board of Education* v. *Barnette*, 319
U.S. 324, 1943) "by forcing him to make what is to him an
empty gesture and recite words wrung from him contrary to
his religious beliefs is overshadowed by the desirability of pre-
serving freedom of conscience to the full."

II

Three major Supreme Court decisions turning upon the religion clauses of the First Amendment were handed down in 1952, the campaign year which set the stage for the Eisenhower presidency. Of these, two—*Burstyn* v. *Wilson* (343 U.S. 495) and *Kedroff* v. *St. Nicholas Cathedral* (344 U.S. 94)—gave no comfort to the godly folk who believed, with Pastor Docherty, that the religious component in the American way of life could formally and constitutionally be expressed through the American system of government. The third—*Zorach* v. *Clauson* (343 U.S. 306)—was more ambiguous.

The Miracle, a motion picture by Roberto Rossellini, was the touchstone for *Burstyn* v. *Wilson.* A poor peasant girl (played by the great Anna Magnani) is seduced by a passing stranger whom she has confused with St. Joseph; pregnant and deranged, identifying herself with the Virgin Mary, she enters a church and has her child. The film critic for *L'Osservatore Romano,* the ably edited daily newspaper of the Vatican, while acknowledging that "questions may arise—even serious ones—of a religious nature" from this movie, paid tribute also to its "passages of undoubted cinematic distinction," and concluded: "We continue to believe in Rossellini's art." Less genially, the Vatican's Catholic Cinematographic Center found the picture "an abominable profanation"—but did not avail itself of its power to censor. Neither did the Italian government; the film was shown freely throughout Italy, to mixed critical reviews.

What would play in worldly-wise Rome, however, did not fare so well in equally urbane—but Cold-War-haunted—New York. In the fall of 1950 the Metropolitan Opera offered, for its history-making first Opening Night telecast, a splendid revival of Verdi's *Don Carlo*—a musical melodrama which at one point has a villainous king of Spain confess to the Grand Inquisitor, and get absolution *in advance,* for a murder he intends to commit. The opera was greeted by picketers, who proclaimed it "anti-church and anti-state"–as indeed it was. The Met's tough-minded new manager, Rudolf Bing, ignored such nuisances, and the show went on to several repeat performances later in the season. However, although Grand Opera might get by as capital-A Art, a mere movie—even one in a foreign language, with subtitles— could expect less tolerance. *The Miracle* opened in Manhattan on December 12 that same year. The city license commissioner attacked it as "officially and personally blasphemous," and on February 16, 1951, the New York State Board of Regents decided that the exhibitor had committed—not indecency, nor immorality, nor incitement to crime, nor other legally recognized grounds for censorship, but *sacrilege*. New York's appellate courts agreed, and Rossellini's forty-minute film went to the U.S. Supreme Court.

Ducking the question whether the state might censor motion pictures on other grounds (i.e. obscenity), Justice Tom Clark, a rather conservative Truman appointee, went right to the heart of the constitutional-religious issue: "Under the First and Four- teenth Amendments a state may not ban a film on the basis of a censor's conclusion that it is 'sacrilegious.'" More long-windedly, as was his wont, Justice Felix Frankfurter traced the derivation of the word "sacrilege" back through successive editions of the *Encyclopaedia Britannica* and the great commentators on the English common law to Saint Thomas Aquinas; concluding that, technically, the only definition of "sacrilege" that would remain actionable in modern law would be its etymological meaning of theft or physical injury to church property. Otherwise, Frank- furter reasoned, the term "sacrilegious" as used in the argument over "The Miracle"—as a rough synonym for "blasphemous" or "profane"—had become too inflated to enforce: "Conduct and beliefs dear to one may seem the rankest 'sacrilege' to another." So much for the under-Godders' argument that there is a specific normative religious belief, however minimal, which one must profess in order to be accounted a good American.

Even more striking was the Court's decision in *Kedroff* v. *St. Nicholas Cathedral* an explicit rejection of Cold War religious norms. Ever since 1872 (*Watson* v. *Jones*, 13 Wallace 679), the

Supreme Court had taken the prudent position that when a dispute arises *within* a church, any secular court should abide by the decisions of the church's own judicial authorities; they are the experts on their own beliefs, and they know their own rules. Unfortunately for logical symmetry such disputes often involve tangibles such as church treasuries, trust funds, and buildings—matters on which secular authority *does* have the final say—and intangibles of ideology which tempt it to interfere.

Kedroff involved, as rival claimants to their Cathedral headquarters in New York City, the Russian Orthodox Archbishop of New York, Metropolitan of All America and Canada—and the Patriarch of Moscow, in his capacity as Archbishop of the Diocese of North America and the Aleutian Islands. The Russian church, like much else, had split at the time of the October Revolution. Russian-descended North Americans and White Russian exiles wanted no part of a parent church that existed by permission of the Communist government in Moscow and which asked its overseas co-religionists to abstain "from political activities against the U.S.S.R." The Patriarch of Moscow, who was recognized as fully legitimate by the other traditional Eastern Orthodox Patriarchs, of Constantinople, Alexandria, Antioch, and Jerusalem, had never relinquished hierarchical control of his North American mission, begun back in the eighteenth century when Russian priests first evangelized the Alaskan Eskimos. And that, to North American Cold Warriors, would not do. "The Bolshevik Revolution may have freed the state from the grip of the church, but it did not free the church from the grip of the state," Justice Robert Jackson cried. "To me, whatever the canon law is found to be and whoever is the rightful head of the Moscow Patriarchate, I do not think New York law must yield to the authority of a foreign and unfriendly state masquerading as a spiritual institution."

But Justice Jackson was in dissent. "Under our Constitution it is not open to the governments of this Union to reinforce the loyalty of their citizens by deciding who is the true exponent of their religion," his colleague Frankfurter snapped. For the

Court as a whole, Justice Stanley Reed ruled that the state could not, without breaking the wall of separation, interfere with the Moscow Patriarchate's traditional ecclesiastical control of its North American province—not even "to free the American group from infiltration of . . . atheistic or subversive influences." Congressman Rabaut, in a speech justifying his amendment of the Flag Pledge, told the House of Representatives that "the unbridgeable gap between America and Communist Russia is a belief in Almighty God"; yet here was such a bridge, and Americans and Russians were crossing it. Nothing in American jurisprudence, as the courts understood it in 1952, could stop them.

The issues in *Zorach* v. *Clauson* were more finely drawn. Pious school boards and PTA's for years had been experimenting with "released time"—a scheme whereby school children would be excused from regular classes in order to receive religious instruction. The reasoning had been that the state, although barred from preferring one sect at the expense of another, does not violate the Constitution by giving aid and comfort impartially to *all* religions. However, in *Illinois ex rel. McCollum* v. *Board of Education* (333 U.S. 203, 1948), the high court had ruled that such reasoning could not be stretched to allow religious teachers to come regularly into tax-built classrooms during school hours, "substitute their religious teaching for the secular education provided under the compulsory education law," and take attendance, with absences to be reported—and, presumably, punished—in the usual secular way. Illinois in using "the state's compulsory public school machinery" to help church groups fill their classes with students, Justice Black summed up, was clearly on forbidden territory; such action "falls squarely under the ban of the First Amendment."

Nothing daunted, religious educators regrouped. If the Court had forbidden the State of Illinois to allow sectarian instruction on school property and during school time, New York City would allow school children to be dismissed early and sent off the campus for such instruction. The catch was that students who did not participate in the religion classes were not simply turned loose. They had to stay in study hall—and the "released" students, as in Illinois, were marked absent if they did not show up for class. Opponents promptly argued that the differences between such an arrangement and the Illinois plan were insignificant. In New York, as in Champaign, Illinois, "the weight and influence of the school is put behind a program for religious instruction"—a program, moreover, which public school teachers were required to police. Challenging the city school system, dissenting parents sought legal redress, in an action which came on appeal to the U.S. Supreme Court as *Zorach* v. *Clauson.*

They met a Court whose temper had considerably changed since 1948. Already, dissenting in the *McCollum* case, Justice Reed had expressed misgivings about the direction in which constitutional interpretation seemed to be going. "The prohibition of enactments respecting the establishment of religion do not bar every friendly gesture between church and state," Reed had cautioned. "It is not an absolute prohibition against every conceivable situation where the two may work together." Otherwise, logically, the houses of Congress would have to dismiss their chaplains; so would the armed forces, which from earliest times had commissioned and paid clergymen to conduct religious worship "ashore and afloat, employing for the purpose property belonging to the United States"; the G.I. Bill must cease financing the education of veterans who were training for the ministry; Annapolis and West Point would have to abolish compulsory chapel; and the District of Columbia schools would be obliged drastically to abridge their opening exercises, which included both Bible reading and the Lord's Prayer. Such a sealing off of public society behind Jefferson's wall, carried to its deductive conclusion, would hardly have left room for the children in those schools to profess allegiance to a flag "under God."

III

The *Zorach* v. *Clauson* decision in effect reversed the *McCollum* ruling. By a vote of 6–3, the Supreme Court upheld the New

York released-time program. Justice William O. Douglas—writing the opinion of the Court—agreed with Reed's argument in *McCollum*. If the First Amendment were construed to say that "in every and all respects" there should be a separation betwen church and state, then "policemen who helped parishioners into their places of worship would violate the Constitution," Douglas reasoned. "A fastidious atheist or agnostic could even object to the supplication with which the Court opens each session: 'God save the United States and this Honorable Court.'" It would be pressing the concept of separation to just such logical extremes, Douglas argued, if the Court should strike down the New York released-time law on constitutional grounds. For the state to adjust a schedule of public events to believers' needs was merely to follow the best of the nation's traditions, by recognizing Americans' basic nature: "We are a religious people whose institutions presuppose a Supreme Being"—an acknowledgment, Mark DeWolfe Howe has argued, "that a *de facto* establishment of religion prevails throughout the land."

Militant civil libertarians were outraged. It particularly hurt them that Douglas, a sturdy champion of unpopular liberal causes—as recently as 1951 dissenting, for example, from the conviction of U.S. Communist party leaders under the Smith Act (*Dennis et al.* v. *U.S.*, 341 U.S. 494)—should have written such an opinion. Indeed, Justices Douglas and Black, who so often stood together in the fifties in dissent for civil liberties, sometimes against the entire rest of the Court, were on opposite sides this time; for Hugo Black found no essential difference between the Illinois religion classes the Court had previously struck down and the New York program it now upheld. In both cases, Black observed, "the school authorities release some of the children on the condition that they attend the religious classes, get reports on whether they attend, and hold the other children in the school building until the religious hour is over. . . . This is not separation but combination of church and state." With a touch of poetry, Black argued that Americans' religious decisions in the past had been "as free as the choice of those who answered the call to worship moved only by the music of the old Sunday morning church bells." And their right to choose, logically and necessarily, implied the right not to choose: "The First Amendment has lost much if the religious follower and the atheist are no longer to be politically regarded as entitled to equal justice under the law."

Justice Black was politely firm; Justice Jackson, also in dissent, was angry. He made short work of Douglas's argument that "no one is forced to go." If the public schools had been taking up so much of the children's time as to encroach upon their religious opportunity, they could easily have simply shortened everyone's school day—but that proposal had been rejected, "on the ground that if they are made free many students will not go to the Church." What really made "released time" effective, therefore, Jackson argued, was "the truant officer who, if the youngster fails to go to the Church school, dogs him back to the public school room," which then "serves as a temporary jail for a pupil who will not go to Church." The majority, whom the Justice sarcastically labeled "my evangelistic brethren," had confused objection to compulsion with objection to religion; and "we start down a rough road when we begin to mix compulsory public education with compulsory godliness." Prophetically, eighteen years before anybody used the term "Moral Majority ," Justice Jackson warned: "The day that this country ceases to be free for irreligion it will cease to be free for religion—except for the sect that can win political power."

Such, then, was the strangely mixed constitutional status of religion in America at the advent of Dwight Eisenhower, as interpreted by the highest court in the land. Americans were a religious people whose institutions presupposed a Supreme Being (*Zorach*), yet their laws could recognize no specific offense as sacrilege against such a Being (*Burstyn*). They could neither interfere with control of an American church by a hierarchy located in a foreign, hostile, and ultimately anti-religious country (*Kedroff*), nor compel fellow-Americans to repeat a pledge of national unity that clashed with their own religious convictions

(West Virginia v. *Barnette)*. In short, the harder one looked at
that "definitive factor in the American way of life" which Reverend
Docherty so confidently proclaimed, the less definitive it appeared.

   Dwight Eisenhower was, and is, often criticized by intellectuals
precisely for this lack of definitiveness, in religion as in much
else. "One might say," wrote William Lee Miller in 1953, "that
President Eisenhower, like many Americans, is a very fervent
believer in a very vague religion." To some extent, however,
that vagueness may have been forced upon Ike by the nature
of the role he was called upon to play. George Washington had
included in his inauguration address a supplication "to that
Almighty Being who rules over the universe," and Eisenhower
had opened his own inaugural with a prayer; almost all presidents,
with the scrupulous exception of Thomas Jefferson, have functioned from time to time as *pontifex maximus*. They have also
had to preside over a nation that has become plural in lifestyles
and cultures beyond Jefferson's wildest imaginings. Caught between his personal family piety and his responsibility of stewardship for so diverse a nation, Eisenhower, in one of his most
quoted and often laughed-at lines, found words that constitutionally split the difference between Justice Douglas's grand
pronouncement and the other Justices' spirited dissents: "Our
government makes no sense unless it is founded in a deeply
felt religious faith—and I don't care what it is."

   When the Confederate founding fathers wrote their new
Constitution in 1861 they had changed the preamble of the old
Federal document to avoid this religious vagueness. Between
"secure the blessings of liberty to ourselves and our posterity"
and "do ordain and establish this constitution" they had inserted
the words "invoking the favor and guidance of Almighty God."
Their new nation—unlike the Union then being defended by
the worldly, materialistic Yankees—conceived in liberty of a
sort, but certainly not dedicated to the proposition that all men
are created equal, was at least declaring itself to be a nation
under God. The parallel with the Union's formal religious
confession in 1954, aimed at the materialistic Russians, is close

enough to be embarrassing. The Southern Confederacy was not the only part of America where protest arose from time to time against the U.S. Constitution's careful eighteenth-century secularity. Soon after the disastrous Northern defeat at Bull Run in 1861, liberal Protestant theologian Horace Bushnell, in a sermon preached in that staunchly Yankee capital, Hartford, Connecticut, had also proposed amending the Preamble to recognize that all authority is derived from God.

From time to time during and after the War between the States such an amendment had regularly been presented, and Congress just as regularly had tabled it. In 1946 a Christian Amendment Movement emerged, proposing yet again that the Constitution be altered to include: "This nation devoutly recognizes the authority and law of Jesus Christ, Saviour and Ruler of Nations, through whom are bestowed the blessings of Almighty God." To word it that way seemed a bit much. Nevertheless, militant evangelicals kept on proposing such an amendment, or a milder version that would not be so specifically Christian, throughout the fifties. Three decades afterward it would still echo in the rhetoric and proposals of a self-proclaimed Moral Majority.

Dwight Eisenhower, measured thus, would not have qualified as a Moral Majoritarian. "I do not care whether you be Baptists, whether you be Jews, whether you be Catholics or Protestants or whatever," he told the audience during a speech in Harlem during his 1952 campaign. He might have cared had they been atheists; "There must be that feeling that man is made in the image of his Maker," Ike continued. But in his genial, all-inclusive fashion he did not press the point. For Cold Warriors more zealous than Eisenhower, religious rhetoric like the President's presented a dilemma. If Americans were seriously trying to distinguish "our" way of life from "theirs"—the Russians'—in religious terms, they could not very well make the disclaimer that they didn't care what it was.

On the other hand, the moment they started spelling it out in any detail, they began unwittingly testifying that America's

religious way of life was not one, but many. Militants who might
have worked together as secular ideologues were driven apart
by their own ancient sectarian feuds. In particular, Protestant
and Catholic right-wingers who were in basic agreement on
many political issues—anti-subversion, anti-UN, anti-welfare,
anti-foreign aid—cherished underneath that agreed-upon program a long-standing mistrust of each other.

IV

"There is only one force in the universe that can destroy
Communism, and that is the Catholic Church," thundered Father
Richard Ginder, an ultra-reactionary who had hoped Douglas
MacArthur would be the Republican nominee in 1952 and who
believed Dwight Eisenhower to be no more than the Communists'
American errand-boy (*Our Sunday Visitor*, August 31, 1958).
Such Catholics, clerical or lay, were prone to argue that Protestantism is next to Liberalism, which is one step away from
socialism, which easily slides into Communism. Since the Communist Manifesto first appeared in 1847 the Popes, in countless
encyclicals, pastoral letters, and addresses from St. Peter's Square,
had spelled out the Church's stand against it. Therefore we
know the Catholic Church is anti-Communist, the zealots contended; but we can't really trust the Protestants. In another of
his weekly "Right or Wrong" columns on October 23, 1955, in
the widely-circulated *Sunday Visitor*—which one could find in
many Catholic parishes piled up in stacks at the church steps
after Mass—Father Ginder quoted with approval the dictum of
J.B. Matthews, who had formerly worked for both the House
Un-American Activities Committee and for Joe McCarthy's Senate
subcommittee, that "the largest single group supporting the
Communist apparatus in the United States today is composed
of Protestant clergymen." Since 1949, Catholics who voluntarily
"profess, defend and spread" Communist doctrine had automatically suffered excommunication; could any such purgative

discipline exist in the easy-going, disorderly world of Protestantism?

Conversely, militant Protestant anti-Communists found it hard to form a common front with their ancient foe in Rome. Rev. Carl McIntire, who from his pulpit in Collingswood, New Jersey, regularly denounced liberals, government spenders, one-worlders, and other standard villains as defined by the ultra-Right, published a poster early in the fifties that graphically expressed his *Weltanschauung:* a cartoon vision of Satan with his arms outstretched over the world. The left arm was the Kremlin—the "international Communist conspiracy"—and down from its hand came strings, which led to little marionettes labeled as New Deal functionaries, leftist college professors, radical labor leaders, and the like, all busily doing the Devil's work. But the right arm of this same menacing figure was the Vatican, and the puppet-strings descending from that hand were attached to inquisitors, parochial-school teaching sisters, and Jesuits. The Red and the Black here on earth might be ranged against each other, but ultimately both were controlled from Hell.

Obviously, for Protestants of that crusading sort, Joe McCarthy posed a real problem. Yes, he *was* pursuing the common foe of all religion—but he was a Catholic! Later in the fifties, when McCarthyism was emerging again in a more sophisticated guise (e.g. Robert Welch's plausibly documented "Eisenhower is a Communist" tract *The Politician*), Catholic and Protestant extremists seemed to be burying the hatchet; but the old hostility smoldered just beneath the surface. Not long after the fall of Cuba to Castro in 1959 Helen Wood Birnie, a former Communist Party organizer who had "got religion" in the Protestant evangelical sense of that term, spoke in a number of Pentecostal churches along the circuit from Minneapolis to Seattle where she had formerly recruited disciples for Stalin. Introduced as "Sister Birnie" by one youthful, smiling local pastor at the climax of a typically fervent Assembly of God evening service, with old-time gospel hymns and prayers punctuated by "Praise the Lord" and "Amen," this ex-Communist planted herself on the platform, with a grim frown like that of the severe farm wife in Grant Wood's painting *American Gothic,* and talked on the theme "I was an Angry Young Woman for thirty-three years." In the thirty-fourth year she had seen the light, and now she denounced not only Communism but Modern Republicanism, the UN, and the godless public schools from which she had removed her children lest they be taught the theory of evolution.

Questions popped out from the audience afterward: was Fidel Castro a Communist? Were there Communists in the Republican Party? And, inevitably, "What did you think of Senator Mc-Carthy?" Sister Birnie paused for a long time. The tension in the air was electric. Then, slowly, she said she thought Senator McCarthy had done America a lot of good, even though he *was* a Catholic. In the back of the church a conservative young Republican student from Vermont, who had just recently become a convert to Catholicism, muttered, "There goes the whole ball game."

McCarthy himself may have been intuitively aware of this pitfall. "Both his admirers and his detractors admitted that McCarthy made few, if any attempts to exploit his religion for political purposes," writes Donald Crosby, S.J., a careful student of McCarthyism. Even when he spoke before all-Catholic audiences, as in an address before the Catholic Press Association on May 25, 1950, the Senator took pains to state that "Protestants, Jews and Catholics" had come to the defense of one of his anti-Communist committee witnesses, and that Communism sought to destroy "all the honesty and decency that every Protestant, Jew and Catholic . . . [had] been taught at his mother's knee." Indeed, Father Crosby noted in his excellent study of McCarthy titled *God, Church, and Flag,* when the liberal Catholic journal *Commonweal* condemned McCarthyism the Senator declared that it was being more helpful to the Communist cause than the *Daily Worker.* Otherwise, when Joe McCarthy identified religion of some sort with "the American way of life," his language was usually as vague as Eisenhower's.

Nevertheless, there was an important Catholic component in

Joe McCarthy's popular support. After his death in 1957 the Catholic War Veterans sponsored an annual Joe McCarthy Gold Medal Americanism Award, and beginning in 1959 yearly pilgrimages to McCarthy's grave in Appleton, Wisconsin, with a memorial Mass, speeches by conservative politicians, and a graveside recitation of the rosary, kept alive the memory of his crusade. Catholics split on McCarthyism as they split in varying proportions on other secular issues, as did non-Catholics; but in some regions the Senator's ethno-religious identity blotted out the usual lines of political division in America.

Massachusetts in particular, as partisans of a Massachusetts Senator with acute presidential ambitions realized to their dismay in the early fifties, had "the highest proportion of McCarthyites in the land." The classic great political gulf in Boston for years had been between Yankee Protestant Republicans (Harvard, Back Bay, and the old investment banking houses) and Irish Catholic Democrats (South Boston, the Church, and organized labor). John Kennedy's Senate race against Henry Cabot Lodge in 1952 was a classic Bay State political contest; indeed, it was a rematch, both candidates' grandfathers having run for the same office thirty-six years before. But the Kennedy forces were deeply anxious lest Joe McCarthy come into the state to campaign for Lodge. McCarthy had qualities many Catholic Bostonians, including Senator Kennedy's own father, admired—except that he was a Republican. "After all," Father Crosby sums up, "some of the Boston Irish may have thought, a man whom the *Christian Science Monitor* and Harvard disliked so much could not be all bad."

When the McCarthy subcommittee in 1953 went after a Harvard physics professor who admitted his own former Communist activities but declined to inform on other people he had known, a censure proposal against Harvard was introduced in the Massachusetts legislature, *supported* by Democrats—i.e., by Boston machine spokesmen for whom Harvard was the epitome of WASP oppression—and *opposed* by Republicans; i.e., by white-collar and elite elements for whom Harvard symbolized civili-

zation. Some Boston Catholics of Irish descent, deciding that
Joe was one of their own despite his unfortunate affiliation with
the GOP, managed to incorporate him into their traditional
political folklore. McCarthy, not his terrorized targets, was the
victim of oppression; "They"—the Protestant English-Americans
who controlled the banks, the media, and the Ivy schools—had
persecuted "our good man, Al Smith"; and now "they"—the
same They!—were persecuting Joe McCarthy.

What McCarthy had malignly accomplished was to combine
and confuse the "liberal" cause of equal opportunity for historically penalized Catholics and immigrants with the "conservative" cause of rabid anti-subversion. For a time this fusion
was powerful and effective. It was not "the less fortunate or
members of minority groups" in America who had turned radical,

What McCarthy had malignly accomplished was to combine and confuse the
"liberal" cause of equal opportunity for historically penalized Catholics and
immigrants with the "conservative" cause of rabid anti-subversion. (He is
shown here with Senator John McClellan of Arkansas.)

the Senator maintained in his notorious Wheeling address in 1950, but "bright young men . . . born with silver spoons in their mouths"; beneficiaries of wealth, good education, and family prestige. Such members of the old Protestant elite were not merely snobs, McCarthy insisted; they were disloyal. Furthermore, they were ultimately irreligious. Their arch-leader Dean Acheson's defense of Alger Hiss, which the Senator interpreted as a proclamation "that Christ on the Mount endorsed Communism, high treason, and betrayal of a sacred trust," was a "blasphemy . . . so great that it awakened the dormant indignation of the American people." Evidently, no matter what the Supreme Court had said in *Burstyn* v. *Wilson,* in the McCarthyites' minds it remained legally and politically possible in America to commit sacrilege.

V

It was an evening in Lent, that season in Boston when the butcher shops laid out so appetizing an array of slippery fresh fish that dining on them instead of meat seemed hardly a sacrifice. In the upstairs office of the Hotel and Restaurant Employees' and Bartenders' International Union, AFL-CIO, Local 186, near the Charles Street MTA stop where the subway trains emerged from their winding tunnels to clatter across the river into Cambridge, a group of new union members had gathered to be initiated into the ranks of organized labor. Three and four stops away on the MTA, at MIT and Harvard, beleaguered professors at about that same time were girding for scheduled encounters with HUAC and with Joe McCarthy.

The union officials—the business agent, the president of the local, and a secretary—were in no hurry to get started. On the wall opposite the folding wooden chairs where the new recruits chatted and fidgeted was a television set, and above the TV was a crucifix. Shortly the relationship between liturgic symbolism and the electronic tube became clear. Promptly on the hour someone snapped on the set, and shortly the screen was filled with the charismatic presence of Bishop Fulton J. Sheen.

Fulton Sheen was no ordinary clergyman standing in front of a camera. Like his contemporary Billy Graham he had mastered the electronic media. Both clerics had previously been successful on radio; Graham with his *Hour of Decision* program, Sheen with *The Catholic Hour*. As TV erupted across the American landscape, both moved easily into the new medium, convincingly demonstrating that ancient doctrine can mesh comfortably with modern technology. Billy Graham developed a format for telecasting his evangelical crusades, with the Bible as his only stage prop and the cameras ever alert to pick out an intent face from the crowd; down into the 1980s it would remain highly effective as television theater. Similarly Fulton Sheen, playing with all the skills of a good actor to a live audience that laughed and applauded, in a conventional video program format complete with breaks for commercials, quickly emerged as a major television star. In the race for the Nielsen ratings the Catholic prelate in 1953 defeated a formidable prime-time opponent, the madcap, much-loved vaudevillist Milton Berle.

Fulton Sheen had been a philosophical opponent of Communism for many years. Indeed, he had converted several prominent ex-radicals, notably Louis Budenz of the *Daily Worker,* to Catholicism. Usually he refrained from witch-hunting, however, and most of the time during the McCarthy rampage Sheen kept his distance from the scruffy Senator. But occasionally his religious and patriotic enthusiasm carried him away, and tonight was one of those times.

On this particular Lenten program the sermon topic was the betrayal of Christ by Judas. In the union office beside the Charles River the little gathering was seized by the speaker's rhetorical gifts, including his knack for the sentimental ("Think of it—he could have been *Saint* Judas"). Then the bishop moved smoothly from religion to politics, comparing the forsworn apostle's treason to his Master with American Communist sympathizers' treason to their country. In order to get rid of a plague of rats one did not have to burn down the barn, the cleric cautioned—a back-handed knock at McCarthy's "methods"—but it was necessary, nevertheless, to "get rid of the dirty *rats!*"

As he punched out the last syllable, his eyes flashing, the devout listeners in Boston murmured approval. Then the program ended, and shortly the union secretary was explaining to the new members how their monthly dues would enable the local to "fight the bosses" for better wages and working conditions. Clearly this kind of anti-Communist militancy was not, as political liberals so often naïvely assumed, a defense of reactionary Republican capitalism.

From a *religiously* conservative standpoint, however, there was something bothersome in Fulton Sheen's warm-hearted Americanism. A heresy-hunter of another kind might have gone after the bishop himself, for having dared thus to liken the American commonwealth to the Body of Christ. With zealous Under-Godders the tempting pitfall was always there: if the distinguishing essence of the "American Way of Life" was religion, and if one could not spell out the details of any particular religion without giving offense to others who also wanted to defend the common way of life, one logical way out of the dilemma was to affirm in effect that *America* was the religion. But that claim ran smack into the ancient ban, "thou shalt have no other Gods before Me." No wonder Eisenhower was content to say merely that "the Almighty takes a definite and direct interest day by day in the progress of this nation," and let it go at that.

All patriotism, from a transcendent religious point of view, runs the risk of turning into idolatry. A decade earlier the United States and its United Nations allies, including Russia, had fought and defeated two powerful nations both of whose governments, in different fashion, had equated the State with God. For Catholic patriots, in particular, the necessary theological check against political excess was reinforced by their awareness that the apex of the visible form within which they worshiped lay not in Washington (or Boston) but in Rome. Even such an

extreme national chauvinist as Richard Ginder had to take account
of "exaggerated nationalism of the sort denounced by Pius XI"
in the encyclical *Quadragesimo Anno*. American nationalism,
however, Father Ginder insisted, was not that kind at all. Rather
than conceiving the religio-civic alternative to "godless Communism" as an ideological-nationalistic "way of life," Ginder
explained it in terms of what we would nowadays term a life
style. "There is something about an American that speaks to our
heart," the militant priest wrote in his "Right or Wrong" column
for October 16, 1955:

> If he didn't play on the high school team, he played in the band.
> He can talk about the Yankees and the Dodgers . . . He is as open
> and trusting as an airedale pup and so big hearted that the whole
> world takes advantage of him. He showers every day and insists
> that even his blue-jeans be immaculate . . . And while your Eng-
> lishman has his own peculiar charm and the Italian his, the Amer-
> ican, with all his human dignity, has even more than that. He is
> a brother. . . .
> We Americans love everybody—but we're never going to be
> so foolish, because of that, as to fork over the title to our own
> country.

In such words Father Ginder unknowingly anticipated the
turmoils of the sixties, when the way people dressed and behaved
would be fully as much an issue as the political stands they took.
His regularly showering, clean-blue-jeaned American represented
the "culture" against which other Americans would pose a
"counterculture." Nor need any Protestant, Jew, Black Muslim,
or atheist have found anything peculiarly "Catholic" in such a
description of the normative American. Here at last was a basis
for burying the traditional animosities of Protestant and Catholic
political right-wingers and here, I suggest, is the real root of
what later came to call itself the Moral Majority.

VI

People who judged governments by their godliness or god-
lessness were likely to extend that judgment to international

organizations as well. Many who detested atheistic Communism disapproved also of the religionlessness of the United Nations. "The UN has persistently excluded God from its activities and undertakings," Father Ginder wrote on August 23, 1953. "Unlike every session of Congress and all American legislative bodies, no UN Security Council or General Assembly meeting is permitted to begin with a prayer"—even though the UN had its headquarters in the U.S. and received 35 percent of its budget, ultimately, from godly American taxpayers. Space at the Assembly for a prayer or meditation room (of an artistically and theologically noncommittal kind) had finally been found in 1951, "although from the very beginning the UN could afford plenty of space and money for one of the largest bars in the world with tax-free liquor." U.S. membership in the world organization gave an "appearance of endorsement" to UN atheism, and if equally godless Red China became a member and took over the Chinese seat on the Security Council it would then be time, Ginder concluded, "for all Americans to demand that we get the U.S. out of the UN and the UN out of the U.S."

President Eisenhower obviously did not agree; somehow, the American civic faith he professed was compatible with the humane and hopeful, if formally nonreligious, purposes of the United Nations. And, in addition to the UN's efforts to create a pattern of civilization that would rise above humanity's nationalistic chaos, a parallel movement toward international order was taking concrete form in the churches themselves. In 1948, at Amsterdam, delegates from 44 countries representing 147 religious denominations—29 of them American—founded a World Council of Churches. Its first six co-presidents included a Greek Orthodox prelate and the Archbishop of Canterbury; *they*, at least, could not be accused of godless Communism. But another of the presidents was a U.S. Methodist Bishop, G. Bromley Oxnam, who regularly tangled with the House Un-American Activities Committee—and who, unlike most Committee victims, after years of its badgering challenged HUAC to what amounted to a public debate, in which he confronted the Committee with the evidence against him (rather than the other way around, as was usual) and confounded it utterly. Oxnam's presence high in the World Council of Churches was evidence to militant Under-Godders that that body, like the UN, was also infected by atheistic Communism.

The Council had to wrestle with centuries-old theological divergencies within its ranks: Protestant versus Eastern Orthodox concepts of church authority, Anglican versus Baptist views of the ministry, Lutheran versus Reformed ideas about the sacraments. But it was acutely aware that its own religious dividedness existed in a setting of secular schism as well. "We are divided from one another not only in matters of faith, order and tradition, but also by pride of nation, class and race," the First (Amsterdam) Assembly of the World Council confessed in its message to the World. Nevertheless, "We intend to stay together."

Staying together, if it had merely meant going to church together, might have given no offense. But the Church throughout its history had conceived its mission far more comprehensively. "We have to learn afresh together to speak boldly," the Assembly message went on, "both to those in power and to the people, to oppose terror, cruelty and race discrimination." So far, no conflict with a religiously conceived American Way of Life; except perhaps the U.S. white South, which was already girding for the segregation battles of the fifties. But the message went on "to ask God to teach us together to say 'No' . . . to every system, every programme and every person that treats any man as though he were an irresponsible thing or a means of profit"— a blow, however softened, at the foundations of capitalism— and "to the defenders of injustice in the name of order," a description that fitted any number of governments calling themselves Christian.

The same Cold War that poisoned the amateur, non-nationalistic Olympic ideal and echoed noisily at the UN also broke into the World Council's theological deliberations. The founding conference in Amsterdam was marked by a memorable debate between Josef Hromadka, a Czech theologian who in 1958 would win the Lenin Peace Prize, and U.S. delegate John Foster Dulles, a Presbyterian layman—an argument not unlike the Vyshinsky–Lodge interchanges at the UN. The World Council, however, ended its debate by spanking both sides in the Cold War. "The Christian Church should reject the ideologies of both communism and laissez-faire capitalism," the conference report on economics concluded, "and should seek to draw men away from the false assumption that these are the only alternatives. Each has made promises it could not redeem."

The Russian Orthodox Church in Russia had not yet become a member of the Council (it joined in 1960), but Protestant churches in the East European satellite countries belonged from the beginning, as did the old German Lutheran former state church, which was struggling against incredible odds to remain one religious body in a physically and politically divided Germany. Its great theologian-statesman Otto Dibelius, Bishop of Berlin, was elected to the next slate of presidents by the World Council's Second Assembly, which met in 1954 at Evanston, Illinois. The *Chicago Tribune* in its typical fashion took editorial note of all those bearded, caped and coped foreigners meeting out on the North Side and condemned their one-worlding, Red-lining un-Americanism.

At a more profound level, nationalist exclusivism like the *Tribune's* ran against the American grain. The self-righteousness of America, conceiving itself as innocent and virtuous while it confronted "a corrupt, devious, and guileful Europe and Asia," Will Herberg pointed out in 1955, was complicated by the fact that "virtually all Americans are themselves derived from the foreign parts they so distrust." In a country where the old North European Protestant hegemony had started to break down, as the 1960 presidental election would show, the same was true also of sectarian barriers of a kind which had once disrupted families, shattered marriages, and prompted mutual persecution.

The formation of the World Council of Churches was followed in 1950 by the establishment in the U.S. of the National Council of Churches, an integration of previously existent Protestant interdenominational agencies. The total constituency of the American denominations that entered the Council—25 Protestant, 4 Eastern Orthodox—amounted to thirty million church members and included most of the old, long-established "mainstream" churches, both WASP and Black. Addressing "the People of the Nation" early in 1951, the National Council declared that "the American Churches, of which the Council is one of the visible symbols, are in their true estate the soul of the nation."

This was quite a different idea, however, from the minimal, essentially noninstitutional, civic religion which was usually meant when people spoke of piety as an element in the "American Way of Life." Nor did the Council mean that these churches that were the nation's soul constituted a kind of collective State Shinto. "When those Churches take their true course," the statement continued, "they draw their standards not from the world around but from the guiding mind of Christ. The Church is not the religious phase of the civilization in which it finds itself; it is the living center out of which lasting civilizations take life and form." Then-current, now perhaps dated, theological ideas breathe through this manifesto; it has echoes of Paul Tillich and Arnold Toynbee. Those ideas, however, gave the churchmen who proclaimed them a healthy distance from any notion that religion can simply be equated with nationality. That way lies simple tribalism or, as Toynbee would have put it, idolatry.

The tendency to huddle together in a tribe and worship its totem is never greater than during a war, and the National Council's message went out "at a moment when clouds arising from the war in Korea threaten to darken the entire sky." Nevertheless, the Council summoned the American people to "live and, if need be, die" not simply as national patriots but as "loyal members of the world community," upholding a standard for which nonreligious humanitarians and even some of the anti-religious radicals could also have lived and died—"without hysteria, without hatred, without pride, without undue impatience, without making national interest our chief end, but shaping our policies in the light of the aims of the United Nations, without relaxing our positive services to the other peoples of the world, and in complete repudiation of the lying dogma that war is inevitable."

It was a large and demanding agenda that the National Council leaders thus implicitly held up for their constituents as the needful public policy for getting through the fifties: don't cut foreign aid, stick with the UN, reject McCarthyist heresy hunting, and don't stampede toward war no matter what the macho hawks say. If these member churches were "in their true estate the soul of the nation," their task was not passively to celebrate that nation's way of life but actively to criticize it by a standard higher than its own—and where necessary, labor to change that way. Such an approach was a very long distance from the concept of the "nation under God" held by people like Sister Birnie and Father Ginder, but it was fully as logical an inference as theirs. To be sure, "Under God" may be taken with the narrow meaning, given it in a Joan Baez protest song of the sixties, as merely a pompous nationalistic claim to have "God on our side." It may also be taken, however, as a penitent acknowledgment that a nation stands under judgment.

America's last great lay Calvinist theologian, Abraham Lincoln, who had first publicized the term "under God," had understood it so. Black religionists had never forgotten this prophetic insight, and by the mid-fifties Martin Luther King, Jr. was dramatically putting an ethic and tactic of nonviolent revolutionary love into practice, with the hope that the "American Way of Life" as it then existed in race relations might be transformed. As for those white Protestant clergymen whom the investigating committees were trying to nab as Communist agents, most of them were only trying to carry out what they perceived as the practical implications of their faith—a mode of religio–political activism long domesticated on the American scene as the "social gospel." Religion, so often perceived in the fifties as a prop for the status quo, had always within it the potential for social change, as the sixties would again show. When clergy and lay people linked arms to march against war, racism, and other uncharitableness in the name of their God, singing "We Shall Overcome"—itself an old gospel song—they would march in the conviction that they, not their Rightist opponents, were the real moral majority.

CHAPTER SIX

History, Mystery, and the Modern World

I

THE visiting cleric had come to a state university campus for "Religious Emphasis Week," an observance that has developed in U.S. colleges and universities as one result of educators' constant shadow-boxing with the religion clauses of the First Amendment. On some campuses such weeks are celebrated by inviting Catholic, Jewish, Mormon, and various Protestant speakers to lobby for their respective religious brands, on the political model of the radio and TV doctrine of "equal time." At other schools such gatherings are organized on "interfaith" or "non-sectarian" lines. This particular instance, in the fall of 1956, was billed as an Ecumenical Conference. The rostrum was in readiness with its reading lamp, pitcher of water, and microphone; the university's music auditorium, tastefully modern with blond wood paneling, held rows of neatly dressed students politely waiting to be inspired.

The student conference coordinator stepped up on the stage to introduce the speaker—who, instead of joining him on the platform, walked informally over to the front row of folding seats. After a brief, softly delivered ritual greeting the visitor put his hands on the back of the nearest chair, gazed earnestly at his audience, and said: "When I look into your empty, apathetic faces—*I get scared.*"

There was an awkward silence. Then their distinguished guest began to declaim a long soliloquy from an avant-garde play by Samuel Beckett, *Waiting for Godot,* which had perplexed drama critics the previous Broadway season almost as much as it perplexed these students now. This was not the kind of pious edification they thought they had come to hear! As the incomprehensible words rolled over their heads they stirred restlessly in their seats; they murmured; one whispered "What's going on?"; a few laughed in embarrassment. Seeing the effect he was creating, the speaker broke off, told them he was going to read them some more poetry, and launched into "Vanity of vanities, all is vanity . . . and there is no new thing under the sun" (Eccles. 1)—a passage closer than most in the Bible to the mood of the two tramps who fare through the darkness and chaos of the universe in Beckett's play. Then, as the light of recognition dawned in some of the faces before him, the unconventional interpreter announced that he was going to read them another poem—and came right to the heart of his evangel, with I Corinthians 13: "Though I speak with the tongues of men and of angels, and have not love." From then on he had the audience completely in his hands.

"Something has happened in our time," the theologian Paul Tillich wrote in 1952, "which has opened up many people in such a way that we can again speak to them and participate in their situation." An iconoclastic cultural movement had arisen in the Western World, variously expressed in names like *The Wasteland, No Exit, The Age of Anxiety,* or *Encounter with Nothingness,* which confuted the easy progressive optimism of the previous century and expressed "anxiety about the meaning of our existence, including the problems of death, faith, and guilt." To the troubled student in the fifties who could not buy the bland comforts promised by a self-celebrant "American Way of Life," and who might be reading and discussing with friends the unsettling insights of Nietzsche and Sartre, not to mention those

of Marx and Freud—all the while asking the eternal undergraduate question "Me: why?"—a religious advocate who came
at him or her with *Waiting for Godot* might have an impact far
more profound than that of a more conventional evangelist.

It was a radically different approach from that of Billy Graham
and Fulton J. Sheen, both of whom tuned their oratory to their
listeners' general American, culturally bourgeois expectations.
But the social upheavals of the twentieth century, which many
perceived as threatening to religion, could also be taken as a
missionary opportunity. "Today there are many people," Tillich
asserted, "who have become aware of their human existence in
such a way that they ask the question to which we"—the defenders
of traditional faith—"can give the answer."

Paul Tillich was especially interested in the way the fine arts,
revolutionized by a modernist consciousness—painting, sculpture,
architecture—could become vivid instruments for the articulation
of that question and answer. He had been pondering the subject
at least since 1919, when he gave an address "On the Idea of
a Theology of Culture" before the Kant Society in Berlin, in
the course of which he first put forth his later much-quoted
axiom: "Religion is the substance of culture; culture is the form
of religion." Driven into exile in 1933 by the Nazi government
like so many other German and Continental intellectuals, a
group whose members have greatly enriched their adopted
homeland in America, Tillich—a U.S. citizen since 1940—had
learned much from his American hosts: "the spirit of the English
language," he once confessed, "has demanded the clarification
of many ambiguities of my thought which were covered by the
mystical vagueness of the classic philosophical German." In return
this fine-honed German intelligence, schooled at Berlin, Breslau,
and Halle, had much to give Americans—and especially to religious Americans, many of whom enjoyed "positive thinking"
but were not especially addicted to *hard* thinking.

It was jarring, if you were an American of conventional aesthetic
preferences, to hear this refugee professor praise (for example)
Pablo Picasso's *Guernica*—a great, wall-spanning picture that

had been provoked into existence by the brutal bombing of a small town during the Spanish Civil War—as a religious painting; indeed, as a *Protestant* painting, which exemplified "man's finitude, his subjection to death, but above all, his estrangement from his true being and his bondage to demonic forces." The relationship between religion and the arts had never been easy. Art, when following its own genius, tends willfully to go its own way; when it does not, it tends to become hopelessly tame. In England and America, in particular, religious art in the nineteenth century had largely become "calendar art," didactic poster-narrative or prettified portraiture. In the meantime, secular art had begun to part company with popular taste altogether. Few Americans, probably, really liked "modern"—post-Armory Show—painting and sculpture. It was hard enough for a Middle American to be asked to enjoy Picasso, that shatterer of the human frame, whose abstract "peace dove" symbol had become an icon of the Communist-sponsored (and therefore, presumably, godless) wing of the peace movement, without also being asked to learn theological lessons from him!

Tillich struggled valiantly against the philistinism of his adopted compatriots. In December of 1954, for example, young painters and sculptors in the New York area mounted an art show within the grey Gothic walls of Union Theological Seminary, to which pious little old ladies came in quest of the Christmas spirit and went away offended at the artworks' (from their point of view) ugliness, incomprehensibility, subversiveness, and downright blasphemy. To enhance the show Professor Tillich gave an informal gallery talk, insisting in his warm, winning, heavily-accented English that "anything which points toward the ultimate Ground of our being is entitled to be called religious art."

Critics of this "theology of culture" wondered whether the tactic was quite fair. Campus clergy who drew points of orthodox doctrine from the Theater of the Absurd, or from abstract-expressionist painting, or from existentialist philosophy in order to win friends among the unconverted sometimes seemed only to be chasing after bandwagons in order to sprinkle holy water on them. Calling something religious did not necessarily make it so, and the would-be baptizers' efforts to be trendy sometimes only made them look ridiculous. Tillich was robustly aware of this pitfall. "If religion had only the word everybody has—every newspaper, every radio, every speaker," the emigré scholar declared in 1942, "it would have no word at all worth listening to"; and it would not become more worthy of attention simply by extending its quest from the mass media into the art museums. "If religion gave only a little more enthusiasm, a little more certainty, a little more dignity to something that would be done anyhow, with or without religion, then religion would have no significance at all."

Tillich also realized that for many of his contemporaries the darker side of man as traditional, Judaeo-Christian religion pictured him—fallen, corrupt, and lost—seemed far more convincing in the age of Hiroshima and Belsen than the brighter portrait of a being who had been made in the image of God and placed only a little lower than the angels. It was the "*negative-*Protestant character" of Picasso's *Guernica* that seemed "obvious" to Tillich; what the painting "put before us with tremendous power" was "the question of man in a world of guilt, anxiety, and despair." To look at painting and sculpture was to realize that attempts to re-create religious art in the modern world had led to the rediscovery of symbols which mostly expressed "the negativity of man's predicament," Tillich wrote in 1957. "The symbol of the Cross has become the subject matter of many works of art—often in the style which is represented in Picasso's 'Guernica.' Symbols, such as resurrection, have not yet found any adequate artistic representation, and so it is with the other traditional 'symbols of glory.'"

In a grim world overshadowed by the nuclear bomb, secular thinkers who were not practicing Catholics, Protestants, or religious Jews had no difficulty with theological terms like *estrangement, alienation,* or even *the demonic,* a term Tillich defined as "the mythical expression of . . . the structural, and therefore inescapable, power of evil." They could believe, in some sense, in *sin;* they were unmoved or embarrassed by a word like *grace*. A hard-headed atheistic disciple of Sigmund Freud would have had no difficulty explaining St. Paul's cry "For the good that I would I do not: but the evil which I would not, that I do" (Rom. 7:19); the Freudian would have said that that's just the way neuroses work. But he would have had great trouble giving voice to the question people like Paul Tillich really wanted him to ask (verse 24): "Who shall deliver me from the body of this death?"

II

"Today," Tillich wrote in 1952, "the meaning of original sin, its universality, its tragic role in history, can be emphasized in a way that it could not be twenty years ago." Since the eighteenth century this had been "the most attacked of all doctrines;" believers in rational progress had indignantly rejected any idea that the human course, through history and in individual lives, is one of recurrent and inevitable failure. In modern, metropolitan, bureaucratic, war-making civilization, however, the situation had come to seem quite different; there were not only sociological but also theological reasons to assert that the human condition in the fifties was one of "growing up absurd":

> A profound insight has been developed in modern literature [,] namely, that one of the fundamental expressions of sin is to make the other person into an object, into a thing. This is perhaps the greatest temptation in an industrial society in which everybody is brought into the process of mechanical production and comsumption, and even the spiritual life in all its forms is commercialized and subjected to the same proceess.

Reinhold Niebuhr, Paul Tillich's teaching colleague at Union Seminary for two decades—American-born, but nurtured in the same German theological tradition from which Tillich came—had seen the human consequences of that mechanical process as a young inner-city pastor in Detroit during and after the First World War. Theologically liberal in his youth, Niebuhr had moved on from that liberalism to a chastened restatement of more orthodox doctrine, while retaining many of the distinguishing marks of the *political* liberal. In the fifties, for example, he chaired the Greater New York chapter of Americans for Democratic Action, and in 1952 both he and Tillich, like most other academicians, were ardent partisans of Stevenson against Eisenhower. Theologically, however, Niebuhr and Tillich stood considerably to the Right of other intellectual New Dealers.

"The Christian faith undoubtedly survives in a so-called 'modern' age in which scientific development is supposed to have invalidated it," Niebuhr wrote in *The Self and the Dramas of History* (1955). "It survives, in part, because all the testimonies of philosophers and scientists against it can not avail against the inner witness of the human self." To Fundamentalists and skeptics alike it seemed outrageously contradictory to assert, as Niebuhr did, that the story of Adam and Eve and the apple is both "mythical" and "true." Niebuhr's neo-orthodox gospel puzzled seekers after logical symmetry, who assumed that anyone who seriously asserted the Fall of Man must also believe that the earth is no more than six thousand years old and came into existence in seven calendar days. However, "the influence of this myth upon the Christian imagination is not primarily due to any literalistic illusions of Christian orthodoxy," Niebuhr declared (in *Faith and History,* 1949). "The myth accurately symbolizes the consistent Biblical diagnosis of moral and historical evil."

Much of Niebuhr's work, especially after the Second World War, was an attempt to take the drama of personal and existential theology into the larger theater of history. Groups, as well as individuals, did not the good that they would and did the evil which they would not; nations, races, classes, governing elites, were as prone as private selves to rationalize, excuse, justify, and explain away. To project the ego upon a larger social entity, and worship it, was as much an idolatrous act as to turn inward in self-absorbed narcissism. Reinhold Niebuhr would have so interpreted the "social ethic" of Whyte's Organization Man, and he was not at all surprised by the appearance in modern times of Hoffer's True Believer, whose self is "so conscious of its finiteness as an individual that it finds no opportunity to assert the ultimate significance of itself in history except by asserting the significance of the collective self." Progressive rationalists had hopefully believed that that kind of submergence of the individual in the mass was "a phase of history," now long past; however, "the recrudescence of religious nationalism and the pseudo-universalistic Messianism of communism have instructed us that this idolatry . . . is not merely due to the limits of a primitive imagination."

But Reinhold Niebuhr did not fall into the Under-Godders' trap of complacently contrasting the Soviets' disguised-nationalist messianism with the "free world's" crusade for the one true God. The trouble with the Cold War division of the world into categories of "we" (good) and "they" (bad), for someone who really took the doctrine of original sin seriously, was that sooner or later one had to face the question "—and who the hell are *we?*" Marxist ideology and republican-capitalist doctrine, Niebuhr argued, were similarly unselfcritical and idolatrous; "both creeds imagine that man can become the master of historical destiny." In the collective life of humankind, this activist theologian summed up (in *The Structure of Nations and Empires,* 1959), "most evil arises because finite men involved in the flux of time pretend that they are not so involved. They make claims of virtue, of wisdom, and of power which are beyond their competence as creatures. These pretensions are the source of evil, whether they are expressed by kings and emperors or by commissars and revolutionary statesmen."

Niebuhr did not contend that the *results* of all such pretentious claims are equally deplorable. "The Marxist and the bourgeois property ideologies are equally indiscriminate," he argued in *The Irony of American History* (1952); however, "the Marxist ideology has proved to be the more dangerous because, under the

cover of its illusions, a new society has been created in which
political and economic power are monstrously combined while
the illusion is fostered that economic power has been completely
eliminated." On the hither side of the Iron Curtain, in ironic
contrast, the U.S. has achieved a society with a tolerable degree
of fairness to its citizens largely by *disregarding* its own formal
economic creed! "Our success in establishing justice and insuring
domestic tranquillity has exceeded the characteristic insights of
a bourgeois culture," Niebuhr contended. "Frequently our success
is due to social and political policies which violate and defy the
social creed which characterizes a commercial society."

By his own logic, Niebuhr could not in turn elevate this relative
social and political success into a new focus for idolatry. That
would have been to align himself with "the blind fanatics of
western civilization who regard the highly contingent achievements of our culture as the final form and norm of human
existence." Niebuhr was acutely aware that he might be committing the heresy which Marxists term "American exception-
alism": the doctrine that America is somehow exempt from the
historical processes the rest of the world must undergo. America's
achievement in pragmatically averting the rise of a home-grown
revolutionary socialist movement might, he admitted, "be due
primarily to our highly favored circumstances . . . the wealth
of our natural resources, the unity of a continental economy
and the efficiency of our technology." The post-New Deal government's strategy of preventing a struggle over who gets the
largest slice of pie by simply baking a bigger pie would not look
so effective in the energy-pinched eighties, when the technology
looked less efficient, the resources were less abundant, and inflation seemed to be shrinking the pie to the dimensions of a
cupcake.

Under changing historical circumstances—and historical circumstances always change—Americans might come to regret
the aborting of a native radical tradition from which they could
have learned much: "In so far as the absence of a Marxist
challenge to our culture has left the institution of property

completely unchallenged," the theologian prophetically warned, "we may have become the prisoners of a dogmatism which will cost us dearly in some future crisis." We had already, in Herbert Hoover's reluctant response to the Great Depression of 1929, learned that "the lip service which the whole culture pays to the principles of *laissez-faire* makes for tardiness in dealing with the instability of a free economy;" and the future might not grant the culture the needed margin of time before it had to act. Yet action carried its own dangers. As the welfare state evolved, the question would have to be raised "whether the scope of bureaucratic decisions may not become too wide and the room for the automatic balances of unregulated choices too narrow." These and other misgivings must confront every modern democracy, "since there is no neat principle which will solve the relation of power to justice and of justice to freedom." Nevertheless, Niebuhr concluded, "With these reservations we may claim that the unarticulated wisdom embodied in the actual experience of American life has created forms of justice considerably higher than our more articulate unwisdom suggests." Reluctantly, here and there, in his footnotes, the neo-orthodox prophet and Adlai Stevenson partisan conceded that such unarticulated wisdom could be embodied at times even in the experience of American life under Dwight Eisenhower.

III

People could enjoy and use a book like *The Irony of American History* who did not share its author's theology; there was in fact a substantial fellow-traveling fringe whose members one wit referred to as "Atheists for Niebuhr." It did not require a commitment to conventional religious faith to believe that the rational hopes of the eighteenth-century Enlightenment had been premature, that the course of human history was not automatically and inevitably progressive, or that the human animal was characterized by ingrained orneriness. Critics in the fifties, both religious and nonreligious, made full use of Reinhold Niebuhr's insight into the moral ambiguity of historical and personal existence. "We have met the enemy," said Walt Kelly's cartoon character Pogo, "and he is us."

Sometimes such critics overdid it. When a writer for example insisted in 1951 that "one of the essential marks of decency today is to be ashamed of being a man of the twentieth century," or when a speaker at a college alumni-faculty seminar in 1959 on "The Distrust of Reason" cried out that people "no longer believe that education will make them wise, that science will make them healthy, that law will make them peaceful, that freedom will make them happy, or that love will make them good," the natural counter-urge was to tell all such moaners and groaners to go pull up their socks. "Humanity has always been in a crisis," remarked a friend of the philosopher Irwin Edman in 1953. "The only special thing about the current one is that it *is* current." One of the things that made theirs an age of anxiety, he suggested, was the to-do that was made about anxiety itself: "It is enough to have things to worry about without worrying about the fact that we are worrying. I'll leave that to the psychologists who talk like theologians and the theologians who talk like psychologists."

"Most ages that aren't completely smug tend, after observing themselves, to run themselves down," Louis Kronenberger observed in 1951. "Hamlet is perhaps most neurotic, most modern, most timeless, for exclaiming 'The time is out of joint.'" To be sure, in certain important respects the time *was* out of joint. "An age that saw an intolerable regime bring on a catastrophic war, that has produced in turn not even a nominal peace, is not likely to be an age of reassurance," Kronenberger conceded. "The intellectuals of this age do have some cause for thinking that they have been assaulted and disrupted beyond the common measure." Nevertheless, "if it is the great delusion of moralists to suppose that all previous ages were less sinful than their own, then it is the delusion of intellectuals to suppose that all previous ages were less sick." Intellectuals in the fifties, like other people, demonstrated once again the truth in the old adage that the only thing man learns from history is that he doesn't:

> However shocking the pillage, rape, and murder statistics of the Middle Ages, we somehow see the inhabitants as heartily sustained by a faith in God. However widespread the excesses and pestilences of the Renaissance, we see its inhabitants as hale and whole through their faith in themselves. However incessant villainy may have been in the eighteenth century, or however endemic the vapors, we somehow see the Augustans as integrated and healthy through their faith in reason ... I am far from optimistic about today's world or tomorrow's; but I suspect for all that, that lots of people in the Middle Ages or the Renaissance or the Enlightenment were quite as sick as ourselves.

In fact, argued Wallace Douglas in an essay on "The Solemn Style of Modern Critics" (1953), to write about "the long, dark and fairly dismal drama" of modernity might in some cases be only a ploy to give that writing an aura of significance it did not deserve: "The critics have inflated their language and turned their business into melodrama in order to give importance to an otherwise inconsequential occupation." Usually misunderstanding both Reinhold Niebuhr's sense of the irony of history and Paul Tillich's concept of a theology of culture, literary analysts in particular seemed prone to be "always drifting off into attacks on the eighteenth century, because it was rationalistic; or the nineteenth century, because it was optimistic; or the Renaissance, because it forgot the medieval heritage; or Protestantism, because it isn't at least Anglo-Catholicism; or the American liberal mind, because 'it has no idea of its own momentousness or of its own tragic career.' " American liberal minds could properly have retorted that to voyage successfully through the turbulent seas of modern mindlessness and chaos might require more, not less, of the spirit of eighteenth-century rationalism, nineteenth-century optimism, and Renaissance humanism.

"Since the war years, the optimistic, rational faith has obviously been losing out in competition with more tragic views of political and personal life," C. Wright Mills wrote in *White Collar: The*

American Middle Classes (1951). "Many who not long ago read
Dewey or Marx with apparent satisfaction have become more
vitally interested in such analysts of personal tragedy as Søren
Kierkegaard or such mirrors of bafflement as Kafka." Perhaps
indeed their sense of tragedy, and of despair in reason—the
quality which was the prime tool of their trade—was only a
romantic projection of their own powerlessness. Although they
celebrated the death of reason while politically supporting that
highly rational verbalist Adlai Stevenson, this seeming inconsistency might be resolved unconsciously by their sense that
Adlai, in this murky, world-weary *Weltanschauung* of the fifties,
had to be a loser. Mills, who managed to fare through the fifties
with his radicalism intact against all the fuzzing and blurring
influences of corporate prosperity and against all the inhibitions
born of the Cold War, gave such intellectuals a good spanking.
"Alienation," he charged, as that word was used in contemporary
"middle-brow circles," did not mean the kind of estrangement
from the vulgar pretensions of bourgeois culture that had characterized intellectuals in the Roaring Twenties. It was, rather,
"a lament and a form of collapse into self-indulgence, a fashionable way of being overwhelmed."

Speaking sociologically—and nobody did more to spark the
revival of theoretical sociology in the fifties than C. Wright
Mills—the author of *White Collar* argued that this newfound
tragic sense of life, although experienced by many "as a personal
discovery and a personal burden," was at the same time "a
reflection of objective circumstances"—circumstances which engendered in such people "the political psychology of the scared
employee." Much in this indictment is, sadly, quite true. Academic
halls in the fifties were filled with scared employees.—scared
not so much of Joe McCarthy as of their own department heads
or deans—who, in the pursuit of that elusive magic talisman
known as tenure, wouldn't say or do anything to rock the boat.
And living off the bounty of the communications industry were
other scared young people, who daily committed exactly the
kind of "doublethink"—misrepresentation and creative forgery,

while denying even to oneself that that is what one is doing—
which is the way the fictional Winston Smith makes his living
in *1984.*

There is always, however, as Emerson observed long ago, a
minority unconvinced: "some protester against the cruelty of
the magistrates to the Quakers . . . some defender of the slave
against the politician and the merchant; some champion of first
principles of humanity against the rich and luxurious . . . some
pleader for peace; some noble protestant, who will not stoop
to infamy when all are gone mad." In the emergent new white
collar society described by Mills, where "between the intellectual
and his potential public stand technical, economic, and social
structures . . . owned by others," such an objector's job might
have become harder. He or she could not, for example, pam-
phletize en masse in the manner of Tom Paine. Nonetheless,
as Mills himself conceded, "the independent artist and intellectual
are among the few remaining personalities presumably equipped
. . . to unmask and smash the sterotypes of vision and intellect
with which modern communications swamp us." Some of them,
at least, drawing upon native American traditions of stereotype-
smashing (e.g., Thorstein Veblen, Henry Thoreau, Mark Twain)
if not upon the prophetic religious principle expounded by
Tillich and Niebuhr, were willing to give it a try.

IV

Such independent artists and intellectuals could not, however,
simply go back to the debunking stance of the Jazz Age. The
expatriate intellectuals of the 1920s had been caught off base
by history. They had attacked the American culture they knew,
calling it provincial, materialistic, philistine, and barbarous; which,
to a large extent, it was. Many of them had contrasted it with
cosmopolitan European, or at least Parisian, enlightenment.
Then in the thirties they and their successors had seen—and,
in the forties, fought—against a power that swept across cos-

mopolitan Europe and for six dark years reorganized it under
the ultimate in racial and national provincialism, in the process
committing barbarities unmatched by any nation since the ancient
Assyrians. And if that power's deeds were barbarous, its words
were philistine: "When I hear the word 'culture,'" Propaganda
Minister Paul Joseph Goebbels once cried, "I reach for my re-
volver."

By such a standard of comparison, U.S. culture didn't look
so bad. Furthermore, although postwar Soviet culture—espcially
after the death of Stalin—was not as blatantly lowbrow as the
Nazi regime had been, still from time to time it humiliated a
Boris Pasternak and drove out an Alexander Solzhenitsyn or a
Mstislav Rostropovich, to join the earlier stream of European
refugee artists and intellectuals like Toscanini and Einstein who
had decided that in modern times the place to pursue a vocation
that would be "Western, purposeful, and whole" was the United
States of America.

It was no accident that the Jefferson Memorial in Washington,
commemorating that most reflective and cultivated of all presidents, was completed in the wartime year 1943 under President
Roosevelt. An appreciative intellectual-folkish interest in U.S.
culture and in its past had begun under the New Deal; it burst
into full flower after the war, in a vogue for "American Studies"
and for American intellectual history. In contrast, the more
severe critics in the twenties would have denied that America
had an intellectual history.

No doubt some of this vogue was put on, a case of "anything
they can do, we can do better," including culture. "Not one
American in ten thousand had ever heard of Van Cliburn until
he won the first prize of the Tchaikovsky Piano Competition,"
Abram Chasins bitingly observed soon afterward (*Reporter,* May
19, 1958), even though the young Texas pianist by the time he
was nineteen had already won *five* other, equally severe piano
competitions in the U.S., one of them formidably juried by the
likes of Rudolf Serkin, Eugene Istomin, and George Szell.
Nevertheless, to move from a situation in which even an artist

of Cliburn's ability, representative of "the American standards that have produced musicians of the first caliber year after year," had to scratch for the opportunity simply to do his work, to a situation in which "neither social prestige nor any speculator can pry loose a seat for the concerts of an American concert pianist in his own country," was a great gain—however suspect some Americans' motives might be for trying to get those seats. Surely it wasn't *all* Cold War one-upmanship; conceivably it might even portend a Cold War thaw, for while Van Cliburn was winning standing ovations in the USSR, the Moiseyev Dance Company from Moscow was drawing the greatest ticket demand in Madison Square Garden's entire history.

In 1949, the first year of Truman's elective presidency, Oliver Larkin brought out a comprehensive study of *Art and Life in America*. In 1960, the last year under Eisenhower, the book appeared in a revised and enlarged edition. In the meantime, as such books go in the marketplace it had done very well, even though to speak of *art* and *life* in the same breath was mentally and emotionally as unsettling, for many Americans, as it had earlier been to pronounce together Darwin's two words *origin* and *species*. "We cannot take art in our stride," wrote Louis Kronenberger in a perceptive essay on "America and Art" (1953). Historically, Americans had confronted the fine arts as "frank, unblushing ignoramuses or comically solemn snobs . . . they either tend to hold back lest they commit howlers; or to go into raptures lest they be taken for clods; or to pooh-pooh the whole business lest they seem longhaired and sissified." As critics, they went at art "like a race of antique-shop dealers for whom everything is either magnificently authentic or the merest fake. We are not a people," Kronenberger concluded, "for whom, at any level, art is just a natural and congenial aspect of existence." But in the age of Eisenhower that mind-set was at last beginning to break down. The reception of performers like Van Cliburn and creators like those depicted in Larkin's book was a sign of the times.

If the fifties marked the advent of Elvis, they were also the heyday of the long-playing phonograph record, which had made it possible to hear the longer works of classical music without the five-minute interruptions that had formerly plagued all recorded operas and symphonies. The fifties were a time when long lines of people stood waiting to see a Matisse show at the Museum of Modern Art or a Cézanne show at the Metropolitan, and when high school bands played, increasingly, music that both challenged them technically and demanded interpretive insight. Perversely, however, as the public began gingerly to approach the arts some of the artists backed away. "The social realist wants to charm you or win you over," one prominent avant-garde painter conceded in 1957. "But the abstract expressionist says to the public (more honestly): 'You're stupid. We despise you. We don't *want* you to like us.'" Larkin noted that many art critics mystified the public far more than they enlightened it, by writing "comments which were the literary equivalent, rather than the clarification, of complex and difficult paintings and sculptures." And the musicologists were, if anything, even more baffling.

Such critics tended also to slight the entire heritage of the artistic past in order to dwell upon the fads of the present. A gallery guide at the Chicago Art Institute once allowed a class of high school teachers, who were studying the history of U.S. art at a nearby university, only one grudged, cursory glimpse of an early American portrait before he hustled them away through the corridors past treasured nineteenth-century paintings by George Inness and Winslow Homer, ignoring all their objections of "Hey, we'd like to stop and take a look at *that*" in order to plant them for a long look at one of the museum's currently fashionable showpieces, a drizzled-upon canvas executed in the fifties by Jackson Pollock.

Against such prejudice—and it *was* prejudice, generated in reaction against the opposite and older bias that had put down all art as frivolous unless it was out of date—the new "American Studies" movement asserted that the American past cannot be studied only in terms of political, economic, or even (as usually conceived) social history. Just as one would not study the politics of Periclean Athens without taking note of the Parthenon, so one ought not to study the politics of Jefferson's young republic without paying attention to Jeffersonian architecture. American history was also American art, American literature, American religion, American philosophy. A U.S. sailing ship at sea in the nineteenth century could and should be looked at as an agency of the nation's expanding commercial power, but it would be well to pay attention also to the scrimshaw work its sailors were carving in their leisure moments up in the forecastle. Such an approach to American civilization did run risks: of dilettantism, of national provincialism, and of bourgeois self-celebration. "To *study* something means to study it critically," Arthur Bestor warned in 1955, "and it is terribly difficult to be critical about ourselves." Properly done, however, a program in American studies had the potential, Bestor believed, for "a new flowering of humanistic studies, equal in grasp and profundity with the great works of the past, and more alive, perhaps, to the man of the present age."

Formal or "high" culture was admittedly at some disadvantage when studied this way, because the further one moved into the past the more it merged into the imperial shadow of its British parent. Informal or "popular" culture had the same problem, complicated by the inevitable disappearance of much of its source material. At the same time, however, American folk art was winning enthusiastic converts among the kind of European—especially French—intellectuals who in another time would have condemned all U.S. culture as hopelessly raw and juvenile. Although some such savants still did not know, Sidney Alexander charged in 1951, "that Texas has symphony orchestras as well as Stetsons," Joseph E. Baker noted in 1957 from his experiences as an exchange professor in France, that in many ways Parisians had come to "look upon America as Americans look upon Paris; for example, as a source of styles (for French men), of dramatic entertainment . . . of dancing (such as the Charleston and *le jitterbug*), of music *(le jazz hot)*." Gallic cultural journals treated

Frank Sinatra as a serious artist and praised America's western films. Professor Baker reported that his students in Auvergne had taped all the square-dance records he and a French professor of chemistry had brought with them from the U.S., cherishing these *danses folkloriques américaines* along with New Orleans jazz and the American dance tunes of the twenties, which in France were often played at the original tempo. "The French can value such things that come down to us from our past," the American visitor concluded ironically, "even when some unhappy Americans have themselves abandoned them."

Prior to the post-Stalin thaw at least, Eastern Europe's official reaction to American folkloric dances was to denounce them. One American observer thought it "a stroke of genius" when an announcer in the German Democratic Republic, during a Bach concert that was conducted by Dmitri Shostakovich and broadcast over East German radio, declared: "This is our answer to the American 'Kulturbarbaren': Bach or boogie-woogie—take your choice." It may not have been a stroke of genius at all. Americans could have made three possible retorts to the DDR announcer's question: Yes, we can play Bach, or at least Tchaikovsky, as Van Cliburn is showing you; or, So what's wrong with boogie?; or, We can do both. To the second response the young people of the Soviet Union, as they risked chastisement by purchasing U.S. phonograph records on the black market, were giving their own answer.

V

As with the heritage of the arts, so with the history of ideas; the fifties—so often stereotypically thought of as "anti-intellectual"—were a time for American cultural enrichment. "One of the most interesting things in my teaching experience," one eloquent and erudite teacher-scholar reminisced in 1968, was "the passion for intellectual history that seized the generation that was post-Nazi." This had been, however, Carl Schorske

thought, "a not altogether healthy symptom" of American political
and cultural development in the postwar years:

> When I was first teaching right after the war, the fields of eco-
> nomics, politics, sociology and the like were the popular fields
> and people in history were generally motivated toward *that* kind
> of socially-oriented historical inquiry. . . . Then there came a real
> desertion of these areas, [and] a lot of kids start to opt out and
> lean way over on the other side—to literature, philosophy and
> the like . . . Where previously there'd been a strong current of
> democratic idealism or Marxism, there arose an interest in the
> tragic view.

Professor Schorske, who in the course of his teaching experience at Wesleyan, Berkeley, and Princeton trained a good
many able young intellectual historians, in this response to an
interviewer's question sounded somewhat like C. Wright Mills
in *White Collar.* In explaining this shift from a "social sciences"
to a "humanities" orientation, Schorske took note of "the increasing neutrality of the conceptual disciplines of economics,
political sciences and the like"—a neutrality dismissed in *White
Collar* as "an academic cult of the narrowed attention"—in contrast
to such disciplines' previously conceived "normative or social-
critical role." Both Schorske and Mills took account also of the
oppressive presence of the Cold War and of McCarthyism as
contributory causes of "flight from social engagement." Unlike
Mills, however, Schorske did not equate a tragic sense of life
with the mere political psychology of a scared employee.

In his own teaching during the fifties and sixties he developed
an appropriate strategy for reaching his students at their own
existential moment in history. "In my teaching, I shifted to a
more intensive focus on specific figures who might be real culture-
heroes to the students," Schorske explained. "I tried to show
how, as thinkers, they were coming to grips with their own
society even when they were saying nay to it or denying the
meaningfulness of history." Carl Schorske's own work in intellectual history lay in Europe, rather than America; he found
his potential culture-heroes in the waning years of the Austro-

Hungarian Empire. But intellectual historians could also find in the American past specific figures who had come to grips with their society even when they said nay to it; crying with Thoreau, for example, that under a government which imprisons any unjustly, the proper place for a just person is also a prison, or with Tom Paine that against all national established religions one's own mind must be one's own church. And such culture heroes were available in abundance. That the U.S. "should have produced a Carnegie, a Rockefeller, a Vanderbilt, a Ford, an Edison, an Eads, a Roebling, a Mahan, or an Eisenhower was natural enough," Henry Steele Commager wrote in *The American Mind* (1950), "but that it should also have produced in the same time-span a Henry Adams, a William James, a Louis Sullivan, a Thomas Eakins, a John Dewey, an Edwin Arlington Robinson, an Oliver Wendell Holmes, a Vernon Louis Parrington, a Thorstein Veblen, a Willard Gibbs, was more surprising."

Even more important than what such artists and thinkers said nay to, for their heirs in the 1950s, was what they affirmed; those beliefs which emerged among them, as Ralph H. Gabriel expressed it, "to serve as guides for action, as standards by which to judge the quality of social life, and as goals to inspire humane living." Tacitly rejecting the idea, then regnant in many graduate history departments, that the historian for fear of contamination must abstain from "present-mindedness," Professor Gabriel in revising his book *The Course of American Democratic Thought* in 1956 declared that the objective of the new edition was the same as that of its earlier (1940) version: "to achieve such insights as may be gained in a study of the past to illumine partially a present that, like all presents, is obscured by shadows."

To illumine that present, American intellectual historians strove to recapture for present use certain aspects of the American past which previous generations of U.S. intellectuals had neglected, or had even sought to live down as a bad memory. Nothing benefited more from this revaluation than Puritanism; the pioneering work on Puritan religious and secular thought that had been begun by Perry Miller around 1930 was reinforced in the fifties by a host of able younger scholars. No longer was it possible, Edmund Morgan affirmed in *The Puritan Dilemma,* a biography of John Winthrop (1958), to condescend to seventeenth-century Massachusetts as "a preposterous land of witches and witch hunters, of kill-joys in tall-crowned hats, whose main occupation was to prevent each other from having any fun and whose sole virtue lay in their furniture." A seventeenth-century Puritan like Winthrop, as he admonished his compatriots on the way to Boston in 1630 that "we must be willing to abridge ourselves of our superfluities, for the supply of others' necessities; . . . we must delight in each other, make others' conditions our own, rejoice together, mourn together, labor and suffer together; always having before our eyes our commission and community in the work," proclaimed a gospel that spoke to the condition of Americans three and a quarter centuries later, if they cared to listen.

From the standpoint of progressive political witness and action, however, there were losses as well as gains in this new appreciation of Puritanism. To play up John Winthrop was, in effect, to play down Roger Williams; to focus sympathetically upon the problems of a governing elite was subtly to downgrade the historic role of dissent. For example, the many undergraduate students who learned about political and social controversy in early New England from Perry Miller's paperback *The American Puritans: Their Prose and Poetry* (1956) got Governor Winthrop's version, which was (to say the least) biased, of the conflict between the Bay Colony's magistrates and Anne Hutchinson; not until the sixties had taught historians to be alert for more radical roots of the national culture would it become possible to perceive Mrs. Hutchinson as the first American champion of women's liberation.

Moreover, in spite of Americans' renewed intellectual interest in theology as shown in the vogue for Niebuhr and Tillich, there remained a good deal of religious illiteracy in the U.S.; and some of the most pious, as may be inferred from chapter 5, were among the least literate. But the same lack of basic information about religion also existed for many who were less pious but more scholarly. Teachers and students glibly described as "Puritan" all kinds of traits and ideas which the founders of New England had shared with other, non-Puritan Englishmen; or with Continental, non-puritan Protestantism; or even with that part of Christendom which remained Catholic. One contemporary definition of "Puritanism," as "that spirit in religion which has driven men at all times to seek a purer way of life, one that was simple and good as opposed to the insincere conventionalities and corruptions in the world about them," could just as well have been applied to the flower children of the sixties, who had no great affinity for intellectual history (or any other kind) and would have been horrified to be thought of as Puritans. "The definition is not without charm," comments Emil Oberholzer, Jr., "but it is hardly helpful to the historian," especially to the historian seeking to discern the roots of a specifically American national culture. As with Puritans, so with much else that "American Studies" people and American intellectual historians studied (for example, Social Darwinism): the description of a distinctively American phenomenon tended either to distort it by ignoring its European context or, the opposite error, to dissolve it into an aspect of Western civilization as a whole.

VI

When American Puritans took time out from fighting Indians or arguing theology or trading with the Dutch, and wrote history—some of which was very good history indeed—they gave the major credit to God for the way it had happened. "I shall crave leave," wrote Governor Bradford toward the end of the sixth chapter in his classic history *Of Plimoth Plantation,* "that their children may see with what difficulties their fathers wrastled in going through these things in their first beginnings, and how God brought them along notwithstanding all their weakness and infirmities." Bradford and other American Puritan historians regularly worte of "special providences;" as when a "lusty young

man" aboard the *Mayflower* was rolled overboard in a heavy sea
and "it pleased God that he caught hold of the topsail halyards"
and so was saved. (Presumably it also pleased God that in the
first winter at Plymouth, half the *Mayflower* passengers should
die.) Here, most of the American intellectual historians working
in the fifties had regretfully to part company with the Puritan
Calvinist intellectuals whom in so many other ways they admired.

Historians since the thirties had been engaged in what Henry
May has called a "recovery of American religious history," rescuing a dimension of human affairs which they had theretofore
neglected in favor of economic and other considerations. However, to "recover" religious history, in America or elsewhere,
did not necessarily mean to accept all of its traditional premises.
Marxist historians in East Germany, for example, engage in
exhaustive study of the German Reformation without thereby
becoming converted either to the literal Biblicism of the German
Anabaptists or to the formal tenets of Luther's Small Catechism.
In the West, the "scientific" historiography of the late nineteenth
century, followed by the subjective and relativistic historical-
philosophical assumptions of Croce and Becker, had led to a
situation in which—as Albert Outler put it in 1965 in a presidential
address to the American Society of Church History—"The notion
of 'providence' has simply dropped below the mental horizon."
Taking as one homely example a sharp turn in both religious
and secular history that happened in 450 A.D., when the Roman
Emperor Theodosius II was thrown from his horse and killed,
Outler contended that it would be "preposterous" nowadays to
argue that "it was God who spooked that horse."

For a theologian to write *about* history, as Reinhold Niebuhr
was doing, seemed a reaonable enterprise. To *base* empirical
history upon theology was quite another matter. "All historical
interpretation proceeds under the strictures of a methodological
principle of radical uncertainty," Outler insisted, and such uncertainty compelled skepticism. Outler's colleague, Georges Florovsky, America's leading Russian Orthodox church historian,
agreed: "The purpose of a historical understanding," Father

Florovsky wrote in 1959 (in a collection of essays honoring Paul Tillich), "is not so much to detect the divine action in history as to understand the human action—that is, human activities— in the bewildering variety and confusion in which they appear to a human observer."

Thus, the same historians who could derive insight from a religious culture-critic like Tillich or a religious critic of society like Reinhold Niebuhr were deeply suspicious of a religious system-builder like Arnold Toynbee. Toynbee's philosophy of history had enjoyed a considerable vogue in America in the late forties, when the first six volumes of his *Study of History* appeared in a one-volume abridgment that got a substantial media play (e.g., in *Life* and *Time*). Like his predecessor Oswald Spengler, Toynbee believed it possible to discover and generalize the laws that govern the historical behavior of civilizations: their genesis, growth and downfall. Unlike Spengler, he believed that the ultimate motive power in their rise and fall was human free choice ("challenge-and-response") rather than a natural, or- ganically recurring cycle. Spengler's metaphor for a civilization was a plant that springs up, flowers, and dies; Toynbee's was a rock-climber scaling a cliff, who will most likely slip and fall but could possibly make it to the top. At the same time, Toynbee rejected the materialistic historical philosophy of Karl Marx; the goal of human history was a heightened spirituality, and the ultimate source of all the challenges to civilization was some- thing very like the Puritans' divine providence. Toynbee's phi- losophy of history was understandably popular in some quarters; it was pious, it championed free will, and it was anti-Marxist. Nevertheless, professional historians by and large detested it.

Graduate students coming into the large Ph.D. degree-mills that major academic history departments were becoming in the fifties commonly were exposed to a course of some kind in historiography. Typically they heard lectures, often from dis- tinguished scholars, on "older and newer viewpoints" in the history of the French Revolution, or the English monarchy, or the Civil War and Reconstruction in the U.S. They were exposed to economic history, military history, intellectual history. They were taught the difference between primary and secondary sources, and the nature and limits of inference from documentation. They were warned against "present-mindedness." And then someone would come in and throw at them the Toynbee lecture, or rather the anti-Toynbee lecture, telling them that Toynbee's philosophy of history was riddled with inaccuracies, pseudo-scientific, elitist; it was theology (or mere preaching) in the guise of history.

Sometimes the vehemence of this lecture was so strident that it may well have tempted some of the less meek among the graduate students to go to the library and *read* some Toynbee! Any useful insights Toynbee's system might have given the students were swept aside by their teachers—and there *were* such insights; it has been cogently suggested that even if Spengler's and Toynbee's concept of a comparative morphology of civilizations did not qualify them as the Galileo and the Newton of a comprehensive philosophy of history, they might at least be regarded as its pioneering Aristotle. Even Marx didn't get this treatment. Marxism, to most historical mentors in the Cold War years, was merely mistaken; Toynbee was somehow threatening.

He was threatening, such mentors would have said if asked, because he generalized and systematized, and history simply can't be done that way. But a deeper, intuitive/emotional basis for the rejection of Toynbee existed, and it went far beyond the bounds of graduate school. In 1954 the last four volumes of *A Study of History* appeared—again receiving a one-volume abridgment; life's too short to read them all—and something became evident that readers of Toynbee's shorter essays, which were published in the forties under the title *Civilization on Trial*, had suspected all along. The openness of choice that lay before a cliff-climbing civilization, as it went through the dialectic of "challenge-and-response," was more apparent than real; toward our own civilization in particular divine providence had darkened into divine judgment, and from Toynbee's own premises and

point of view it appeared virtually certain that *Western Civilization
had already broken down.*

"In the middle of the twentieth century the principal questions
in dispute among Western intellectuals seem to be whether the
West can be saved, and if it is worth saving," observed the
shrewd radio news reporter Elmer Davis in 1953. "The two
most popular of recent historical philosophers both think the
Western world is going downhill, and one of them"—Toynbee—
"seems to feel that it won't be much loss." To which Davis,
looking at the "moral nihilism and intellectual rigidity" of the
most obviously available alternative to Western civilization, Stalin's
USSR, cried: " If we aren't worth saving, who is?"

Not only Spengler and Toynbee but other speculators had
"dealt with our predicament in terms of what befell civilizations
of the past; and these analyses, however embellished with facts,
or conjectures, from Chinese and Mayan and Sumerian history,
all rest pretty much on the one case about which we have tolerably
complete information—the decline and fall of the Roman Empire." But the modern West had something going for it that
the intellect of Greece and Rome at their most glorious never
quite achieved: "the scientific method and above all the freedom
of the mind that makes it possible." And we, despite all the
frightening parallels to our own situation that one can discern
in the late Roman republic, are not Rome. "Is not every civilization
bound to decay as soon as it penetrates the masses?" Rostovtzeff
had asked thirty years before. "We can only say," Davis retorted,
"that we shall in due course find out. We have started in that
direction and we can't turn back."

CHAPTER SEVEN

The Inmates of the Academy

The World of Worthal and Snarf

I

"THE evolution of the ancient world has a lesson and a
warning for us," Michael Rostovtzeff wrote at the end
of his monumental *Social and Economic History of the Roman Empire*
(1926). "The main phenomenon which underlies the process
of decline is the gradual absorption of the educated classes by
the masses and the consequent simplification of all the functions
of political, social, economic, and intellectual life . . . Our civilization will not last unless it be a civilization not of one class,
but of the masses." For many generations, political thinkers like
Thomas Jefferson, educational politician-statesmen like Horace
Mann, and a host of sturdy frontier schoolmasters and Yankee
schoolma'ams had been accepting that challenge for America.
They had affirmed that the way to forestall the process of decline
was to let the masses *become* the educated classes. In the nineteenth
century this battle was fought at the level of universal, tax-
supported elementary-school education, and won. But all members of each generation are born into the world as barbarians,
and no battle for culture is won forever. As the fifties began,
the ground that had been captured for the Three R's was under
furious counterattack.

"Through the years we've built a sort of halo around reading, writing, and arithmetic," an Illinois junior high school principal observed in 1951; however, "we've made some progress in getting rid of that slogan." This was not a sign of the absorption of the educated classes by the masses, as Rostovtzeff had feared. It was almost the reverse; it showed that the masses could be led into intellectual oblivion by their ostensibly better educated mentors. "When we come to the realization that not every child has to read, figure, write and spell," the Illinois school administrator cheerfully continued, "then we shall be on the road to improving the junior high curriculum":

> Between this day and that a lot of selling must take place. But it's coming. We shall some day accept the thought that it is just as illogical to assume that every boy must be able to read as it is that each one must be able to perform on a violin, that it is no more reasonable to require that each girl spell well than it is that each one shall bake a good cherry pie.
> We cannot all do the same things. We do not like to do the same things. And we won't.

Undermined though it was by educational philosophers such as the foregoing—people who, as Richard Hofstadter observed in 1963, "would do anything in the name of science except encourage children to study it"—the movement for universal education had in the meantime marched on to new territory. Between 1890 and 1940, high school enrollments nearly doubled every decade; one-third of American seventeen-year-olds were in school in 1910, two-thirds by the end of the fifties. Also, proportionately more of them each year were going onto further education. One out of ten Americans of college age in 1940 was in college. Two decades later—fueled by the G.I. Bill of Rights, by postwar affluence and upward mobility, by fear of the draft, and by increasing demands from business, science, and government for people with academic degrees—the figure was one in three. The offspring of the baby boom who then bulged the walls of every kindergarten and grade school in the land could be expected shortly to be knocking on the doors of university admissions officers; "In the generation just ahead of us," George Williams prophesied in 1958, "every family in America, and almost every individual in America, will be, at some time, immediately and personally involved in the life of some college."

In retrospect, this claim was obviously overstated. Of the fifty million poverty-stricken Americans disclosed in Michael Harrington's *The Other America* (1963) a very high proportion clearly were not, and were not about to be, involved in the life of any college. Nevertheless, the long registration lines each September during the fifties, and the chaos in the campus bookstores, showed that a university youth generation was rising in numbers such as the U.S. had never known before. Dormitories with noisy reverberant corridors and paper-thin-walled rooms sprang up to house them, and freshly minted Ph.D.'s—that rearguard of the G.I.-Bill-financed host which, instead of entering the workaday world in the late forties, had gone on to graduate school—were conscripted to teach them.

Collegians were not yet insurgents; that would not happen until the sixties. In the fifties, "classrooms were quiet fields of neatly combed heads bent over spiral notebooks," writes Peter Filene. "Even when they talked, they moved on mental tiptoe," like the student who, when her opinion was challenged by one University of Wisconsin instructor, meekly answered "I take it back." In another era such students might have resisted, and developed an underground intellectual culture of their own, learning from books other than those prescribed in class. To some extent this did happen in the fifties. *The Second Sex* seems to have circulated in such a fashion, and from time to time a Marx-reader put out a mimeographed pamphlet or wrote a letter to the student newspaper. Science fiction also, not yet fashionable in the classroom, had its academic closet devotees. But a Gallup poll taken in 1950 indicated that American college students by and large didn't read much of *anything*. And indeed, one thoughtful librarian wondered, why should they? "There are no books in our libraries that can tell the youth of 1958 how to shape their lives around sex, marriage, military service, a system of business that professes traditional honesty but practices trickery and frivolousness, a religion they cannot understand, or a civilization that may be blown up at any moment," Ralph Ellsworth wrote. "The young must decide these things by talking with one another. And this they do. The student union building rather than the library has become the heart of the campus"— except, of course, just before finals.

Professors only a little older than such students, who had personally been formed not by postwar affluence and Cold War paranoia but by prewar penury and wartime hopes, had a hard time finding the range of a generation which the media over-simplifyingly labeled "silent." Silence does not necessarily imply consent. It can also be a reverse-English way of saying "No!" to everybody who has an axe to grind, including one's professors. Students who had responded, orally or in an exam blue book, to some teacher's invitation to "express your own opinion freely,

A generation which the media oversimplifyingly labeled silent.

even if it disagrees with mine," and had then had their heads
chopped off, were understandably wary and cynical. Mc-
Carthyism, so often blamed for the classroom silence of the
collegiate young, really had very little to do with it. Long before
McCarthy came and long after he was gone liberal arts professors
played this game with their captive audiences, often blissfully
unaware that they were doing so. "A thousand times I have
heard professors declare, 'I don't like students who merely remember. I want students who will THINK,'" Professor George
Williams of Texas observed. But when one pressed such a professor to explain what he meant by *thinking*, "you find that he
always means that the student should . . . come to the same
conclusions that the professor has reached . . . Let any student
do a little *thinking* to the contrary, and the professor will tell
him, 'you are just not *thinking!*'"

From time to time in the fifties a politically activist journalism
staff wrested control of a student newspaper from the fraternity-
sorority element and, as one skeptical sophomore wrote in a
letter to his own campus paper at one ivied Eastern U.S. university
in October of 1954, "embarked on a great editorial crusade to
arouse students from their apathy, give courage to timid souls,
and regenerate the American Left." But before they all "progress[ed] backwards to the thirties," he cautioned, they should
consider whether those bold old days were in fact so colorful
and radical as older people remembered them. He concluded
that they were not: writers safe and secure on the WPA artists'
program had merely written *as if* they were starving workers,
and rich boys—they must have been rich to get to an Ivy campus
at all in those days—had merely taken out "their peeve on daddy
by mussing their hair and wearing a red tie." Bound in the
present, the writer could not anticipate the situation that was
coming in the sixties, when effective radical student leaders with
equally mussed hair and wearing no ties at all were going to
arise from the very heart of the Affluent Society:

> Socialism is not a toy for rich boys and intellectuals, nor is it

a convenient expression of individualism. Socialism is the tool of a poor or propertyless class. . . . America is now a middle class country; workers, even in the present recession, are not suffering from lack of property, but strangling from an excess of time-payment ownership.

In contrast with the thirties, . . . student politics are now genuine and realistic . . . Our present day students are well-fed; they honestly reflect their class, and this is a better sign than anything in the thirties.

Even the military draft, which a decade later would fuel some of the most furious of student protests, seemed to this under-graduate a fact of life to be faced with resignation: "Only one-third of those from twenty-one to twentty-eight (draft age) vote," the writer concluded his letter, noting also that neither U.S. political party was committed to a smaller army. "There is nothing to be done about this by voting, nor is there anything to be done by parades. The thing to do is wait, and wait as comfortably as possible."

II

Both of the foregoing interpretations of the American college student in the fifties —as the cautious, professor-pleasing book-worm or as the equally cautious would-be radical placing himself or herself on "hold"—assume such students' basic rational se-riousness. For the majority of U.S. university-goers in any era that is probably to assume too much. The words George Santayana wrote in 1920 about the Harvard he remembered from the 1890s can be repeated, with a smooth sense of fit, about college life in the 1950s—or for that matter, in the 1920s or the 1970s: the students, Santayana recalled, "were keen about the matters that had already entered their lives, and invincibly happy in their ignorance of everything else." What paralyzes radicalism, most of the time, on American campuses may be neither McCarthyism and police repression nor wealth and careerism, but rather a real philosophical unawareness that anything not bound by the personal pronoun "I" really exists:

> A gentle contempt for the past permeated their judgments . . . they instinctively disbelieved in the superiority of what was out of reach. About high questions of politics and religion their minds were open but vague; . . . the fluent and fervid enthusiasms so common among European students, prophesying about politics, philosophy, and art, were entirely unknown among them. Instead they had absorbing local traditions of their own, athletic and social . . . Life, for the undergraduates, was full of droll incidents and broad farce; it drifted good-naturedly from one commonplace thing to another.

The Daumier of this "haphazard, humouristic existence" was Richard N. Bibler, who drew the "Little Man on Campus" cartoons that were syndicated to many college newspapers in (and after) the fifties. Bibler, like many creative artists, started young; he drew his first cartoon at the age of fourteen. It was a comment upon one of the New Deal-era "sitdown strikes," and appeared in the Wichita (Kansas) *Eagle*. Two aunts, one of whom (Bess Neathery) had had her own cartoons published in the jazz-age magazine *College Humor,* influenced the style and scope of Bibler's work, as did Tom Hudson, a cartoonist noted for his antic, bulbous-nosed pen-and-ink characters in the *Saturday Evening Post*. During World War II Dick Bibler was field artist for the American enlisted-men's magazine *Yank*, Pacific Edition; he came to college, therefore, with the throng that matriculated and graduated just *before* the fifties, financed by Public Law 346—the "G.I. Bill of Rights." There was thus a short, subtle "generation gap" between Bibler and the high-school-graduates-turned-freshmen who figured in so many of his cartoons; perhaps that personal divergence from the hitherto traditional academic pattern helped give Bibler the sardonic perspective that was so manifest in "Little Man On Campus."

As a freshman at the University of Kansas in 1945, Bibler won a cartooning contest and was then asked by the college newspaper to draw one cartoon a day, which he did for four years. His satire was pointed enough to provoke administrative wrath; the artist remembers having been called in three times by the president of the university for complaints about his cartoons. "I planned to quit drawing the cartoon after college," Bibler told one interviewer in 1968, "but many people wrote and told me to keep drawing"; and so, while the cartoonist went on after his Kansas Bachelor of Fine Arts degree to earn an A.B. at Colorado State (Greeley) and an M.F.A. from Stanford, "Little Man On Campus" continued to spring forth from his drawing board. The little men and women on campus who peered up at readers from the pages of the literally hundreds of university and college newspapers that carried Bibler's cartoons in the fifties included fussy deans and stern housemothers, affluent if slow-witted football players and their job-insecure coaches, fatuous alumni and eager Army recruiters. Especially, however, the artist chronicled the doings of Worthal, pledge and brother in a fraternity appropriately named Signa Phi Nothing, and his arch-nemesis, Professor Snarf.

"My first meeting with Professor Snarf was a bitter one," wrote Jeffrey Smith of the Stanford faculty in 1952. "I had just come from a class in which I had given a heavy end-of-the-course assignment. I opened the Stanford *Daily*, and there was Snarf, with a pile of books on his desk, saying almost exactly what I had said, and grinning maliciously not only at his class but at me." *Almost exactly what I had said;* that is the secret of Bibler's comic impact. Like any other effective satire, his bold drawings with their outrageous captions were a humorous caricature of a painful reality. Rather than lecture his audience on sexual harassment or intellectual sloth, Bibler simply drew the lank-haired, baggy trousered Worthal—the ultimate "frat-rat"—ineffectually drooling at an elegant young woman or sweating out an ingenious evasion of studying. The joke was on Worthal and/or Snarf, but it also struck at anyone who, however loosely, answered their description. As the misquoted adage had it in the fifties, "If the shoe fits, lie in it"; Bibler, Jeffrey Smith contended, "through his chosen instruments, Worthal and Snarf, has put the finger on us all. Doesn't he know that what we all want is constructive criticism, or, to put it more precisely, praise?"

Worthal may have been a transient figure on the American campus. In the sixties his brand of madcap hedonism would have been out of fashion, and his successors in the seventies and eighties would have been far more smooth (i.e., "preppy")— or else, in the *Animal House* tradition, simply gross. (He wasn't bright enough to have qualified for *Doonesbury.)* Professor Snarf, however, pre-existed "Little Man On Campus" and has long outlasted the fifties. Today he may lack the pointed teeth Bibler gave him (so reminiscent of those fanged sergeants who hassled "The Sad Sack" in one of the great cartoon series of World War II), but he continues to cringe before administrators, browbeat and humiliate his students, and indulge in what would be power trips except that they occur on so petty a scale. A graduate student, for example, who has been misdirected into the wrong line of comprehensive exam study by a professor, and then savaged on his or her orals, might object that the real-life equivalent of a Snarf is not actually very funny. On the other hand, neither were the real-life equivalents of Ebenezer Scrooge in *A Christmas Carol* or Führer "Hynkle" in Charlie Chaplin's the *Great Dictator.* Entrenched power (great or little) can easily shrug off moral indignation directed against it; satiric laughter, however, cuts it down to size.

One campus newspaper in 1968, at the crest of the radical sixties, stopped running "Little Man On Campus" because it wanted the space for political cartoons. "It is kind of sad that everything students think about has to be serious," said Bibler. "I feel that I'm a little behind the times." But the vigorous drawings of "Little Man On Campus" *were* political cartoons; for politics—in its primordial sense of "who gets what, when, where, and how"—happens in all of life: in a union local or a business office or a Sunday school or the counselors' lodge at a summer camp, quite as much as at the command posts of the mass media or in the corridors along the Potomac. Academic life had always had a high degree of pretentiousness; and, as

From Little Man, What Now? *by Richard N. Bibler. Copyright © 1959 by Richard N. Bibler. Used by permission of Mr. Bibler.*

From Little Man on Campus, *by Richard N. Bibler. Copyright © 1952 by the Board of Trustees of the Leland Stanford Junior University. Used by permission of Mr. Bibler.*

university life in the U.S. swallowed up more and more people for ever-larger fractions of their lives, its tendency to pomp and self-inflation increased proportionately. Well it was in the fifties that an impish jester with a drawing pen could reduce it to its rudiments as an institution run basically on sex, sadism, and greed.

III

Professor Snarf, had he thought about it at all—and in Bibler's cartoons he is a most unreflective sort—might have argued that he only tormented his students for their own good, like a hard-driving athletic or music coach who pushes his or her players to the top of their form. One venerated senior professor, a fictional character in a 1958 detective story by Isaac Asimov, candidly answered the question whether his own former students loved him by saying that they most certainly did not: "Looking back on it, they may think now they did, but they didn't back then . . . A research professor, if he's any good, is the plague of his students' lives. A student, if he has any spirit, hates his professor until he finds out later on how much good the plaguing has done him." (Incidentally, an academic environment is an admirable milieu for murder mysteries; the general level of malice is sufficiently high that *everybody* is a potential suspect.)

But this fictitious slave-driver contended that his own attitude—"It wasn't love I wanted; it was work. And I got it"—was exceptional: "Research has become a game. A Ph.D. is a consolation prize awarded for inhabiting a laboratory for a couple of years while the professor spends his time in his office composing applications for grants." Such a grantsman—and he existed in growing numbers in the fifties, the beneficiary of the growing corporatization of academic life—was educationally a cut *below* Professor Snarf, whose terrorism at least jolted a student from time to time into opening a book. And a book, once opened,—the right book, at the right moment—can have a mind-enlarging impact even on a Worthal. The problem, as librarian Ralph Ellsworth pointed out, was that quite often the required reading in a university course could not by any stretch of imagination be considered the "right" book for that purpose: "The materials read are sterile and lifeless. They do not have in them the magical quality of generating intellectual curiosity . . . They are not the books one takes to bed to read."

The favorite educational rallying cry of the fifties was "excellence." To listen to commencement speeches, Phi Beta Kappa luncheon addresses, or inspirational talks to incoming freshmen in those years one would have imagined that all the professors were holding up against the onslaughts of barbarism the standards of the Good, the Beautiful, and the True. Probably some of them were. Others, however, were frittering away their time, thought, and conversation; trading gossip about how Professor Zilch had had an offer from Great Eastern University but the administration wouldn't match it, or laughingly (and condescendingly) comparing notes on student examination-paper bloopers and howlers—and rationalizing the essential bleakness of their own situation by blaming their troubles on the Dean, their students, the off-campus anti-intellectuals, the Eisenhower administration, or each other. The back files of the American Association of University Professors *Bulletin* for the fifties make depressing reading, both as to the reality of the problem they faced—for the civilizing of this great insurging student mass *was* a staggering educational task—and as to the elitism of the way they faced it. Many, in those days when the drudge work was still being done by beginning instructors with, or just short of, the Ph.D. rather than being shoved off onto T.A.'s, fled from the mind-numbing horror of two or three hundred un-grammatical, badly scrawled "blue books" at exam time into the library stacks; others, drained of all zest for further hard schol-arship by the exhausting trauma of their own graduate school experience, fled from the stacks to their students. Hence the false quarrel between "teaching" and "research," which has di-vided university departments from that day to this.

"There are factions in all faculties," sociologists Theodore Caplow and Reece J. McGee wrote in *The Academic Marketplace* (1958), "and at least some of the factions are the same every-where." In any academic department at each of the ten prestigious universities they studied, the lines of schism were easy to trace. In addition to "teachers," who were said to neglect their schol-arship, and "researchers," who were said to neglect their stu-dents—frequently both charges were true—Caplow and McGee took note of "Young Turks" versus "Elder Statesmen," "Pro-administration" versus "Anti-administration," "Generalists" versus "Specialists," "Humanists" versus "Scientists," "Inbred" versus "Outbred," and "Conservatives" versus "Liberals." To a reader a quarter-century after this investigation these lineups sound discouragingly familiar—discouraging because one would like to believe people capable of benefiting enough from experience to make changes in their situation. Labels do change; in the course of the sixties the "Liberals" and "Conservatives" in some departments were replaced by "Marxists" and "anti-Marxists," for example—but the animosities, apparently, do not. The authors of *The Academic Marketplace* reported "instances . . . of fights which began almost twenty years ago and are still being carried on with great vigor, although all the original participants have departed from the scene!"

The focus of the Caplow-McGee study was on jobs: how vacancies in the professorial ranks occurred, how the replacements were recruited, and how the positions were eventually filled. These researchers wrote with a light touch unusual in sociology (less unusual in the fifties than in other eras, as noted in chapter 4), and they livened their expository text with quotations, many of which would be cuttingly funny—as is also the case with some of the captions on the Snarf cartoons—if the reality they disclosed were not so appalling:

"He would rather publish an error than let a colleague find one in his manuscript."
"We had parties twice a month, played golf, etc., all the time. We also had a lousy department."
"It was clear that his really tremendous work with this student group hadn't been weighted at all in the consideration of his promotion . . . It caused the rest of us to decide that if this kind of activity was not what was honored . . . then we'd do what was honored, namely sitting in the library and writing weighty papers, and let their goddamned student group go to hell, which it has."
"It's like choosing a wife; you want one that other people will admire too. It's hard to tell exactly how good they are; the opinions of others are presumably related to promise as a scholar. We're also influenced by apparent brightness and possibilities of stimulation for us—and they're supposed to be able to teach, I guess."
"We take a good look at their letters and then when they're down here we look at them and talk to them and then we take a good look into our crystal ball and pull out the best man."
"She had the M.A. and was working on her doctoral dissertation and we would have very much liked to have gotten her, but when she saw the Dean, he turned her down. He . . . thought she was too stylishly dressed."
"He played the recorder. That was the reason we hired him." [interviewer]: "Because he played the recorder?" "Yes, we thought that would be nice."

Jacques Barzun, in a brief foreword to *The Academic Marketplace*, remarked on "the radical ambiguity of a profession in which one is hired for one purpose, expected to carry out another, and prized for achieving a third"; respectively teaching, research, and prestige. Supposedly the prestige was based on the research and (more rarely) the teaching. In practice, Barzun pointed out, scholarship was "judged by a survey of opinion rather than a survey of published work; the printed material gathered or submitted for that judgment is looked at but not read." And the products of this irrational and haphazard selection process were supposed to foster and further a civilization that would be "western, purposeful, and whole"! *Growing Up Absurd* was not the end of it; for some, the absurdity would continue until they were emeriti.

In their closing chapter Caplow and McGee offered some simple, sensible proposals for reform. Except for transitory reformist flurries during the sixties, few of these proposals have been implemented anywhere. Perhaps that was inevitable. The sociological folkways of the profession these investigators described "enforce upon its members a tradition of secrecy, ignorance, and self-deception," Barzun wrote. Since *The Academic Marketplace* dealt with the professors' most fundamental vocational concerns, therefore, "it is likely that the last persons to hear about it will be the academic profession."

If that profession was incorrigible from without and unreformable from within, then why didn't its younger, more openminded members leave it in droves? Inertia, perhaps; the investment of four undergraduate and at least that many graduate years in preparation bound the psyche into a pre-programmed course of action. Comfort; the shabbiness of the academic lifestyle by comparison with that of its business-world equivalent was mitigated by such features as its long vacations (who else besides teachers got them?) and the sense—not entirely illusory—that in spite of all the harassments and frustrations one was working on one's own time. Fear; to have been penalized in typical American grade and high schools as "greasy grinds" (the slang term constantly changes, but the image remains the same) and then to have been rewarded with "A's" as soon as they got to college, bred in the kind of youths who became professors "an abiding scorn for that old nonintellectual world that had ignored and rejected them so long," George Williams wrote. "Usually this scorn prevented any subsequent understanding of the viewpoints of the non-intellectual, nonbookish world, or even developed into outright hostility toward that world."

Yet a young professor during the fifties had another possible motive for seeing it through. That non-intellectual, nonbookish world, as Goodman and Whyte were showing (and as Thorstein Veblen had shown a long while before), had its own absurdities, and they were more dangerous than any in academia. Those of the young who came from that "outside" world into university laboratories and classrooms were the hope of the future (even Worthal!), just as commencement speakers said they were; at any rate, the young were the only future there was. Even the nonteaching researcher who ignored them, but might be a viable role model for some of them, was contributing toward that future; for against the disintegrative forces in that other world they would need all the intellectual and cultural resources they could get. It was still, as H.G. Wells had put it long before, a race between education and catastrophe.

IV

Organization or Other-Directed Man was as rampant on the campus as in that other, "non-intellectual, non-bookish world"; perhaps more so, since the university's primary traffic is in verbiage and so many of the cues and counters that Organized the individual, or attuned him to the Others, were words. The teacher-scholar in the fifties who aspired to be a runner in that race between education and catastrophe, therefore, commonly took a careful look around to make certain that at least a few of his colleagues were running on the same track. "Asked what

they would do if the school president arbitrarily banned a debate
on Red China or a speech by Owen Lattimore," in a survey of
The Academic Mind by sociologists Paul Lazarsfeld and Wagner
Thielens (1958), more than half the respondents (in a sample
of 2500 professorial social scientists from 165 colleges and universities) declared that they would "protest vigorously" to the
president—but often added qualifications, such as "If two or
three people got together, I'd protest." To Lazarsfeld and Thielens "the clear, if unconscious, implication is that the initiative
would have to come from someone else."

And no wonder, if George Williams's more personal and
impressionistic *Some of My Best Friends Are Professors* is at all
representative of academic reality . "I have seen famous professors
all atremble before going to have a routine interview with the
university president," Williams recalled:

> I have seen friends by the dozen desert a professor who incurred
> the displeasure of the administration; I have seen faculty com-
> mittees pledge themselves to support a certain policy, and have
> seen most of the members abandon their pledge instantly on
> finding that the administration opposed the policy . . . Then there
> was the time, in faculty meeting, when I made some fairly harmless
> proposal of which, as it happened, the administration did not
> approve. The next day one of my colleagues . . . came to the door
> of my office, looked up and down the hall to see that nobody
> was watching, plunged inside, quickly closed the door after him,
> whispered, "I don't see why on earth anybody could have opposed
> the motion you made in meeting yesterday," and then plunged
> out the door again.

Williams was quick to add that he did not think professors
"any worse in this respect than most people in the business
world," who he thought were even less likely to oppose *their*
bosses. "I am merely saying that it is a mistake for the professors
themselves, or for anyone else, to think of the professor as a
high-minded intellectual, whose actions and opinions are always
influenced by rational and courageous considerations." Professors
in the fifties who assigned their students the great essay by
Henry David Thoreau on *Civil Disobedience* often proclaimed

their admiration for its author's dictum that one man more right than his neighbors is a majority of one already, but in their personal and professional affairs they seem rarely to have taken Thoreau's advice. To learn of this timorousness would have disappointed regular readers of Dick Bibler's cartoons, who might have expected from Snarf at least, in such situations, some show of spunk.

For the rough-and-tumble of an encounter with Senator Joe McCarthy, or his like, timid souls like these were ill prepared. Sociologist David Riesman suggested that the hesitant anti-McCarthyites in the universities were moved not so much by rational fear for their careers as by the fear of "public embroilment with a bully, which can become an unbelievably harassing full-time job. Many of us"—the kind of Americans who had become professors—"can recall, or prefer not to recall, our dismal encounters with bullies in high school or earlier." When the Young Republicans at one university in 1954 invited McCarthy to speak on campus and suggested that one of the politically liberal professors debate with him, the liberals were dismayed: "Though we dared not admit it, we were afraid that logic and argument would be so much chaff in the wind before the brutal insistence of his mindless repetitions," one such liberal confessed. "We were afraid to face McCarthy because we had no confidence that reason would stand up against his sub-rational appeal."

And that, Robert Langbaum reflected a year after the episode, had been the liberals' mistake with McCarthy all along. "To lose the sense of one's power is in fact to lose one's power," this chastened professor summed up. "To believe the enemy powerful is to make him powerful. If there is one lesson to be learned from the recent collapse of the McCarthy myth," Langbaum wrote in the wake of McCarthy's Senate censure, "it is that the inventors and sustainers of that myth have been not those who admired McCarthy but those who feared him." Much has been made, from a civil liberties standpoint, of McCarthy's targets as having been helpless victims: so much, indeed, that sight has been lost of an important psychological truth.

In anticipating a visit, or raid, by Joe McCarthy at their campus "we talked each other into a fever," Langbaum recalled. David Riesman, writing when the McCarthy balloon had not yet burst, made the same point: "Intellectuals who, for whatever reason, choose to regard themselves as being victimized contribute to the very pressures they deplore":

> The naming of evils, intended as a magical warding off, can have the opposite effect. It is easy to imagine a group of academic people or civil servants sitting about in the hot summer of 1953 and swapping stories about who got fired from the Voice of America because he subscribed to *The Nation*, and how so-and-so was not rehired at Benton College because his wife had once joined the League of Women Shoppers—each capping the other's whopper of the reactionary menace. What is the consequence? A stiffening of spines? A clearing of the mind and will for action? I doubt it.

Quite so, responded historian Peter Gay; some American intellectuals "get a gleam in their eyes when they tell you the latest horror about McCarthy—a tell-tale gleam that reveals the awful truth that they are thoroughly enjoying themselves." Nevertheless, the historian thought the sociologist's polemic somewhat off target. "The scare stories are all Mr. Riesman says they are: they are masochistic, they partake of the self-fulfilling prophecy, they are often excuses" for not taking a stand one did not want to take anyway. "But they are also something else— they are, by and large, true." Professor Gay did not have a prescription for solving the dilemma Riesman posed. "To retail those stories may mean that we join the men who spread the very climate of fear that they are deploring," he conceded. "But is not the failure to tell them equally dangerous?" Newsman Elmer Davis agreed. "I regret that I have to mention McCarthy. I regret that he exists," he told the Vassar college community in 1953. "But he does exist, and not to mention him would be as if people in a malarial country refused to mention the anopheles mosquito."

Archibald MacLeish, the unrepentant liberal poet, who had

launched this intramural professorial discussion of McCarthyism with an eloquent address on "Loyalty and Freedom" (*American Scholar,* Autumn, 1953), insisted on putting first things first. "The open-mindedness for which Mr. Riesman pleads is noble enough, but there are some things as to which an unwillingness or an inability to make up one's mind is not noble." The American Revolutionary generation's supreme achievement, MacLeish declared, had been its resolution of "the most difficult of all constitutional problems," namely, "reconciliation within one society of the conflicting human desires for freedom and for community. It may well be the ultimate shame of our generation that with us that resolution fails." Against that ultimate shame it remained true, in one veteran New Dealer's mind, that the only thing Americans had to fear was fear itself.

V

Military tradition has it that the best defense is a successful offense. If the sterotypical intellectual was popularly judged to be at best ineffectual and at worst un-American, one highly effective way to confound that stereotype might be for an intellectual publicly and conspicuously to put his or her nimble brain to work for some laudable purpose, such as making a great deal of money. In the fifties, one of the most dramatic methods by which a sharp-witted young American might amass a quick fortune was to appear on a television quiz program.

Charles Van Doren, when he became such a contestant in November of 1956—in the wake of the Hungary and Suez crises, and not long after Eisenhower's election to a second term—hardly seemed to be the kind who needed to prove himself in such a fashion. From any standpoint other than the purely pecuniary he seemed a person who already had it all. He came of a distinguished American family; his mother a novelist and editor of the *Nation,* his father a beloved Columbia professor whose luminous lectures on comparative literature regularly

drew twice as many people to his class as were enrolled in it
for credit, his uncle a respected critic and biographer. Charles
had studied at the select Manhattan High School of Music and
Art, at St. John's College in Annapolis, at Cambridge University,
and at the Sorbonne. Unlike some young people who languish
in the shadow of famous elders, young Van Doren showed every
sign of having the industry and talent to make it on his own.
Many talents, in fact; he was an accomplished clarinetist, actor,
and mathematician. When he settled down in Columbia University's English Department in the mid-fifties with a predoctoral
instructorship in English he was pronounced "an able and exciting
teacher" by Grayson Kirk, Eisenhower's successor as president
of Columbia.

The university's $4500 salary was adequate; Van Doren was
single, and he lived alone and simply in a small Greenwich
Village apartment. He thought he had his next four years planned
out. The plans did not include TV quiz games; in fact, the
young instructor did not even own a television set. "But you
know these are the Eisenhower years," Van Doren explained
later to an interviewer; "there's money lying around everywhere.
I wasn't aware of it." So he went downtown, took a 100-question
screening examination, and within a week learned that he had
been selected as a contestant on *Twenty-One.*

The television quiz programs had evolved from radio's, with
proper adjustment for the explosion in the money supply since
the forties. Master of Ceremonies Phil Baker's modest invitation
at the climax of the radio show *Take It or Leave It,* " Will you
try for the $64 question"—the largest sum a contestant could
win on that program—became transformed in the fat fifties
into an attempt at *The $64,000 Question,* a show which first aired
on June 7, 1955, and by early August had hooked forty-seven
and a half million viewers. Media success breeds imitation. *The
$64,000 Question* soon shared time on VHF with other quiz and/
or game shows: *The Big Surprise, Tic Tac Dough,* and a clone
from the parent program called *The $64,000 Challenge.* The
maw of television was insatiable; it constantly needed new ma-

terial—and out there among the masses, TV critic Jack Gould pointed out, was a "bottomless reservoir of intelligent people to draw upon." Besides, such shows were cheaper to produce than almost anything else the medium did. They did not need to be, as TV people say, "production rich." Fundamentally all you needed was a studio, a frenetic M.C., someone to do the encyclopedia research, and two contestants sweating inside their "isolation booths" as they groped for the Big Money.

Twenty-One derived from blackjack, except that instead of playing cards the bank dealt the players questions, each worth a given number of points (at $2000 a point). As in the card player's version of the game, one could stand pat at 19 or 20 points and hope that one's opponent did not reach 21. It had the advantage over blackjack that one ran no risk of being "busted" by being dealt a card that put the total over 21 points; the dealer simply put into play a question worth the necessary point or points to make the total 21. It had the disadvantage that the contestant, isolated inside the soundproof booth, did not know the opponent's strategy until so informed by the friendly M.C. Such was the game Charles Van Doren was to play, against current champion Herbert Stempel—who, producer Al Freedman told him, was unpopular and unbeatable, and therefore hurtful to the show. And at that point the young Columbia instructor learned that the program was fixed. What it needed, Freedman explained, was a series of exciting tie games between Stempel and Van Doren, after which Stempel would be told in advance that he had to lose the next game.

Van Doren hesitated. This was the normal practice on television, Freedman assured him; "by beating Stempel, and becoming a winner on the contest, he would be doing a great service to teachers." *Again, the devil taketh him up into an exceeding high mountain, and sheweth him all the kingdoms of the world, and the glory of them.* The next day Van Doren met with Freedman to go over the questions he would be asked on his first show:

He told me the questions I was to be asked, and then asked if I

could answer them. Many of them I could. But he was dissatisfied
with my answers. They were not "entertaining" enough. He instructed me how to answer the questions: to pause before certain
of the answers, to skip certain parts and return to them, to hesitate
and build up suspense . . . He gave me a script to memorize, and
before the program he took back the script and rehearsed me
in my part.

Truly, there was no business like show business!

Charles Van Doren went on the air, tied Herbert Stempel
three times as scheduled, and became an instant folk hero.
Before their second telecast Stempel was told he would have to
"take a dive," as he himself put it; miss an absurdly simple
question (the name of one of his favorite movies) and thus be
retired from the show. There was subtle snob appeal in this
arranged victory of Renaissance Man from the Ivy League over
a chubby ex-GI who was working his way through City College;
"now," someone said backstage as Stempel was leaving his isolation
booth for the last time, "we have a clean-cut intellectual as
champion instead of a freak with a sponge memory." The clean-
cut intellectual was so popular that NBC moved *Twenty-One* into
the time slot opposite the most universally watched television
program ever aired, *I Love Lucy*. The money rolled in; so did
two thousand personal letters every week, one fourth of which
were reported as having come from "a teacher, a parent, or a
student thanking Van Doren for the worthwhile image he proj-
ected toward education and the value of studying"—a seeming
vindication of Al Freedman's Iago ploy.

In due course an attractive opponent was found for another
exciting series of tie games, and on March 11, 1957, after failing
to identify the current king of Belgium, Charles Van Doren
stepped out of the booth for the last time with record winnings
of $129,000 ($28,000 after U.S. and New York income taxes)—
but not out of show business. NBC signed him on for five years
at $50,000 a year; "the network," Kent Anderson concludes,
"could not let such a charismatic and now-familiar face drift
away unpurchased." He ended up on the network's morning

Today show. In a lengthy article for *Life* on September 23, however, Van Doren rejected his earlier rationalization. Education and quizmanship really had very little to do with each other. The educated person and the quiz show contestant were "moving rather rapidly in opposite directions." The world of the educated was "full of mysteries," and the more you learned the more you realized you did not know. "Opposed to the dim uncertainty of the world of the educated man is the bright little circle of light in which the quiz show contestant basks in his isolation booth," where "all is certainty." It certainly was.

Even before Van Doren got safely outside that circle of light, Herb Stempel had begun to talk. At first such talk was taken as the sour grapes of a disgruntled loser, and the *New York Post's* libel lawyer advised against printing Stempel's accusation. But there were other programs, other contestants, and other newspapers. The mass-circulation magazines *Time* and *Look* pointedly asked "Are the TV quiz shows rigged?", and on August 28, 1958, two now-defunct New York City newspapers, the *Journal-American* and the *World-Telegram and Sun,* at last broke the true story of Stempel's downfall. His opponent and the network denied everything, and a year later Charles Van Doren received his Ph.D. and became an assistant professor at Columbia. A painstaking district attorney, Frank Hogan, kept the issue alive, however, and a Congressional subcommittee became interested. Still Van Doren insisted he had never been assisted in any form on *Twenty-One.* Then, on November 2, 1959, he appeared before the Committee and confessed everything: "I have deceived my friends, and I had millions of them."

Although Columbia and NBC both promptly fired him, the confession generated a new wave of sympathy. "For some years, Americans have seen their public figures tarnished with the same sins many of them would like the opportunity to enjoy," Jay Bentham and Bernard Rosenberg summed up in the New Left journal *Dissent.* "That is why the rite of public confession increasingly creates sympathy and success—for those who confess totally, dramatically and on time." And in the American political economy, Murray Hausknecht wrote in the same journal, the quiz shows *had* to be fixed, because "rigging is an important means of controlling the risks inherent in a 'free market.' " The superseding of one sort of contestant by one of another kind was a form of planned obsolescence, like that of automobiles; an economic necessity, even when it required involving a college instructor from a noted literary family in "an idiotic show fundamentally subversive of the meaning of intellectual work." The American corporate economy which spawned those idiotic shows could then afford also to tolerate a degree of meaningful intellectual work, however; Van Doren, in due course, wound up as an editorial vice-president in the executive offices of the *Encyclopedia Britannica*.

VI

Television had not yet extended its tendrils as far as Antarctica. The eighteen men at America's South Pole station, the first humans in history to have "wintered over" at the bottom of the world, watched no TV quiz programs. On September 23, 1957, they cheered the first sunrise they had seen in 186 days; autumn in New York is springtime at the South Pole. But until the first of the new season's mail and supply planes arrived from the edge of the Ross Ice Shelf they had not much else to do except shovel away the snow from the entrance to their tractor garage, "amble about"—at − 70° or 80°F.!—"appreciating the beauty of the sastrugi in its myriad fantastic wind-sculptured forms," or search futilely for the black tent Roald Amundsen had pitched when he came on foot to the South Pole in 1911. Then, on October 5, 1957, the outside world with its Cold War concerns broke into their isolation: Americans on the vast and empty polar plateau heard the triumphant "beep-beep-beep" of *Sputnik I* as it orbited the Earth.

South Pole base leader Paul Siple, who had been coming to Antarctica since he was a Boy Scout with Admiral Byrd in 1929, organized an around-the-clock watch to tape-record and count the Soviet satellite's pulse rate, audible periods, and signal intensity. Both the orbiting Russian transmitter at the edge of outer space, and the Americans watching and listening below, were there on behalf of a quite un-Cold-War-like common cause; since July 1 the U.S. and the USSR had been participants in an intensive world-wide study of our planet's ways, the International Geophysical Year.

Rockets and Sputniks were a planned part of this scientific enterprise, and their purpose was by definition not exclusively national; the satellites intended to be launched as part of the American IGY program, U.S. Antarctic program director Laurence Gould pointed out beforehand, "will orbit around the earth without regard to any nation's rights to air space above territories, and no questions will be raised." The same would, of course, be true of craft launched from the USSR. Paul Siple, as he logged the Soviet messages from space, took the Russian exploit calmly enough; prior to joining the Antarctic IGY program Siple had participated in discussions of America's own satellite program, and now he mildly "wondered why ours wasn't up also." Back at home the reaction was not so calm. *The Russians had beaten the Americans into space.*

It is noteworthy that although some Americans tried to minimize the achievement, saying that the Russians had merely tossed a piece of iron into the air, nobody tried to argue that this was just another Moscow propaganda trick. The reality of that saucy little basketball-sized space ship was inescapable. Nor could Americans rationalize that the secret of space flight had been stolen from them, as some contended had been the case with the atomic and hydrogen bombs. "Those Russian spies must be *really* good," science fiction editor John Campbell jibed; "they stole a secret we didn't even have yet." No; this was humiliating in the same way that being defeated in the 1956 Olympics had been humiliating: the USSR had bested the USA in something at which Americans were supposed to excel. "The Russians have beaten us in our own special field," Campbell summed up; "they solved a problem of engineering technology faster and better than we did."

If the spies could not be held responsible, then whose fault was it? The rival armed services were blamed to some extent. The Army, the Navy, and the Air Force had all had their separate rocket development programs, and each service's entrepreneurial bickering, instead of stimulating a healthy rivalry, had had the effect of slowing down the progress of the others. Another factor was bureaucratic refusal to face unpleasant reality, in the spirit of the ancient king who is said to have executed any messenger who brought him bad news. Campbell gave an example of a friend, engaged in rocket research since the V–2s first started rising from White Sands, who had lately been fired for stating the truth that the U.S. rocket program was not going well. In many people's minds, however, the prime culprit was U.S. education. To the existing polemical literature on *Why Johnny Can't Read* was added a new kind of exposé, detailing *What Ivan Knows That Johnny Doesn't,* and for the moment Americans stopped hearing that it wasn't really necessary that all their children learn to read, figure, and write.

"There's nothing like a good, hard kick in the pants to wake up somebody who's going to sleep on the job," science fictionist Campbell observed. The Russians had done the Americans the inestimable service of delivering the kick. All at once the sleazy downgrading of people who lived by books and words as "eggheads" sounded archaic. "Suddenly the national distaste for intellect appeared to be not just a disgrace but a hazard to survival," Richard Hofstadter wrote afterward; and even though many people's concern "seemed to be for producing more Sputniks, not for developing more intellect," clearly the atmosphere had changed. The Congressional shadow-boxing over federal aid to education which had been going on since the early New Deal years—with opponents of such aid regularly defeating it by adroitly fusing the biases of Southerners who didn't want the aid to support desegregation, urban Catholics who didn't want it to go only to public institutions, and Republicans who didn't want education to be an activity of the national government—yielded to Congressional approval of a National Defense Education Act, which the federal legislature passed with unwonted speed. You could get away with quite a lot of federal aid to education, it turned out, as long as you called it defense education.

Here, as humankind poised at the edge of the gulfs of space, *could* have begun a profound transformation of the life of the mind in America. Imagine all the Snarfs and Worthals remodeling themselves as they lifted their eyes to the stars! Sadly, it was not to be. For one of the factional categories that divided American academic departments in Caplow and McGee's analysis, the Scientists versus the Humanists, news such as *Sputnik I* only threw fuel on the blaze. And their conflict had implications far more momentous than those of Young Turks and Elder Statesmen, administration backers and administration opponents.

The U.S. was not the only nation afflicted by this crippling feud. Sir Charles Snow, who as a practicing scientist and novelist firmly straddled the gulf between science and the humanities, gave a BBC lecture in 1959 (amplified from a 1956 essay in the *New Statesman*) which vividly described a schism between what Snow called "The Two Cultures"—"a gulf of mutual incomprehension—sometimes hostility and dislike" that divided scientists, to whom the entire literature of the traditional culture seemed either regressive or not relevant, from "the literary intellectuals, who . . . while no one was looking took to referring to themselves as 'intellectuals' as though there were no others." Incomprehension readily turns into moral disapproval; "the feelings of one pole become the anti-feelings of the other," Snow warned. "If the scientists have the future in their bones, then the traditional culture responds by wishing the future did not exist." Both sorts of prejudice were, he thought, "dead wrong"— but that of the humanists was worse. Many scientists had at least *some* acquaintance with the humanistic culture (e.g., Einstein playing the violin); but few humanists had any conception of the splendid intellectual edifice modern science was creating.

"As with the tone-deaf, they don't know what they miss," Snow chided:

> They give a pitying chuckle at the news of scientists who have never read a major work of English literature. They dismiss them as ignorant specialists. Yet their own ignorance and their own specialization is just as startling. A good many times I have been present at gatherings of people who, by the standards of the traditional culture, are thought highly educated and who have with considerable gusto been expressing their incredulity at the illiteracy of scientists. Once or twice I have been provoked and have asked the company how many of them could describe the Second Law of Thermodynamics. The response was cold; it was also negative. Yet I was asking something which is about the scientific equivalent of *Have you read a work of Shakespeare's?* I now believe that if I had asked an even simpler question—such as, What do you mean by mass, or acceleration, which is the scientific equivalent of saying, *Can you read?*—not more than one in ten of the highly educated would have felt that I was speaking the same language.

Sir Charles spoke from a British perspective, and he looked wistfully at the U.S. and the USSR—both of which, he felt, managed this "two cultures" business better than did the U.K. Alas, the grass is always greener on the other side of the fence. The chief executive officer of the American Association for the Advancement of Science, Dael Wolfle, reported in 1959 that "it is not uncommon to hear someone say with smugness and even a touch of pride, 'I don't know a thing about science.'" According to James R. Killian of M.I.T., at one American university's faculty meeting that was deciding the fate of students who were failing one or more of their courses, "when it was announced that a student named Cicero was failing in Latin, everyone laughed. A little later, when it was announced that a student named Gauss was failing in mathematics, only the scientists laughed."

In the shrinking, ever-changing planetary society of the fifties, that kind of unawareness was no laughing matter. As Elmer Davis noted, the scientific outlook was one resource modern society possessed which the foundering Roman Empire had lacked—and the dangerous social simplifications of which Rostovtzeff had warned need not rise from the masses. To say "I don't know a thing about science," Wolfle went on, was to say that one "knows nothing and cares nothing about the methods of thought that are responsible, more than any other, for changing the world." Science had become that world's "chief instrument of power," and no democratic society's citizens would be able to make wise decisions about the use of that power "unless the men and women who make them understand something about the forces with which they are dealing." Yet non-scientist professors balked at encouraging in those citizens—including themselves—any understanding of such forces, beyond a grudging concession to their scientific colleagues that college freshmen be required to take, in addition to English Comp., P.E., and Western Civ., something the freshmen themselves contemptuously referred to as "Bug Science." Historically, however, this anti-science bias was a gross distortion of the liberal artists' own humanistic tradition. It was a peculiar vision of the intellect that could lead so many intellectuals to argue that toward science, at least, Ignorance is Strength.

CHAPTER EIGHT

The Movies Said They Were Better than Ever

I

"THERE'S New York," said a young actor just returned to the big town from a successful spring tour in 1952, "and there's San Francisco. And in between—there's a vast wilderness. Part of it is natural, and some of that part is rather nice. But most of it is man-made . . ." The voice trailed off in a dignified shudder.

Rome has always felt this way about the provinces, and the provinces have always found it infuriating. They have also always paid the capital the compliment of imitation. They too, if affluent enough, have built their forums, circuses, and baths, in order to show the Romans that "Everything's Up to Date in Kansas City." And sometimes they have had the last laugh. In the waning years of empire the city of Rome, abandoned by its own emperors, dwindled into the second rank, while erstwhile provincial centers like Alexandria and Byzantium enjoyed a flourishing economic and cultural life. From the standpoint of a theater- and concertgoer in Manhattan in the fifties, however, this historical parallel would have seemed a dismal one. Alas, America's Alexandria was not San Francisco but Los Angeles; and its political capital— its Byzantium—was notoriously not a good show town. In the fifties, as the musical comedy *Damn Yankees* humorously testified, Washington lacked even a presentable professional baseball team.

Nonetheless, that youthful trouper strolling across what he considered a man-made American wilderness had missed something quite important. Had he kept his ears and eyes open he could have found, for example, symphony orchestras in some of those outlying capitals (including L.A.!) that ranked with ones he might then have encountered in Europe. Especially he should have noticed the university and other local groups which were busy creating the very constituency from which his own tour audiences were drawn.

Such stage-struck provincials were taking up and presenting to their home communities a generous amount of the rich and variegated Broadway fare of the fifties. These regionally rooted companies often made up in love and zest for lapses in professional finesse. And they possessed one inestimable advantage: an inexperienced and unjaded audience quite unlike that which was filling most of the choice New York theater seats on corporate expense accounts. When a college troupe early in the sixties took Shakespeare's *Henry IV,* Part I to one locality that was fifty miles up a gravel road from the nearest paved highway and had, literally, *never* seen "live" theater, they discovered to their delighted surprise that Hotspur's bravura soliloquies prompted spontaneous applause. These were fresh, unprimed playgoers; the very kind of people, unskilled in linguistic analysis or literary criticism, for whom the playwright had written that show in the first place. Rather than puzzle over the meaning of Shakespeare's archaically unintelligible lines, they joyfully swung with his music.

Back in the metropolis, however—the proximate source from which the regional companies got their modern material—all was not well. There had been 75 playhouses in operation in New York City in 1929; in 1955 there were 31. Broadway managers during the 1929 season had been able to mount 224 productions; in the fifties they were lucky to reach 70. The chance that a new play would fail, four to one at the end of the Second World War, had widened to seven to one. And the average professional actor's salary was now $790 *per year.* "For twenty-five years the taste for legitimate drama has steadily waned," the *New York Herald-Tribune's* drama critic, Walter Kerr, asserted. "Nothing—not the gradual recovery of the dollar during the 1930s, not the war boom of the 1940s, not the fantastically easy money of the early 1950s—has halted the shrinkage. The general economy may go wherever it likes; the theater goes right on down."

Drama, Kerr felt, had ceased to be something people enjoyed. It had become a kind of medicine you took now and then because it was supposed to be good for you, or a status symbol you occasionally indulged in because the ritual of going out on the town included "taking in a play." And many of the plays, quite frankly, were not worth the traffic hassle and the price. "A familiar nightmare is that agonizing one in which you are desperately anxious to get somewhere but can move only at a semi-paralyzed pace," Kerr began one sarcastic chapter in his book, *How Not To Write a Play.* "The mind darts ahead; the body lags as though deep under water. I don't know what precise waking experience is supposed to set this nightmare in motion, but I can imagine its taking place after almost any visit to the contemporary theater."

The indictment was not quite fair. Broadway in the fifties, if you picked through its offerings, yielded a satisfying harvest: dramas such as *Country Girl* (Clifford Odets), *Toys in the Attic* (Lillian Hellman), *Summer and Smoke* (Tennessee Williams), *Long Day's Journey into Night* (Eugene O'Neill's last, and posthumously produced, play), *The Crucible* (Arthur Miller) and *The Member of the Wedding* (Carson McCullers); delicious comedies like *The Matchmaker* and *Teahouse of the August Moon;* musicals of the calibre of *My Fair Lady, Guys and Dolls, The Pajama Game,* and *The King and I;* and notable European imports such as John Osborne's *Look Back in Anger,* Friedrich Duerrenmatt's chilling *The Visit,* Christopher Fry's *A Sleep of Prisoners,* and (as we have seen in chapter 6) Samuel Beckett's *Waiting for Godot.* "Any regular playgoer of the fifties who could say he was not sporadically seduced or stimulated by the New York theatre," wrote John Gassner, the distinguished professor of playwriting at Yale, in 1960, "was simply not being honest with himself!"

Writing a book in 1960 based on a decade of conscientious playgoing, titled *Theatre At the Crossroads,* Gassner declared at the outset that "this is an optimistic book" because the theater remained "one of the few popular institutions still worth taking seriously," with which "men and women are creatively involved . . . in spite of the extreme pressures of our time and place." But it was "also a *pessimistic* book," he countered himself, because it pointed toward "softness or error, if not worse than error, in the theatre of the Forties and Fifties." The postwar years had "gleaned a lean harvest in the important areas of tragedy and high comedy," and success on Broadway in the decade 1950–1960 had often been achieved "with more than a little help from sensational writing and stage production. Many a successful play has seemed artificially inflated with psychological and social pseudo-significance and has had no more conviction when platitudinously clear than when muddily ambiguous." And yet, the distinguished critic counter-corrected himself, "If the postwar theatre claims our interest in general it is because the melange has been sometimes exciting and even arresting." As usual it was the best of times, it was the worst of times. Theater has *always* been at a crossroads of one sort or another, and ever since the first advent of the motion picture at the beginning of our century, worried prophets have been warning that the legitimate stage was about to die. It never quite does.

But it might, Walter Kerr argued, unless the theater outgrew its elitist, "we happy few" mentality and remembered Shakespeare's groundlings. There was "a risk of vulgarity in turning toward what pleases the common customer," Kerr conceded, but it had to be run because "the theater must continue to shrivel if we do not do it.":

It seems to me, on the available evidence, to be a good risk. The theater was not created by a minority for a minority. It was created—in its Greek, Roman, and medieval beginnings—by a crowd for a crowd. It has, since its beginnings, been at its healthiest when it was closest to the crowd. There is a favorable chance, with the crowd, of arriving at serious art.

But a crowd is neither a Movement nor an Organization. How favorable was the chance of arriving at serious art with an audience that was in the process of blandly transforming itself into a *lonely* crowd?

II

It would never have entered the head of an average American in the fifties out looking for a good time, Walter Kerr dismally concluded, that one "might deliberately choose playgoing over poker, golf, movies, detective stories, or bourbon on the rocks." President Eisenhower and his friends played golf, nurses on night duty read detective stories, grey-flannel-suited status seekers sipped expensive sour mash bourbon, and some professors played poker. Movies, however, were no longer as clear-cut an alternative to playgoing as they once had been, for in all walks of life fewer people were going to the movies than had gone in years before. *The Wall Street Journal,* as attentive to motion picture balance sheets as to those of any other large industry, reported on October 1, 1959 that average weekly movie ticket sales during 1958 had been just under forty million, whereas ten years earlier they had run over sixty-six million. Worldwide box office receipts of U.S. films between 1947 and 1955, the *Journal* noted (January 6, 1960), had dropped by more than half a billion dollars. The days when nearly everybody went to the movies, and when substantial numbers went three or four times a week, were obviously over.

"It is clear," film historian Arthur Knight wrote in 1957, "that in less than a decade the movies have lost more than half their public." The small local theaters had been especially hard hit, Knight pointed out, because they had lost the "habituals" who formerly came regardless of what was being shown. Moreover, three-fourths of the surviving movie-going audiences were teenagers, and although by Depression-year standards adolescents in the fifties possessed awesome amounts of spending money, they did not command anything like the resources of their breadwinning parents who were staying home and watching Arthur Godfrey or Charles Van Doren or, unkindest cut of all, old movies.

What the movies in their day had done to the legitimate stage, television was apparently doing to the movies. The picture business fought back with vigor, declaring—as sellers of any product do when sales are in decline—that "Movies are Better Than Ever." U.S. makers of motion pictures increased, for example, their efforts to win audiences overseas; they dyed heroines' hair to suit local national tastes, shot different and less happy endings for countries they thought would enjoy downbeat themes, and (on the basis of box office draw) ignored protests like that of U.S. Ambassador to Italy Clare Booth Luce, who did not want *The Blackboard Jungle* shown in Italy because it might give Italians the notion that some American classrooms were less than ideal. As the cultural aspects of the Cold War became muted in the post-Stalin thaw in Russia and the post-McCarthy melting here, high-level negotiations produced an exchange of ten U.S. for seven Soviet films; while Americans were seeing *The Idiot, Swan Lake,* and *The Cranes Are Flying,* Russians would be introduced to *Oklahoma, The Great Caruso,* and *The Old Man and The Sea.* (Since the revenues received for the Soviet films would go to the Ministry of Culture, in IRS terms a nonprofit organization, the U.S. graciously waived collecting income taxes on them.) This drive to internationalize, like that of American corporations in other fields, met with some success; 54 percent of the U.S. film-makers' gross in 1958 came from their overseas business, up from 40 percent in 1950. Yet the handwriting was on the wall. Other nations' film industries were producing excellent fare which competed locally with the U.S. imports and had begun to find—beyond the specialized and small populations who attended "art" or "foreign language" theatres—an American audience; for example, the comedies of Alec Guinness and the English-dubbed Japanese monster movies. Still more ominously, in the more affluent of those other nations television antennas were now sprouting.

If you can't lick 'em, join 'em. After strenuously resisting the release for TV use of any but the oldest of old movies, the film-makers not only yielded and began selling rights to their more recent pictrures but also began themselves to produce material directly for television. Warner Brothers made TV Westerns; Desilu, Inc.—surely one of the spectacular growth industries of the Eisenhower era—bought the old, long-unused RKO lot for a mere $6 million in 1955 and turned it into the gold mine from which sprang *I Love Lucy*. But Hollywood and the local film exhibitors also fought to hold or win back their own audiences, or at least to stanch the flow of red ink. Drive-ins in the late fifties, for example, enjoyed a jump in attendance, wooing families by offering diaper service, baby-sitting, playgrounds and mini-amusement parks, and in one case free Bibles. The new drive-ins, with efficient car heaters, were expensive to build, and as mere theaters they were only marginally profitable; well aware that small children in America are both demanding and ravenous, they made their fortunes from their food concessions.

Publicity stunts to attract people back to the movies included free tickets tucked into workers' pay envelopes, barber service on the premises, and personal appearances by chimpanzees. Hollywood paid top dollar for the film rights to best-selling books and successful Broadway musicals and plays, in order to secure a "pre-sold" audience; evidently the legitimate stage, however shaky its own economic life might be, still exerted a strong influence over what viewers of another medium saw. Some of the lures ran to the wonderful and bizarre. Early in 1960, Michael Todd, Jr., picking up a long-forgotten idea first tried out in New York's Radio City Music Hall, refurbished a Chicago movie theater for $50,000 by running a mile of plastic pipe from a basement laboratory to apertures in each of the theater seats, to which on signal from the movie sound track were squirted smells—of horses or flowers, depending on what was showing on the screen. The *Wall Street Journal* saluted the traditional American entrepreneurial spirit as newly manifested in this imaginative enterprise: "Scented Movies Use Hundred of Chemicals in an Effort to Lure Fans Back by Nose."

The "smellies" were not, as they hopefully advertised themselves, the great breakthrough for the industry that the "talkies" had been. Todd's Smell-O-Vision, and its rival Aroma-Rama (which less expensively wafted itself through the theater's ventilating system), soon diffused themselves away. Todd's father, however, Michael Todd, Senior, an impresario who had moved from Broadway to Hollywood with a successful life-long philosophy of giving his customers "a meat and potatoes show" consisting of "high dames and low comedy," introduced a technological weapon of far greater effectiveness than his son's for winning back territory from the all-conquering video tube. TV's picture was coarse and fuzzy, but that could be attributed to the early state of the art; the pioneering "kinetoscope" peep shows of Thomas Edison in the 1890s now look crude also. In time the new medium would improve. The one thing the family-room type of television could *not* give the viewer was size. The opening shots of the cubist canyons of Manhattan in *West Side Story* (1961) are breathtaking; compressed onto a 21-inch screen they become merely pictures in a well-illustrated magazine. The film industry's response to the challenge of the rival that had brought the world into one's kitchen (or into the corner bar) was to fling open a wider window on the world.

"3-D" filming—the simulation of a human being's stereoscopic vision by projecting two images which are optically resolved to give the illusion of three dimensions—is as old as the Stereopticon travel slides one used to find in Victorian front parlors. It has never caught on; American consumers, so docile in other ways, have refused to wear the uncomfortable vision-wrenching glasses. Cinerama, however, introduced in the fall of election year 1952, was an instant success. It achieved the effect of depth perception, if not of true three-dimensionality, by projecting three overlapping images (from three cameras) side by side upon a curving screen, and let the eye's own peripheral vision do the rest. For certain effects, such as the one hundred cannons lined up wheel-to-wheel for the Battle of Shiloh in *How The West Was Won* (1964), the result was spectacular.

Cinerama unfortunately required a heavy investment in its own special equipment and in redesigned theaters, a formidable undertaking for an industry that was economically overextended already. The inventions which really revolutionized film technology in the fifties were those which enabled the wide panorama to be shown through an accessory lens which could be clamped onto an ordinary film projector, either by shooting a wide-angled picture through a camera which squeezed it to the narrow confines of conventional 35mm movie film (Twentieth-Century-Fox's CinemaScope), or by shooting it on double-width film which was then optically reduced to standard width in the laboratory (Paramount's VistaVision), or—more expensively, but less so than Cinerama—by both filming and projecting the image on wide 70mm film (Michael Todd Sr.'s Todd-AO).

For certain kinds of scenes the effect is extraordinary. In the Todd-AO version of Jules Verne's *Around The World in Eighty Days* (1956), as Phileas Fogg (David Niven) and his faithful henchman Passepartout (the splendid Mexican comedian Cantinflas) lift off from Paris "in a charmingly rococo balloon named *La Coquette*," Arthur Knight has written, "one is launched on an enchanted journey":

> At first she drifts leisurely through Paris, hovering uncertainly above rooftops, gliding past the gargoyles of Notre Dame. Then, gathering momentum, she sails out across the French countryside, past castles and rivers, over meadows and mountains . . . The solemn chilling of champagne with snow scooped from a passing alp, the ceremonial toast between master and valet are not only extremely funny but touching as well. The silent shining atmosphere that surrounds the pantomime somehow conveys the gal-

lantry that lies behind all the elaborate rituals of the human comedy . . .

In this brief episode it is possible to glimpse the new medium working with, rather than against, the filmic freedoms. It is a scene that could have been approximated on the old screen, but never so well.

III

That film's problems begin the moment the balloon comes down. Large numbers of people crowd onto the screen, and the only way it seems possible to manage them is to line them up on parade. All wide-screen filming was plagued by difficulties of this kind. By reason of historical and technical accident, motion picture directors since the dawn of movies had been working with 35-millimeter film, one frame of which is about ¾″ high and 1⅛″ wide—a proportion, roughly, of 3 to 4½. That shape was not perfect; Sergei Eisenstein, the great Soviet director and film theorist, criticized it on a visit to Hollywood in 1930 and argued that the ideal frame, capable of incorporating any kind of vertical or horizontal composition, would be a square. However, the 3:4½ ratio *was* equivalent to the confines within which painters in oils and watercolors had worked for centuries; the standard canvas-boards one buys in art stores today are of such proportions. Therefore, movie people early learned to compose scenes in triangles, spirals, or opposed curves in the same way a landscape painter works. (The amateur still photographer whose camera is loaded with 35mm film, upon realizing that his or her viewfinder will not "take in" all of the Empire State Building or the Grand Canyon, ends up doing much the same.) Adding to this traditional painterly style of composition the kinds of pictorial effects the painter (or the still photographer) can *not* get—e.g., the sharp, time-compressing and space-shattering "shock cut" from one scene or camera angle to another that was pioneered by Eisenstein and D. W. Griffith—the pre-wide-screen film-makers had triumphed over their medium's material limitations. Now, all that painstakingly acquired filmic language had to be unlearned.

It was almost as if the movies had gone back into the theater, with its clumsy necessity for scene-shifting. Directors could no longer make the quick, crisp cuts which for fifty years had been their basic vocabulary. "It is both jarring and unnatural," commented Arthur Knight after having viewed several of the new-style films, "to see an actor stretched out 60 feet in length on a screen that only a moment before had held an entire battleship!" Scenes taken entirely in long shots, perhaps with the camera traveling or angling a little to disguise their essentially static character, faded into other such scenes with monotonous regularity. And the director could no longer use the landscape-painter's forms which had lately served him so well. The painter's circle, which carries the eye into and around the picture, had become a squashed ellipse; the painter's stable, base-down triangle had devolved into a cramped parallelogram. Again and again the wide screen had to be filled, side by side, with groups of three, lest the edges of the picture become irrelevant and the center a gaping void. "It is not at all unusual," Knight observed, "to see films these days in which two actors carry on a casual drawing-room conversation from opposite corners of a screen that often spans an entire city block." Even more jarring was what happened to classic older films re-released for the wide screen. The characters inhabiting Charlie Chaplin's carefully composed 3 × 4½ scenes in *The Gold Rush* have their feet and/or heads chopped off; and the cloud of arrows fired into the air by the sturdy longbowmen of Agincourt in Shakespeare's (and Olivier's) *Henry V* simply vanishes above the screen into outer space.

The greatest directors, as always, took the limitations placed upon them not as a barrier but as a challenge. David Lean, using the long horizontal lines of bridge, river, and onrushing train in the incredibly suspenseful pre-climactic scene of *The Bridge Over the River Kwai* (1957), showed what could be done on the new screen; so, in a more fun-poking way, did Alfred

Hitchcock when he staged a chase across the august countenances of the Presidents at Mount Rushmore in *North By Northwest* (1959). More to the point, such films demonstrated that spectacle need not exclude acting. One remembers from pictures like *Kwai* not only its visual pageantry but also Sessue Hayakawa, far transcending the stereotyped Mr. Moto and cartoon Japanese villain roles to which Hollywood had previously limited him, and Alec Guinness making his determined, staggering, proud walk across a sun-drenched prison compound toward his men. Nor were all the films of the fifties primarily pictorial spectacles. The Academy Awards for Best Actor/Actress during those years included, in addition to Guinness, Marlon Brando in *On The Waterfront*, Ernest Borgnine in *Marty*, Susan Hayward's condemned murderess in *I Want To Live* and Joanne Woodward's incredible three schizophrenic personalities in *Three Faces of Eve*. If movies in the fifties were not "better than ever," they were certainly alive and well.

Other constrictions than the new mechanical ones, however, also cramped movies' style. The fifties came hard upon the trauma of the Hollywood Ten Congressional investigation, the blacklist that followed, and the uproar over Communism in the Screen Actors' Guild that turned Ronald Reagan into a politician. Hollywood had always been chicken-hearted about social and political controversy, and it had also always believed that its mass market did not want to be preached at; as Sam Goldwyn is supposed to have put it, "When I want to send a message I call Western Union." The Cold War reinforced these intrinsic tendencies.

But there were liberating counterforces also at work. In 1948, for example, after years of loftily defining the movies as mere entertainment, the Supreme Court finally decided that "moving pictures, like newspapers and radio, are included in the press whose freedom is guaranteed by the First Amendment"; "the line between the informing and the entertaining is too elusive for that basic right" to allow it to be drawn against film (*United States* v. *Paramount Pictures, et al.*, 334 U.S. 131; *Winters* v. *New*

York, 333 U.S. 507). What these decisions accomplished was to
liberate motion pictures, not so much from McCarthyite pressures
at the national level as from the petty nagging of state and local
censorship boards. We have already seen an example of this
liberation in the outcome of the "Miracle" case, *Burstyn* v. *Wilson*
(discussed in chapter 4), which in addition to applying the religious
clauses of the First Amendment reaffirmed the secular freedoms
as well. "That books, newspapers, and magazines are published
and sold for profit does not prevent them from being a form
of expression whose liberty is safeguarded by the First Amendment," Justice Clark ruled in the Court's formal opinion on
Burstyn. "We fail to see why operation for profit should have
any different effect in the case of motion pictures."

Some had always felt that the really serious restrictions upon
movies were not political but commercial. The corporate-board-
room leadership in the traditional Hollywood studio "front office,"
reinforced by professionally routinized camera, art, music, sound,
and processing departments whose heads (Knight points out)
"persist where directors and producers come and go," and whose
standardized methods "determine the physical appearance of
their studio's pictures—the M-G-M gloss, the Paramount sparkle,
the brassy brightness of Twentieth-Century Fox"—these powerful
forces had rolled out film after film which had had about as
much creative individuality as a Detroit car just off the assembly
line. The Supreme Court's *Paramount* decision had direct impact
upon that system. It forbade the "block booking" by which
studios had forced entire packages of films—good, bad, and
indifferent—upon the local exhibitors and broke up the chains
of studio-owned theaters. (Sometimes the U.S. antitrust laws,
about which historians teach students to be cynical, really do
work.) And the fifties saw another major economic and organizational breakthrough: the rise of the independent producer.

There is an old saying that when an actor grows up he wants
to be a director; to which one may add that as he becomes wise
in the ways of the IRS he learns that it is better to incorporate
oneself than to draw a salary, no matter how astronomically

large. United Artists, which had been founded in 1919 in the heyday of Mary Pickford, Douglas Fairbanks, Sr., and Charlie Chaplin (who first saw the taxable implications in what they were doing), but which had lately fallen on financially evil days, made it possible after its reorganization in 1951 to enable such transfigured actors and other "independents" both to fulfill their artistic hopes and to frustrate the tax man. Owning no studios of its own, but merely the means to finance and distribute the films of others, UA picked up a host of properties (high-budget and low, foreign and domestic, bad and good) and sold them around the world; and among those United Artists properties were *High Noon, Separate Tables, The Defiant Ones, The Apartment, Elmer Gantry, The Barefoot Contessa,* and *The African Queen.*

Others picked up the cue; banks, and even the traditional studios—for a percentage—had become willing to advance production money to directors of proven ability (Alfred Hitchcock, John Huston, Elia Kazan) with few strings attached. One day the front office might have a change of heart and yank at those strings; and top-drawing stars, who were now into the picture for a share of the profits rather than as highly paid wage workers, often infringed on the freedom of even the most independent producer by demanding script changes that would bring parts into line with their conception of their own established screen images. Nevertheless, Arthur Knight summed up in 1957, "for the present, it is heartening to note that the Hollywood film is struggling through to the kind of personal expression so admired in European pictures." In the midst of the fifties—the *conformist* fifties—"American production seems to be returning to the individuality and independence that characterized it back in the days when the movies were young."

IV

Individuality and independence have a way of popping up where you least expect them to. Television in America was

College broadcasting: Individuality and independence have a way of popping up where you least expect them to.

introduced—foisted, some would have said—by the masters of corporate radio, who expected the new medium to be merely a continuation of the old: radio with pictures. And the nation-spanning radio networks, airing programs paid for and, in the pre-TV years, produced by corporate sponsors who absolutely dominated the content of their shows, had usually been as void of originality and creativity as the most front-office-ridden of the Hollywood studios. Nevertheless, and despite that unpromising tradition, the "live" telecast theater of the early fifties "when both disaster and magic were only seconds away" is fondly remembered by its makers as having been television's Golden Age.

The odds against this unlikely development were considerable. In addition to the commercial and political inhibitions it inherited from the older media, TV in its first primitive hasty years often lacked the ordinary technical skills involved in making and putting on a show. Typically it suffered under "the kind of direction and camera work," commented mystery story writer Raymond Chandler in 1950, "that would have been considered ridiculously incompetent in the movies twenty-five years ago." Chandler, a master craftsman in another medium (the book), supposed that in a typical crime show on TV the writing was "no worse than it was in lots of radio shows, but by being intrusive it *seems* worse." The video tube "is really what we've been looking for all our lives," the novelist grumpily concluded:

> It took a certain amount of effort to go to the movies. Somebody had to stay with the kids. You had to get the car out of the garage. That was hard work. Sometimes you had to walk as much as half a block to the theater. Then people with big fat heads would sit in front of you and make you nervous. Reading took less physical effort, but you had to concentrate a little . . . and every once in awhile you were apt to trip over a three-syllable word. That was pretty hard on the brain. Radio was a lot better, but there wasn't anything to look at. Your gaze wandered around the room and you might start thinking of other things—things you didn't want to think about. You had to use a little imagination to build yourself a picture of what was going on just by the sound. But television's perfect. You turn a few knobs, a few of those mechanical adjustments at which the higher apes are so proficient, and lean back and drain your mind of all thought. And there you are watching the bubbles in the primeval ooze.

At the flickering signal's point of origin, however, the very primitiveness of the raw new medium was forcing the adroit use of people's brains. In the beginning, *all* television was "live"; what you saw on the tube was being recorded somewhere by a camera at that very moment. Ampex did not introduce its first really practicable videotape recorder until 1956, and the previously-used "kinescope" technique—which consisted essentially of pointing a movie camera at a TV monitor—faithfully reported the ill-focused image it saw, blotches and all. "The movie camera is not as 'forgiving' as the human eye," TV interpreter Stuart DeLuca noted in 1980, "and films at that time were not as sensitive and tolerant as they are now." Electronically synchronized switching from one camera to another, and special-effects generators operated from the control console, gave viewers *some* of the effects they were used to in the movies; but the kind of total control a film director had exercised in the cutting room was out of the question.

In films, comments media historian Eric Barnouw, "the final tempo and rhythm were generally created not by an actor, nor by actors interacting, but by an editor and the director working with him . . . The manipulation of 'film time' offered creative pleasures so beguiling to film makers that they had virtually abolished 'real time' from the screen." Television, in contrast, which in those first years had to show what it saw in "real time," gave viewers a sequence of events that happened in the same way *they* experienced reality; in actual life we do not quick-cut from an office suite in Manhattan to a deck chair on an ocean liner. Furthermore, whereas the wide-screen filming and projecting of motion pictures forced an emphasis on long-shot spectacle, the cumbersome early TV cameras conversely pushed the younger medium to do lengthy scenes in close-up—which resulted in a refreshing discovery, even through the muddied image on the tube, of the expressive possibilities in the human face.

Veteran rubber-faced vaudevillists like Milton Berle and Groucho Marx obviously benefited from this situation; so did warm-hearted, empathetic showpeople like Dinah Shore, as she kissed all America goodnight on the Chevrolet show ("M-m-m-m-WUH!") or Jimmy Durante, who on TV in his sixties as he sang "September" or shuffled away, hat raised under the streetlights, revealed a gentle, bittersweet melancholy few viewers of his comic films had been aware of. But the greatest beneficiary was live TV drama. The empty air was insatiably hungry, and in order to fill it television studios had quickly to work up and broadcast anything they could lay their hands on. Tad Mosel, who was a script writer in the early fifties, recalls having watched the scenes from next week's production—a play of his own, then two days into rehearsal—and murmuring from the depths of his living room armchair, as the announcer urged the audience to tune in, "And good luck to you all, because I haven't finished the third act yet!" At one point *seven* "anthology dramas" (individual self-contained stories, as distinguished from series shows) were on the air each week, "which means the greedy cameras devoured 300 or 400 original plays a year. There were few 'summer repeats.' If young actors, writers and directors were talented and industrious," Mosel summed up, "it was more than possible, it was practically inevitable, that they would be given their chance."

The producer of such a show, unlike a movie impresario in the high Hollywood era, could not order everybody to pack up and move the whole troupe out on location to Yugoslavia or Puerto Vallarta. The fragmentary sets—a telephone booth, a street corner, a park bench—which could be placed in odd corners of a television studio were improverished imitations of the sumptuous Hollywood back lots of yore, where one could have found everything from a fog-shrouded London street to a sun-drenched Arabian Nights bazaar. Poverty was the mother of necessity; shot in kitchens, short-order restaurants, or family rooms, plays *had* to become, in Mosel's words, "quiet, realistic studies of the people who watched them." And there was no need for such tales to be dull; "there is far more exciting drama," wrote Paddy Chayevsky in a preface to the printed version of his own television plays, "in the reasons why a man gets married than in why he murders someone." Counterpoised against the vivid, larger-than-life world visualized on the wide screen was what Chayefsky termed "the marvelous world of the ordinary."

It is easy to discount such accounts of television creativity in the fifties as mere nostalgia. "Much of the excitement," Stuart DeLuca cautions us, "can be attributed to the pioneering spirit that infected the medium, rather than to any imaginary virtues of live performance . . . Most of those fabled 'Golden Age' dramas would bore an audience if they were somehow retrieved and shown again today." But they *can't* be retrieved, and that is exactly the point. The live teleplay shared with the legitimate stage the tense, creative uncertainty of once-and-for-all performance; as in a high dive, a battle, or a risky business deal, once you were committed you had to go through with it. The unsatisfactory footage could not be snipped out.

Quite aside from the danger of blowing one's lines, there were physical pitfalls. A hinged picture on a wall might swing open to allow a through-the-wall camera angle, and not shut again quickly enough to avoid being caught by another camera working from the opposite side of the set; a director might lose lights and/or camera on the air; stage hands might stroll through a disheveled love scene; the set might collapse; "a corpse—his job done for the night—would rise and brush himself off with the cameras still on," Tad Mosel reminisces. "But it was all right." The viewers took their TV drama seriously; a woman once called up Mosel long-distance "to thank me for recounting truthfully the breakup of her marriage and to chew me out for getting my couple back together at the end." And hundreds of talented young people, who in those years might not have found movie work at all, were learning their craft in the best possible way. "In these revisionist days, it is fashionable to say the 'golden age of television' is a misnomer because not *all* the plays were good," Mosel concedes, "but that is to miss the point. A monster medium had been dumped on the world and nobody knew what to do with it, so they let us do whatever we wanted."

V

The owners of the monster medium were uncomfortable with all this feisty freedom manifest in their employees. The first script Tad Mosel sold, in 1953 (after 30 rejections!), was a teleplay about adultery and suicide—"two very taboo subjects in those days." Television raised anew all the issues of restraint and censorship that had plagued the movies in their own early days; raised them more acutely because TV came directly into the home, so that every program had to be plausibly describable as a "family picture." Moreover, alert young people who were aware of contemporary social reality were more than likely to create shows that would be politically controversial; a play that satirized business values, for example, or a depiction of a schoolteacher falsely accused of Communism. And there was a subtler objection to low-key, realistic, plebeian drama of Paddy Chayevsky's sort, as Barnouw perceptively points out:

> Most advertisers were selling magic. Their commercials posed the same problems that Chayevsky dealt with: people who feared failure in love and business. But in the commercials there was always a solution as clear-cut as the snap of a finger . . .
> Chayevsky and other anthology writers took these same problems and made them complicated. They were forever suggesting that a problem might stem from childhood and be involved with feelings toward a mother or father. All this was often convincing—that was the trouble. It made the commercial seem fraudulent.
> And then these non-beautiful heroes and heroines—they seemed a form of sabotage, as did the locales. Every manufacturer was trying to "upgrade" American consumers and their buying habits . . . But "the marvelous world of the ordinary" seemed to challenge everything that advertising stood for.

And so, in 1954 and 1955, the hands that held the strings began to twitch them. The producer–director connection became, quite regularly, an adversary relationship. Where the censorious minds did not suppress shows outright, quite often they gutted them—or tried to. An intriguing example that backfired was *Thunder on Sycamore Street,* based on an actual episode in which white homeowners in Cicero, Illinois, had combined and conspired to keep a black family from moving into their neighborhood. It was aired on CBS-TV's *Studio One*—but only after the network, the sponsor (Westinghouse), and the ad agency had all agreed that the new neighbor would have to be not Negro, but "something else!" The writer, Reginald Rose, yielded and made the stranger an ex-convict—and added dramatic suspense by revealing the basis for the residents' objection to him only at the end of the play. The result, Eric Barnouw noted, was that the play turned into an extraordinary social Rorschach test":

Comments indicated that viewers filled in the missing information according to their own predilections. Some at once assumed he was a communist; others, that he was a Puerto Rican, atheist, Jew, Catholic, Russian or Oriental. The information that he was an ex-convict, mentioned with the utmost brevity in the final act, was accepted as a logical supplementary detail. The sponsors found, with some uneasiness, that they had presented precisely the kind of controversial drama they had tried to avoid.

That particular battle for social candor was, in a sense, won; many more were lost. More important even than ideological pressures, however, was the continuing evolution of television itself. In a time span measurable in months, the same technological and economic processes that had created the free space within which the live teleplay could flourish went on to crowd that space out.

After the movies began to unload their backlist, and especially after the studios began to make movies directly for television, feature-length movies—and TV series shows developed from them—quickly crowded out the one-shot anthology plays. Then, when videotape came into general use, along with new, more light-sensitive and less bulky video cameras, television regained the editorial flexibility it had lost to the movies. Live studio audiences were replaced by canned laughter; the disaster-prone magic of the once-for-all telecast gave way to slick, professionally-shot sitcoms and crime shows in which nothing, technically speaking, could go wrong. In millions of American living rooms audiences ceased seeing programs that brought insight and poetry into situations quite like their own, and settled back for an endless round of explosions, car chases, and people shouting "Freeze!"

Gresham's Law operated in the way it always does. Many a shoestring-operated local TV station closed its studio and reduced its staff to a force small enough simply to run the projectors and read the commercials. Even a metropolitan station like WOR-TV in New York City, which in 1954 enjoyed live drama every night, two years later had *none;* its 1956 schedule was 88 percent film. Of necessity, the youthful talents who had come

into television drama from the starving New York theater world—
people like Paul Newman, Kim Stanley , Rod Steiger, or Joanne
Woodward—now moved on to Hollywood. A teleplay like *Marty*
could, it turned out, also win critical applause and awards as a
movie; and the studios soon realized that pictures made on
scales more modest than those of the wide-screen circuses were
also a good deal cheaper. But they made those "quality" films
for people willing to go into theaters and pay to see them. In
contrast, by the mid-sixties, Hollywood was shooting "made-
for-television" feature-length films, most of which could have
been described as 90-minute B pictures.

That still left, as something at which television was infinitely
superior to the movies, its coverage of *real* events that transpired
in "real time." The newsreels one saw in theaters, days and
weeks old, could not begin to compete with news that was delayed
at most by a few hours, and in special cases—most notably, in
the fifties, the Army-McCarthy hearings—might be seen in the
instant in which it was happening. Radio news had had this
same immediacy, as Edward R. Murrow had shown during World
War II, with the muffled thunder of war in the streets echoing
behind his dramatic "This [pause] is London." Radio, however,
could tell but not show. Even in TV's crudest early years it
became obvious at once that televised baseball, for example,
brought across the game's archetypal liturgy far more completely
than radiocast baseball could ever hope to. If we may take as
representative of radio sport in the thirties ex-sports-announcer
"Dutch" Reagan's humorous account of how, from the studios,
he used to narrate baseball over the radio by translating data
telegraphed to him from the stadium into graphic sports language—and once *guessed* the outcome of a crucial third-strike
pitch when the telegraph line went down!—we logically conclude
that the live video sportscasting that came with nationwide TV
use in the fifties was not only more vivid but also a good deal
more credible.

Politics and athletics, as already noted in chapter 1, are each
a system of customary, ritual-ridden behavior tempered by in-

novative one-upmanship. In the course of the fifties politicians and athletes, and their mentors, learned to change their ways for the benefit of the cameras. Presidential State of the Union messages and World Series games would eventually move into prime time. Sports television invented the instant replay; political leaders discovered the useful possibilities of programs like *Meet the Press* and *Face the Nation*. When Nikita Khrushchev allowed CBS's tangle of cable and bright floodlights into his office at the Kremlin in 1957, said the veteran newspaper reporter Roscoe Drummond, the Soviet leader "played it like a Barrymore"; and it was obvious that much, much more of this sort of thing was the shape of the future. As soon as Khrushchev and Richard Nixon walked into the U.S. trade exhibit in Moscow in the summer of 1959, saw themselves on a color monitor, and fell into their famous "kitchen debate," Barnouw sums up, it was obvious that "the world was entering a period when the planning of television spectaculars was becoming a central activity of rulers."

Ever since this government-as-theater started to happen, both liberals and conservatives have worried lest television be misused to shape and distort people's experience of reality in the interest of an "Establishment"—which conservatives perceive as liberal, and vice versa. However, as Marshall McLuhan and Buckminster Fuller already were aware in the fifties, the proliferating electronic network was itself rapidly becoming an establishment in its own right. It disseminated both information and entertainment, and the line between them—as the Supreme Court pointed out in its *Paramount* and related opinions—had become impossible to draw. In that blurring lay the potential for a distortion fully as dangerous, intellectually, as ideological bias. Radio and TV were at their best as storytellers, and unfortunately not all of reality can be turned into stories. The local TV program director who mandates that each evening news show, to grab the viewer's attention, must open with footage of either an accident or a fire—and there are many such directors!—may be crowding out all the really important news the people in his or her town have both a need and a right to know. The same is true at the national level; to take a more contemporary example, the recent political debate over Keynesian government-investment economics versus "supply-side" economics, in which the monetarists ended up disagreeing with both viewpoints, was supported on all sides with charts, personal testimony, and homely illustrations, but it really could not be reduced to purely visual terms. "What use is the use of a book," thought Alice, "without pictures or conversations?"—but such books, unfortunately, ever since the *Elements* of Euclid, have been among the foundation pillars of civilization.

VI

Alice's ideal books that combined both pictures and conversations had, in due course, evolved into movies and teleplays. But what could the modern electronic civilization of the fifties do with poetry? A scriptwriter might be badgered by the producers, hamstrung by the advertisers, or hounded by the Red-hunters; yet even such tormentors acknowledged, however minimally, the writer's role. Blacklisting is a form of recognition, a grudged concession of importance; one suppresses the work of art rather than exclaim "why bother?" The serious poet operated in quite another social universe. "The public has an unusual relationship to the poet," Randall Jarrell observed in 1959; "it doesn't even know that he is there."

Poets in that era made their living from obstetrics, like William Carlos Williams; or publishing, like T.S. Eliot; or the insurance business, like Wallace Stevens. But most of them made their living by teaching. "Our public is a rich and generous one," Jarrell conceded; "if it knew that the poet was there, it would pay him for being there." And, in a sense, it did. One could make a fair living if one added to the stipend of a university poet-in-residence whatever came in from lecture tours—or, at worst resort, from writers' (i.e., would-be writers') workshops and conferences. "Kepler said, 'God gives every animal a way

to make its living, and He has given the astronomer astrology,' "
Jarrell wryly quoted; "and now, after so many centuries, He
has given us poets students. But what He gives away with one
hand He takes away with the other: He has taken away our
readers." Not the critical readers, to be sure; *they* read the poets,
and busily wrote acute analyses of them for literary quarterlies,
most of which were subsidized by the same kinds of institutions
that paid the poets. But those were not the readers the poets
really wanted. "A writer cannot learn about his readers from
his critics: they are different races," Jarrell insisted. "The critic,
unless he is one in a thousand, reads to criticize; the reader
reads to read." It is significant that Randall Jarrell, who was not
only a poet but also a novelist and himself a perceptive critic,
did not count his *students* among his readers. Students evidently
were in another category altogether; for them, to continue with
the Kepler metaphor, one cast their horoscopes rather than
directing their gaze at the stars.

For most of human history a poet's audience had not been
readers but listeners, so perhaps this particular battle had been
lost with the invention of the printing press. Yet in the USSR—
a country at least as bookish, in its own way, as the U.S.—the
oral performance of poetry was alive and well; the young Soviet
poet Yevgeny Yevtushenko in the fifties was reading his poems
to packed houses, and his appeal quite clearly was to the young.
American attempts to duplicate the feat were not notably successful. The Beat poets who were then flourishing in San Francisco
coffeehouses tried to revive the bardic tradition of Vachel Lindsay,
who (before the First World War!) had been the last American
to be notably successful at poetizing on the road, but it never
quite caught on. One short-lived exotic outgrowth of the fifties
was jazz-poetry, in which a poet or poets recited their works to
the improvised, lightly scored accompaniment of an instrumental
combo. The problem was that the poetry was rarely as good as
the jazz.

Prose fiction, economically at least, was in considerably better
shape. Theaters might be having trouble selling tickets to stage

shows or even to movies, and nobody got rich selling tickets to poetry readings; but publishers seemed to be having no trouble selling books. These included made-for-movies blockbusters (*The Robe, The Egyptian, Dr. Zhivago, Hawaii, Auntie Mame*), as well as other types that the movies would have to clean up a bit before showing (*Battle Cry, Peyton Place*). As for lasting literary merit, the fifties were not, for the American novel and short story, a decade comparable to the twenties or to the fantastic ten years between 1845 and 1855 (the era of Hawthorne and Melville and Poe). Nevertheless, a span of time that included Thomas Mann's *The Holy Sinner* and William Faulkner's *Requiem for a Nun*, John Steinbeck's *East of Eden* and Aldous Huxley's *The Devils of Loudoun*, James Jones's *From Here to Eternity* and Ernest Hemingway's *The Old Man and the Sea* could certainly account itself respectable.

But the fifties produced no *Main Street*, no *Manhattan Transfer*, no *This Side of Paradise*. Part of the problem may have been that a previous literary generation had done its work too well; "it is as though the older novelists had bequeathed to us, in their picture of the First World War and the decade that followed it, a kind of literary country where our novels go on taking place regardless of their ostensible setting," Robert Langbaum suggested in 1955. If you wrote about a more recent war, you used stylistic tricks learned from John Dos Passos or James T. Farrell. If you wrote about a more recent social culture, you still saw it through the eyes of a mentor who had interpreted the society of the twenties; who indeed, if still alive, might still do doing so. "This is how, since Hemingway, young people in novels act: they drink, they are promiscuous, they say profound things in monosyllables, they don't give a damn."

The thirties and forties had added to Hemingway's suffering tough guy a further, pseudo-political-liberal, stereotype of beautiful little people defined as lovable bums (as in, e.g., *Cannery Row*)—and lately, Edmund Fuller argued in 1957, that image had been given a further, sinister twist: "The lovable bum began to slip away, and in his place emerged the genial rapist, the jolly

slasher, the fun-loving dope pusher." Unable to break away
from the heritage of the twenties and thirties, and recoiling
from the grubby moral nihilism toward which Fuller was pointing,
the serious young writer might be tempted to turn away from
fiction altogether, and write literary criticism—"after having
found," Langbaum continued, "that he cannot in fiction escape
the manner of of his immediate predecessors, that he cannot
invent a fable to express what is different" about the fifties; and
so comments learnedly upon the fables of others.

A different kind of writer, not dealing in fiction at all, seemed
to have pre-empted the task of inventing new fables. In the
twenties it had been a novelist who created an American character
whose name entered language as a descriptive term; *Babbitt*
became a common noun, even an adjective, and was sometimes
spelled without the capital B. In the fifties, however, the novelist's
creative torch seemed to have passed to the sociologist/social
philosopher, who conjured up vivid images of the True Believer
or the Organization Man. Meanwhile the blockbuster novels
came, passed, and were remaindered; so were most of the promising first novels that the *New York Times Book Review* extravagantly
praised. Ominously for the literary future fewer works of fiction
were appearing in magazines, either academic or popular, even
though magazine writing had always been a major form of
literary apprenticeship and even of major production; Scott
Fitzgerald,for example, measured by his total fictional output
had been more a short story writer than a novelist. To one
beginning fiction writer in Missouri who wanted to know how
one broke into the field these days, Raymond Chandler gently
replied in 1951 that "the decline of the pulp magazines"—in
one of which, the late great *Black Mask,* Chandler had gotten
his own start—"makes it more difficult for beginners even than
it used to be, and it never was anything but difficult . . . Contrary
to popular belief, it is a very arduous profession and only a
small fraction of those who attempt it ever succeed in making
any kind of a decent income."

To his correspondent's expressed wish to be schooled in the

fundamentals of narrative technique, the mystery novelist replied skeptically that from his own experience "any writer who cannot teach himself cannot be taught by others . . . I take a very dim view of writing instruction in general." The creator of Philip Marlowe made an exception on behalf of "the extension courses of reputable universities," but in this he may have been too charitable. Mary McCarthy reported in 1954 that a young woman student—"a rather simple being who loved clothes and dates"— at "a progressive college" where McCarthy had been teaching had written one short story about which the student's writing teacher was terribly excited. He told her he would help her fix it up for publication; he "is going over it with me," the aspiring writer explained, "and we're going to put in the symbols." *Put in* the symbols? If symbols and archetypes come welling up from the depths of one's unconscious, or arise naturally from one's perception of reality, one *can't* put them in; they're just there. Another student at the same college, asked at her sophomore orals why she read novels, "answered in a defensive flurry: 'Well, of *course* I don't read them to find out what happens to the hero,'" as if that were the worst thing one could possibly do. Analyze your fiction;. search out the Seven Types of Ambiguity; tease at the Greek myths, sexual referents, Biblical overtones. But never, never enjoy.

"At the time, I thought these notions were peculiar to progressive education," McCarthy commented. "But now I discover that this attitude is quite general, and that readers and students all over the country are in a state of apprehension, lest they read a story literally and miss the presence of a symbol." And that attitude was quite capable of killing literature; "at the very moment when American writing was penetrated by the symbolic urge, it ceased to be able to create symbols of its own." Properly, McCarthy argued, the writer does not *impose* symbols but *discovers* them; "the writer who cares about this must be fascinated by reality itself." To do the job properly one "must be, first of all, a listener and an observer, who can pay attention to reality, like an obedient pupil, and who is willing, always, to be surprised by the messages reality is sending through."

This is true, Mary McCarthy might have added, even for the writer who deals in fantasy or whimsy. I much doubt that Doctor Seuss in 1957 was brooding over the Jungian or Freudian origins of fictional feline headgear when he perpetrated *The Cat in the Hat,* a book for a much younger audience than McCarthy's which at once, as one jacket-copy writer for it observed, "dealt a karate chop to the tired old world of Dick, Jane, and Spot." Certain of the children's books published in the fifties hearteningly combined both commercial success and fictional vitality. *The Cat in the Hat* by 1975 had sold 5.4 million copies; *Charlotte's Web,* published in 1952, by the mid-seventies had racked up 4.5 million; *Little House on the Prairie,* dating from 1953, 2.7 million; and *Green Eggs and Ham,* from its initial appearance in 1960, an incredible 5.9 million. Anything that a badgered parent can read to a child over and over again and still find interesting has *something* going for it; perhaps what fiction in America really needed to do was to get away from the academy—and also out of the TV talk-show circuit, where people play at Being a Writer as a substitute for actually writing—and learn again that in the realm of storytelling whosoever shall not receive the kingdom as a little child shall not enter therein.

CHAPTER NINE
"I Have Seen the Future, and It Irks"

I

A S the young research director took his seat at the table in the missile factory's executive conference room, "the thick, opaque presence of middle-aged businessmen billowed up around him; a compound of cigar smoke, deodorant, and black shoe polish." At the head of the table sat the company's chief executive, "fortified by a mighty heap of forms and reports"; across from him sat the plant security chief. They came right to the point. "Your wife," said the young scientist's boss, "has been classified as a plant security risk," and her husband would therefore be denied access to the laboratories in which he had been working for the past ten years. The security officer spelled it out: as a freshman in college in 1948 she had joined Henry Wallace's Progressive Party; in 1953 she had signed a letter protesting against the exclusion from the United States of Charlie Chaplin, "a notorious fellow-traveler"; in 1954 she had spoken at a League of Women Voters meeting in support of the admission of Red China to the UN; in 1956 she had contributed money to the NAACP. "We can't prove Marsha is an agent of a foreign power," the plant's police captain conceded. "And you can't prove she isn't. In abeyance, we'll have to resolve the doubt against her." The Old Man was more blunt: "Until further notice you're suspended from your job. Either bring conclusive evidence to show she isn't a Communist, or get rid of her."

Civil servants and schoolteachers often told such tales in the fifties, but this one occurred half a dozen pages into a paperback science fiction novel. The book, printed on pulp paper and retailing (when it was first published in 1957) for thirty-five cents, looked like countless other such products; it had a garishly colored cover depicting characters in Buck Rogers suits who flee toward the reader from a vast, staring, coarse-eyelashed orb surrounded by stars. When Archibald MacLeish ringingly declared in 1953 that in the struggle for the defense of human freedom everything depended on "the health and vigor of the human things . . . the things of the mind and spirit," it would probably not have occurred to him to include among such things items like Philip K. Dick's vivid story *Eye in the Sky*. Nevertheless, writers like Dick were some of freedom's most vocal allies, and the role played by commercial science fiction in the witch-hunting years was a conspicuously honorable one. During "that miserable decade we look back on as the era of McCarthyism," said the expert science fictionist Frederik Pohl in 1968, "about the only people speaking up openly to tell it like it was were Edward R. Murrow, one or two Senators, and just about every science fiction writer alive."

One such writer, Ray Bradbury, spoke out with a story about "book-burning"; a term which most people in the fifties used figuratively to describe, for example, the removal under McCarthyist pressure of suspect books from U.S. Information Service libraries overseas. Bradbury, however, in his novella "The Fireman" (1951), made it literal. In a future conceived as not being very far off, firemen no longer put out fires; they start them. Their fire hoses spray not water but kerosene, and they burn books. "*Forbidden* books," a fireman's wife insists. Her husband recounts some of the titles he and his crew burned at their last fire call: Plato, Socrates, Marcus Aurelius. "Foreigners?" his spouse asks.

"Something like that."
"Then they were radicals."

"All foreigners can't be radicals."
"If they wrote books, they were."

The strength of Bradbury's satire—which later became a full-length novel and eventually a film, *Fahrenheit 451* (the temperature at which book paper bursts into flame)—was that he did not impute all this future thought control to a malevolent Power Structure. Book censorship in practice, in the fifties and afterward, was very much an activity of ordinary people—local vigilance committees, voluntary library boards, and PTA's. "Don't blame the government," the city Fire Chief tells Bradbury's hero. If blame belonged anywhere, it belonged with the fatuous "life-adjustment" educator who believed that learning to read and write is not socially necessary.

> With school turning out doers instead of thinkers, with non-readers, naturally, in ignorance, they hated and feared books. You always hate and fear an unfamiliar thing. "Intellectual" became a swear word.
> . . . a book is a loaded gun in the house next door. Burn it. Take the shot out of the weapon. Unbreach men's minds. Who knows who might be the target of the well-read man? Books were snobbish things.

But a charge of "subversion" in the fifties could cover far more than simply reading forbidden books, or supporting Henry Wallace, or recommending Red China's admission to the UN. It also lurked darkly beneath the superficial tolerant talk of Riesman's Others and the bland "Social Ethic" of Whyte's Organization Man, as a synonym for frowned-upon personal behavior. Another Bradbury story, "The Pedestrian," described the dismal fate of a man who is caught out walking by himself in the night air instead of sitting at home watching television like everybody else. The police car that arrests him and carries him off to "the Psychiatric Center for Research on Regressive Tendencies" has a back seat handily fitted out as a little jail cell, with bars—and although the car has an "iron voice" with which to hail him, *its front seat is empty.* The "chilling premise" of this tale, commented science fiction editor Anthony Boucher in 1952, "may be less fantastic than one thinks: The city of Beverly Hills already has an ordinance against walking the streets after 10 P.M."

Bradbury's sentient robot squad car was but the tip of a technological iceberg. Science fiction writers, long accustomed to extrapolating from present theory to future practice, well knew that it was becoming possible to snoop in ways undreamed-of by Sherlock Holmes. Just as computers were starting to come in—the big, blinking-light kind one still sees in low-grade TV science fiction—Poul Anderson returned from a summer of youth hosteling in Europe, with its standard requirement (irritating to a footloose young American) that at the end of each day's journey one fill out a card for the local police. He found his homeland in the throes of McCarthyism. With an author's gift for idea-association, Anderson put the police registration, the computer, and the loyalty investigations all into one package, and in his story "Sam Hall" (1953) imagined a future in which "Citizen Blank Blank, Anytown, Somewhere, U.S.A.," when registering for a hotel room automatically hands a punched ID card to a registry machine that reports his identity to Central Records:

> Aluminum jaws close on it, copper teeth feel for the holes, electronic tongue tastes the life of Citizen Blank.
> Place and date of birth. Parents. Race. Religion. Education, military, and civilian-service record. Marital status. Occupations, up to and including current one. Affiliations. Physical measurements, fingerprints, retinals, blood type. Basic psychotype. Loyalty rating. Loyalty index as a function of time to moment of last checkup. *click, Buzz.* . . .
> The clerk—thirty-two years old, married, two children; N.B., confidential: Jewish; to be kept out of key occupations—punches the buttons . . .
> "Front!"
> The bellboy—nineteen years old, unmarried; N.B., confidential: Catholic; to be kept out of key occupations—takes the guest's trunk. The elevator creaks upstairs.

Closely allied to the spirit of censorship and surveillance is the hangup of Security; and science fictionists, well aware that there are no "secrets" of nature which can long be hidden from alert and persistent inquiry, were especially merciless toward that manifestation of the frightened Cold War mind. "Project Hush," by William Tenn (1954), described a secret military research program whose security procedures were a satiric parody—not too exaggerated—of what actually went on in such undertakings:

> A couple of times a week, everyone on the project had to report to Psycho for DD & HA—dream detailing and hypno-analysis . . . Naturally, the commanding general of the heavily fortified research post to which we were attached could not ask what we were doing, under penalty of courtmartial, but he had to be given further instruction to shut off his imagination like a faucet every time he heard an explosion.

The purpose of Project Hush—a bad name, the narrator grumbles; one does not call attention to a project's secrecy, but covers it with an innocuous code name like Manhattan or Dandelion—is to get a manned rocket to the moon before the Russians do, set up an armed base there, and get back to Earth without anyone else knowing about it. The first part of the mission is flawlessly executed. The three carefully picked Army men touch down at the northern tip of Mare Nubium near Regiomontanus, plant the U.S. flag "with appropriate throat-catching ceremony," set up their base, and begin to explore the immediate vicinity. Then they discover another base, of different design from their own. Who built it? The Russians? The Chinese? The Argentinians?—the Martians?

They can't break radio silence and warn their superiors; that would give the game away. One of them must go and scout out the alien fort, while the others stand by in the ship, ready instantly to blast off and spread the alarm—abandoning him to his fate on the Moon, an expendable military casualty. The sacrificial scout departs; in due course he comes back, with news even

more depressing than his comrades had expected. "The other
dome," he tells them, "is owned and operated by the Navy. The
goddam United States Navy!"

II

Guardians of public and political morality who might have
been alarmed or outraged by stories like *Eye in the Sky* or "Sam
Hall" or "Project Hush" were lulled, perhaps, by the circumstance
that such parables after all, were mere science fiction, and therefore presumably not worth the attention of a Senate investigating
committee. The era of the ragged, ratty, raw-colored, glorious
old pulp magazines was not *quite* over; well into the fifties it was
still possible to find on American newsstands cover paintings

The era of the ragged, ratty, raw-colored, glorious old pulp magazines was
not quite over.

that depicted square-jawed, space-suited heroes firing zap-guns across overexposed heroines at bug-eyed, green-skinned aliens. But this situation was rapidly changing. The pulps, as a class, did not survive the decade. The collapse (under anti-trust pressure) of the Union News Company which had formerly distributed them the length and breadth of the land, combined with the longer shelf-life of paperback books (which did not have a soon-outdated month of issue imprinted on them), and with a decline in magazine fiction-reading generally, swept all such publications from the field; not only science fiction but also the detective, Western, romance, and general adventure pulp fiction magazines with which they had formerly shared rack space in cigar and drug stores. The few which survived converted to a more sedate "digest" format, toned down their covers, and otherwise social-climbed toward respectability.

New science fiction periodicals appeared, reaching for a more mature audience—or to a former pulp audience whose tastes had also matured. *The Magazine of Fantasy*, which soon became *Fantasy & Science Fiction*, began life in 1949 under the astute editorship of J. Francis McComas and Anthony Boucher. Its initial covers were quiet planetscapes or catchy abstractions; its typography was discreet, its layout a single-column, book-style page. There was no interior artwork at all. The traditional letter column, a forum for joyous juvenile capering ever since the pulps' earliest days, was sternly abolished. Later on, cover art reverted part way back toward conventional sf themes, and the pages went to two columns; but by that time the new audience had been won. The issue of May 1955 carried a subscription advertisement on its back cover with endorsements by Guy Lombardo, Ben Grauer, Gladys Swarthout, and Eva Gabor. Boucher, by then sole editor, continued gently to prod his writers toward literary finish and humane sophistication.

Galaxy, founded in 1950, physically looked more like a traditional science fiction magazine. But its hard-driving editor Horace Gold—a man writers remember with fondness and fear for having made them sometimes put story manuscripts through

four or five drafts—was just as determined as Boucher and
McComas to break with the zap-gun tradition. "I am mortally
afraid of retread private eye, western and Congo Sam stories
masquerading as science fiction," Gold wrote in an early editorial
(February 1951), and he was not about to publish such. Gold
was as good as his word; the issue containing that editorial also
carried Bradbury's "The Fireman."

Astounding Science Fiction survived from the pulp era; rechristened *Analog* just after the fifties ended, it persists—nay, thrives—
to the present day. *Astounding,* however, under the tutelage of
John W. Campbell, had begun its evolution out of the pulp
ghetto long before. It had pioneered in displacing bug-eyed
monster covers with accurate, beautiful astronomical art. It had
discovered and developed many of the writers who in the fifties
worked also for Boucher/McComas and Gold; some of them—
Isaac Asimov, Theodore Sturgeon, Lester del Rey—remain major
figures on today's sf horizon. In the fifties Campbell's magazine,
perhaps a victim of its own success, was beginning to spin its
wheels a bit; with occasional brilliant exceptions the stories became
less fresh and pathbreaking, while the editorials grew longer
and windier. Nevertheless, Campbell continued to discover new
writers and to cherish his previously found ones. It was *Astounding,*
for example, that published "Sam Hall."

Cautiously, "mainstream" literati began to take formal note
of the formerly scruffy genre's transformation. "People who
think that their literary I.Q. is too high for them to enjoy the
Magazine of Fantasy and Science Fiction don't know what they
are missing," wrote Orville Prescott, book review editor for the
New York Times, in another of those back-cover ads (September
1958). The austere classical scholar Gilbert Highet, reviewing
his tenure as literary critic for *Harper's Magazine,* took note of
"the steady improvement in science fiction . . . one of the most
interesting general trends" of late (October 1958); and the *Saturday Review*'s Basil Davenport came out of the closet to admit:
"I have been a fan of science fiction all my life."

Professors were, as usual, a little slow to hop up on a bandwagon that had not been set into motion by folk of their own kind. They were a long way as yet from the thriving academic science fiction industry of the seventies, with its college-credit courses, syllabi, conferences, research activities, library acquisitions, and undergraduate anthologies "replete," as Chicago *Sun-Times* critic Roger Ebert put it (October 4, 1972), "with all sorts of dumb Discussion Topics at the ends of the stories." But the water was warming, and a few academicians were testing it. By the end of the fifties, some of the bolder teachers of American Lit. were gingerly dropping into their courses—along with Hemingway, Faulkner, John O'Hara, et al.—an occasional novel of science fiction, sometimes disguising this caper as "a venture into the sub-literary." Typically, as true children of the older of Snow's Two Cultures, they shockingly misunderstood the whole scientific frame of reference; I have known one of them to attempt translating a story plot that turned on a point of mathematical physics into the more congenial language of Freudian symbolism! But at least it was a start.

Early in 1957 four of the leading sf writers of the day—Cyril Kornbluth, Robert A. Heinlein, Alfred Bester, and Robert Bloch—appered as guest lecturers at University College in the University of Chicago. The papers that resulted were published in 1959 as a book, *The Science Fiction Novel: Imagination and Social Criticism*—surely a sufficiently pedantic title—with an appreciative introduction by Basil Davenport: "This book has given me the pleasure, all too rare since my college days, of being a book that I could argue with." Disconcertingly, the authors in assessing the role of social criticism in science fiction had disagreed at some points not only with Mr. Davenport but also with each other; but that, Davenport concluded, "is my idea of a really stimulating and enjoyable book."

Of these four professionals, Heinlein, already moving toward the soapbox role he would play in and after the sixties, had the least doubt of the social significance of science fiction: "It is the most alive, the most important, the most useful, and the most comprehensive fiction being published today." His own platform colleagues spiritedly disagreed. "Should we take science fiction seriously?" Alfred Bester asked. "No more or less than we take television seriously." Science fiction is great when one is in a euphoric mood, but "when I'm most at grips with dramatic reality, I have the least interest in science fiction." What the medium *could* do, Bester interestingly suggested, was provide opportunity for the kind of talk-feasts other cultures made available in pubs, coffee bars, and street cafes. "Nobody talks in American saloons; everybody's too busy trying to imitate Steve Allen or Arthur Godfrey. And anyway, too many American men are compulsives, too driven by their hysterias to be capable of euphoric talk. What other outlet does the thinking man have in his hours of reflection but science fiction?"

Robert Bloch, in contrast, saw science fiction as a literature that consciously confronted society's ills, whether those ills be conceived as mere stuffy conformism or as outright police tyranny. It certainly did so by comparison with recent bestselling fiction, which Bloch saw— with his typical humorous exaggeration—as a mere catalogue of dreary capitulations to the *status quo:*

> There's *The Caine Mutiny,* which teaches us it's wrong to disobey the Captain or go around thinking he's crazy, if we want to get along in the Navy. And *From Here to Eternity,* which doesn't pull any punches—it admits life in the Army can be tough, but the important thing is discipline and learning to love the system. And *Not as a Stranger,* which is about doctors—in fact its plot sounds a lot like a book Sinclair Lewis wrote in the Bad Old Days, except that it shows most doctors are dedicated and live up to all the principles of the American Medical Association, just like it says in *Hygeia* magazine.
>
> And even better, there's those books about businessmen—*Executive Suite* and *The Man in the Grey Flannel Suit* and *Cash McCall,* which prove that big business men really do their best for the country . . . Finally, *The Last Hurrah,* which shows us that so-called "machine politics" and political bosses are pretty darn swell, because you have to be practical about such things.

The science fiction of the fifties, on the surface of it, seemed quite different; "while main-stream fiction glorifies the status quo, science fiction seemingly singles it out as the villain." But that, Bloch insisted, was not enough. In contemporary science fiction "the heroes are too important." Instead of being shown from the lower, or at least lower-middle-class, level where political suffering is the greatest—like that of Julia and Winston Smith in *1984*—the future tyranny is typically portrayed from a position at or near the top. The hero confronts the system at its source, just as in the old pulp days when "the handsome but brilliant young fullback landed on Mars and immediately found himself involved with the Princess, the High Priest and the Emperor." That, Bloch regretfully concluded, was where "some of these books destroy the illusion of reality for me"; in the new sf as in the old, in the course of a couple of hundred action-packed pages, the hero alone and singlehandedly overturns the world.

III

The most sprightly and provocative of these four University of Chicago lecturers was Cyril Kornbluth, who met the challenge of the topic head-on. His chosen title was "The Failure of the Science Fiction Novel as Social Criticism." "As social criticism the science fiction novel is a lever without a fulcrum," the lecturer explained. "The science fiction novel does contain social criticism, explicit and implicit, but I believe this criticism is massively outweighed by unconscious symbolic material more concerned with the individual's relationship to his family and the raw universe than with the individual's relationship to society." Documenting this claim with some pungent and at times hilarious Freudian analysis of some of the cherished pulp sf classics, Kornbluth concluded "that in science fiction the symbolism lies too deep for action to result, that the science fiction story does not turn the reader outward to action but inward to contemplation."

The paradox in this essentially adverse judgment is that

Kornbluth himself, in collaboration with Frederik Pohl, had not long since created one of the sharpest, most effective pieces of social satire ever written in America. Serialized as "Gravy Planet" in 1952, published in book form a year later as *The Space Merchants*, this science fiction novel foretold a future America dominated not by Wall Street, the traditional villain for radicals and liberals, but by Madison Avenue. Eschewing the "long ago in a galaxy far away" approach (which the movies discovered only after book and magazine science fiction had outgrown it), Pohl and Kornbluth inventoried that future in considerable detail and firmly rooted it in the here-and-now. "With almost lunatic single-mindedness," Kornbluth told his University of Chicago audience, "we made everything in our future America that could be touched, smelled, heard, seen or talked about bear witness to the dishonesty of the concepts and methods of today's advertising."

Still more paradoxical was the author's admission, in the face of his own argument that social-critical sf was a lever without a fulcrum, that his and Pohl's opus "did have some effect." It had not been "just another science fiction book which has shot its wad and been forgotten," he asserted; a judgment which has since proven valid: *The Space Merchants* has by now sold three quarters of a million copies, a respectable figure for any book, let alone one narrowly labeled as science fiction. "It stimulated thinking in a lot of places, some of them quite unlikely ones," Kornbluth pointed out:

> There was a full-page review, for instance, in *The Industrial Worker*, the organ of such I.W.W. members, or Wobblies, as survive. I have reason to believe it was read by a lot of people who do not normally read science fiction. It had a vogue in the New York City theatrical crowd, an actor has told me, and I know it was read by broadcasting men across the country. It was read, of course, by the hypersensitive advertising people. In their trade paper *Tide* a reviewer wanted to know whether it was supposed to be good, clean fun or the most vicious underhanded attack on the advertising profession yet. (If he had asked me, I would have told him "Both.")

The Space Merchants had obvious thematic kinship with Frederick

Wakeman's late forties "mainstream" novel (and movie) *The Hucksters,* from which the sf story's savagely conceived scenes around an advertising-agency executive table were probably derived. Being science fiction, however, the Pohl/Kornbluth work could go a step beyond a contemporary-scene satire like *The Hucksters,* by extrapolating some of the *consequences* of advertising, and of the consumer culture which it fosters. Prosperity and progress, as defined in such a culture, require an ever-accelerating use of natural resources; the planet is finite; therefore, the trend of the future is toward shortages—which must, for peace of mind, be defined as something else. "Science," the story's narrator (an advertising copysmith) cheerfully reflects, "is *always* a step ahead of the failure of natural resources. After all, when real meat got scarce, we had soyaburgers ready. When oil ran low, technology developed the pedicab."

That pedicab, depicted on the cover of *Galaxy* for June 1952, with the familiar yellow Checker emblem on the passenger compartment between its forward and aft bicycle sprockets as it wheels across a future Manhattan, seems more a symbol of the energy-conscious seventies than of the apparently affluent fifties. But that is science fiction's pragmatic function: to ask "What if?" or, more ominously, "If this goes on . . . " There is an Underground in *The Space Merchants,* as in so much sf of this kind, whose members are called "Connies" or "Consies"—but they are not the kind of radicals to whom most people paid attention in the fifties. The abbreviation stands for "Conservationists," and they engage in such protest actions as bombing a bulldozer that is about to begin cutting away the topsoil for a strip mine.

In the course of the story its hero makes a pilgrimage through the misery in which, beneath the advertised glitter, America's future underclass must dwell. He spends a harrowing night, for example, among the night-dwellers who solve the overcrowding problem by renting space on the downtown skyscrapers' endless stairs, one step per customer ("Night-dwellers are responsible for their own policing. Management assumes no responsibility for thefts, assaults, or rapes." "Night-dwellers will note that barriers are upped at 2210 nightly and arrange their calls of nature accordingly." "Rent is due and payable nightly in advance at the autoclerk.") And he comes to know, as he tells his boss at the advertising agency, that "The interests of producers and consumers are not identical; most of the world is unhappy; workmen don't automatically find the job they do best"; and "Entrepreneurs don't play a hard, fair game by the rules." But, as T. S. Eliot once observed, humankind cannot bear very much reality. The ad agency tycoon treats the hero's story as a psychotic fantasy and sends him to his analyst! The world of *The Space Merchants* may have seemed a safe distance in the future from the fifties but in another sense it was not very far away.

Pohl and Kornbluth went on to do other satiric extrapolations: of the stock market, which in one of their futures is played by parimutuel gambling machines (*Gladiator-at-Law*, 1955); of organized crime, which in another future has taken over America and given it a government rather *less* repressive than it had before (*Syndic,* by Kornbluth alone, 1953); of conformity, which in yet another world-to-come has bred a population each of whose adult members—of either gender—is exactly six feet tall, gangling, red-haired, blue-eyed, and named Jones (*Search the Sky,* 1954). Other writers in the fifties with this same caustic perceptiveness focused upon the social idiocy they saw around them and turned it into science fiction. Robert Sheckley, notably, suggested that the senseless street violence endemic in urban America might be tamed by making it legal; under strict government supervision, people would take turns at playing Hunter and Victim. "Have a good hunt," one respectable businessman's partner tells him at the beginning of Sheckley's memorable short story "Seventh Victim" (1953); "a good kill will do you a world of good. You've been keyed up." (This, as *Tenth Victim,* also became a film.) More subtly, Wynan Guin proposed in "Beyond Bedlam" (1951) that the logical solution for a culture whose hospitals were increasingly loaded with schizophrenics was to legislate (and pharmacologically carry out) the splitting of *everybody's* personality, so that schizophrenia becomes the hideously enforced norm.

Especially striking, in view of the nuts-and-bolts technological bias which had characterized U.S. science fiction since its infancy, was a considerable retreat from that emphasis in the fifties. In the course of making a case against contemporary society, the traditional futuristic portrayal of ultramodern cities and marvelous machines gave way in some stories to outright pastoralism. "The Climbing Wave," for example, by Marion Zimmer Bradley (1955), brings a spaceship back to Earth after a hazardous voyage of many years. To its captain's dismay there are no longer any spaceports, cities, or government; the voyagers come down into a landscape of "wide plowed fields, scattered toy-like houses, clusters of small buildings." Far away from the inhabited villages eight great starships stand abandoned, "covered from nose to tail with green-growing moss and red rust." To the captain's outraged objection that this is but a slide into decadence, his rustic Earthly host counters with a lecture on the technological burden of modern history:

> The light body-armor of the Barbarian soldier was developed to guard him against the simple weapons of his enemies. But it spurred on the development of more formidable weapons, and finally the armor had to be so cumbersome that the armored man must be lifted on his horse with a derrick. And if he fell down—well, there he was. It helped along the army, as a unit, but it certainly made life a mess for the individual . . . Eventually— well, the knight fell down inside his armor, and couldn't get up again . . .
>
> Then, unluckily for Europe, and also unluckily for the Red Men, the so-called New World was discovered. It's always easier to escape across a frontier, and drive your misfits out instead of learning to live with your problems. When that frontier was finally conquered, man had a second chance to learn to live with himself and with what he'd done. Instead, after wars and all kinds of trouble, he escaped again, this time to the planets. But he couldn't escape from himself . . . And then the crash came. Every man had the choice: die in his armor, or take it off.

Some science fictionists felt that stories like "The Climbing

Wave" were downright reactionary. To reject an organizational, machine civilization, they argued, is to reject also such fruits of that civilization as antibiotics and painless dentistry. Bradley's story, however, hedged against so extreme an "either/or" choice; in an emergency the dwellers on her pastoral future Earth can and do use radio communication, aircraft, and sophisticated medical care. "We use science," one of them explains, "in its proper place."

IV

That science *has* a proper place was something almost all members of the science fiction community insisted on; science fiction, at least until the liberal-arts professors discovered it, had little room for the more extreme pure-and-ignorant disclaimers against science and all its works that were put forth by some partisans in the "Two Cultures" controversy. Furthermore, the heightened social consciousness of 1950s science fiction did not totally displace more traditional sf concerns. Although the disguised horse opera and cops-and-robbers stories were mercifully curtailed in the fifties, there was plenty of room for high adventure, romantic encounter, humor, and the kind of science fiction sometimes called "pure," in which the plot of the story turns on the solution of a scientific problem.

Science, author Hal Clement has pointed out, can be used in science fiction in at least three ways: as a backdrop, "continually affecting actions, motives and problems of the characters but leaving the basic plot essentially 'mainstream'"; as an intellectual ingredient, used "as a mystery writer used clues . . . challenging the reader to beat him to the answer"; or, as the necessary condition "to make possible a story situation that has occurred to the writer." This last category "is sometimes supposed by the uninitiated to comprise all of science fiction," Clement noted in 1976, but it has advanced considerably in sophistication. It is no longer possible to have Buck Rogers walking around in his shirtsleeves on Mars or Jupiter, "regardless of the actual conditions there." On other planets, or in space, the choice is not one of either dying in your armor or taking it off as in Bradley's "Climbing Wave"!

Some writers kept up with the ever-changing pattern of knowledge and devised stratagems to enable Buck to survive on other planets (though probably not including Jupiter); a few, notably Ray Bradbury, continued to write of a shirtsleeveable Mars. Clement's personal preference was to start at the other end of the problem; "I worry about the conditions first and what sort of story they permit afterward." Typically he made up a solar system, populated it with planets, and logically worked out "the chemical, physical, meteorological, biological and other details which may later provide a story background." In the case of his best known story, *Mission of Gravity*—fully as much a landmark of science fiction in the fifties as books like *The Space Merchants*—Clement did not quite make his planet up. He picked a known object which *might* be a planet, and went on from there.

The object was—is—61 Cygni C, discovered in 1943 when Hal Clement was just beginning his work as a writer. It had a measured mass of sixteen times that of Jupiter, making it either an enormous planet or an unusually small star. Unfortunately— or fortunately, for poetic license—it was too close to its brighter primary to allow it to be photographed, which should otherwise have been possible if it shone by its own self-generated light as a star. Therefore, Clement surmised, it could be a planet, cold and therefore invisible; at least, there was no evidence that it wasn't. In addition to its mass, 61 Cygni C's orbit was inferentially known, and that orbit gave the hypothetical planet temperature maxima and minima of -50° and -180° C.; no shirtsleeves there. From that point on, the author was on his own.

Clement wanted to populate his planet with a lifeform that would be viable within those extremes. To power its metabolism he would require an agent other than oxygen—hydrogen would do nicely—and a liquid in its tissues other than water, "a good solvent and reasonably capable of causing ionic dissociation of polar molecules dissolved in it," and stable inside that temperature range. Clement had a pleasant evening discussing with biochemist/ sf writer Isaac Asimov some of the possibilities—ammonia, carbon disulfide, hydrogen fluoride, saturated and unsaturated hydrocarbons, "even a silicone or two"—before settling on methane, which could also constitute the planet's oceans. One idea leads to another; the denizens of 61 Cygni C (rechristened "Mesklin") could then be a seafaring people, and the story's leading character began to emerge: a shrewd, slightly piratical merchant-trader named Barlennan.

But the author wanted more. This was to be a First Contact story, with Earth people visiting the planet and establishing a relationship with its inhabitants. He did not want to beg the question of how such an encounter could be made plausible by inventing some unspecified "gravity screen" to protect the visitors. There was, however, a known, perfectly legitimate way to reduce the effective gravity: "set the planet spinning rapidly enough to make the characters feel as light as I please, at least at the equator," since inertial—centrifugal—effects cannot be distinguished in practice from gravitational ones. "Rapidly enough," given the size of the planet, worked out to a day 17 ¾ minutes long; which added the further complication that the resultant flattening at the poles and bulge at the equator would give Mesklin the figure of a fried egg. Since in the course of the planet's evolution "the rate of spin might be expected to increase to the point where matter was actually shed from the equator," just to cover that eventuality Clement "gave the planet a set of rings and a couple of fairly massive moons."

The mark of a superior writer of "hard" science fiction is that having painstakingly worked out all these data he or she does not simply hit the reader over the head with them. (Historical novelists learn to practice the same kind of self-restraint; they don't flood the story with all the evidence of their work in the library.) Deftly, and deceptively, Hal Clement opened *Mission of Gravity* with a descriptive passage that seems conventional, even "mainstream":

The wind came across the bay like something living. It tore the already wildly turbulent surface so thoroughly to shreds that it was hard to tell where liquid ended and atmosphere began; it tried to raise waves that would have swamped the *Bree* like a chip, and blew them into impalpable spray before they had risen a foot.

The spray alone reached Barlennan, crouched high on the *Bree*'s poop aft. His ship had long since been hauled safely ashore. That had been done the moment he had been sure that he would stay here for the winter; but he could not help feeling a little uneasy even so.

The reader does not yet know that those waves and that impalpable spray are not water; we might be at the beginning of an old-fashioned shipwreck or sea story, in the tradition of Cooper, Kipling, Conrad, or William McFee. But the next paragraph warns us that we are not in that kind of world at all:

Those waves were monsters. They were many times as high as any he had faced at sea [at one *foot* above the surface? Just how big is Barlennan, anyhow?], and somehow it was not completely reassuring to reflect that the lack of weight which permitted them to rise so high [lack of weight? How's that again?] would also prevent their doing real damage if they did roll this far up the beach.

Within the next two paragraphs, Clement's yarn is well launched on its way. Woven into details of character portrayal and seamanship on the good ship *Bree* is the information that Barlennan, at his ship's location near the planetary equator, "weighs about two and a quarter pounds instead of the five hundred and fifty or so to which he has been used all his life"; and that his form is not human: "Barlennan's long body tensed" we are told, at the sight of his first mate "balanced precariously on his six rearmost legs." *Mission of Gravity,* however, which Clement has said is his own bottom-line personal philosophic statement, is a good deal more than just an exotic intellectual puzzle. It unfolds as a story about courage, and cooperation, and the nature of a fair bargain—themes surely germane in the fifties on a small, oxygen-atmosphered, more-or-less spherical planet peopled by quarrelsome, Cold Warring peoples who are basically far more alike than are Clement's Earthmen and the hydrogen-breathing denizens of Mesklin with whom they are able in the story's course to work out a rational, mutually beneficial deal.

V

Some science fiction in the fifties, predicting neither an unsavory future society on the model of *The Space Merchants* nor a logical, inquisitive, and basically humane culture of the kind implicit in *Mission of Gravity*, faced up to the ultimate question of whether human civilization has any future at all. The other planets, if man escaped to one of them in the armor he was unwilling to take off, might serve only as his ringside seat for viewing the home world's end:

> The rolling, rust-red hills of Mars lay in pools of inky shadow under a dark sky in which a shrunken sun and brilliant stars looked down together. A tiny sliver of moon shone high in the rich darkness; another, larger, stood on the too-near horizon. Where the blue disk of Earth should have been was a terribly bright, white star. . . .
> News of the atomic attack had come by radio from the Lunar base when the ship was four days out—yellow-brown mushrooms blossoming over North America, followed by eye-scorching flashes of hot blue light dotting Central Asia. Then the operator's voice had become excited as he told of boiling clouds from the seat and red fire over the continents. A cry of "The bombs set off something else—" and then a crash of static from the ship's receiver and a long silence that remained unbroken.

That description of nuclear destruction—differing in detail, but not in substance, from recent straight-line factual prophecy such as Jonathan Schell's *The Fate of the Earth* (1982)—appeared in 1950. Science fiction, however, had been dwelling upon the theme of atomic apocalypse at least since 1914, when H.G. Wells wrote *The World Set Free*. Before Hiroshima its writers had discussed in their stories such topics as the danger of a runaway reaction in a nuclear power plant; the essential mechanism for detonating a U-235 bomb; and the political and foreign policy implications of developing a weapon against which there could be no defense. They had seen, long before most of their contemporaries, that the release of nuclear energy would abolish traditional Great Power politics and diplomacy at one stroke, and they feared that the lesson would not be learned by enough people in enough time. Their fears and warnings carried over into their fiction: "One man, losing his head and pressing the wrong button, can write the end," says a character in Poul Anderson's story "Wildcat" (1958), "and there are so many buttons." The hero broodingly agrees: "Even if important men on both sides wished for a disengagement, what could they do against their own fanatics, vested interests, terrified common people— against the whole momentum of history?"

Not long after Hiroshima science fiction editor John Campbell, phoned by someone on a New York newspaper who wanted to know what he was doing now that the brand of fiction formerly printed in his magazine had become fact, replied that most of the stories he currently published took place "after the end of the world." His competitor and colleague Horace Gold was getting much the same sort of manuscripts from his own writers. Gold and Campbell both believed that science fiction in the late forties and early fifties was blunting the edge of its prophetic warnings by verbal overkill. "It's a depressing experience to sit at a desk and read story after story filled with pessimism and despair," the editor of *Galaxy* wrote at the end of 1951. "Science fiction has a more important job than to warn of doom."

Some day, Gold argued, the issues of the Cold War and its concomitant balance of terror would be as out-of-date as the issues of slavery, feudalism, or one-piece bathing suits; and it was that eventual future, beyond the present-bound concerns of politicians and journalists, to which science fiction could most usefully address itself. But when anyone in the fifties began to dwell upon the problem of *how* one got from the near future to that farther one, the warning of doom sounded once again, loud and inescapable. Horace Gold, like any good editor, knew when to break his own rules; and so with seeming inconsistency he could publish that same year stories like "Appointment in Tomorrow," by Fritz Leiber, which began with "the first angry rays of the sun"—unpleasantly similar to "the rays from World War III's atomic bombs"—touching "thousands of sleeping Americans with unconscious fear":

> They turned to blood the witch-circle of rusty steel skeletons around Inferno in Manhattan. Without comment, they pointed a cosmic finger at the tarnished brass plaque commemorating the martyrdom of the Three Physicists after the dropping of the Hell Bomb . . . They struck green magic from the glassy blot that was Old Washington. Twelve hours before, they had revealed things as eerily beautiful, and as ravaged, in Asia and Russia.

But there *were* thousands of sleeping Americans, however fearful, to be awakened by the rising sun; Leiber's story went on to chronicle the fate of a few of them. And in the tale just previously quoted there was a man standing on the red soil of Mars to remember and mourn that lunar radio operator's last despairing cry. Woven into the prophet's tapestry of gloom and doom was a modest thread of optimism. If a writer *began* a story with a scene of nuclear disaster obviously the world had not quite come to an end, else there would be no story to tell. Typically—and quite unlike Jonathan Schell's scenario for the end of humanity—the science fiction imagination of the fifties foretold not an ending but a beginning; the world crashes in ruins, but the survivors in those ruins pick themselves up and go on from there, as survivors always have.

They go on, but they carry less baggage; most of the complexities of civilization they leave behind them in the ruins. Science fiction has an entire sub-field of post-Apocalypse stories, which speculate as to just how far human society could fall before it would reach equilibrium. Stone-age savages roaming through the ruins of New York, or dwellers in walled city-states separated by many miles of trackless wilderness, or nomadic tribes like those which formerly dominated Central Asia and the North American high plains—these fictional heirs of a fallen civilization preserve what they can, discard what they must.

What social institutions would they be most likely to keep? Forms of government? Armed forces? Scientific research centers? Or none of these? "In telling future-history," Isaac Asimov has testified, "I always felt it wisest to be guided by past-history." Past-history furnishes one obvious precedent for telling future-history about the kind of society that might be expected after a collapse of civilization: the western Dark Ages following the fall of Rome. Those ages were neither as universal nor as dark as the West's present heirs commonly assume; the "fall of Rome" was felt in India and China as only the faintest of ripples, and in the broken fragments of the Western Empire some people continued to reason by Greek logic and to hand down the law in Latin. Nevertheless, reasoned the author of one major work of science fiction dating from the fifties, the Dark Ages might well serve as a model for the fate of the civilization which rose out of that darkness into modernity, only to annihilate itself through its mastery of the atom about which its ultimate Greek and Roman mentors had speculated. Not the Greco-Roman but the Hebraic strand of that civilization's cultural heritage might outlast the collapse, to interpret to the remnant of its children what had happened:

> It was said that God, in order to test mankind, had commanded wise men of that age . . . to perfect diabolic weapons and give them into the hands of latter-day Pharaohs. And with such weapons Man had, within the span of a few weeks, destroyed most of his civilization. After the Deluge of Flame came the plagues, the madness, and the bloody inception of the Age of Simplification when the furious remnants of humanity had torn politicians, technicians, and men of learning limb from limb, and burned all records that might contain information that could once more lead into paths of destruction.

Such, in the New Dark Age six hundred years hence as imagined inWalter M. Miller's story "A Canticle for Leibowitz" (1955), is the way the eventual outcome of the Cold War is remembered. About all that remains from the fifties, in that future, is an echo of the decade's anti-intellectualism: "Nothing had been so hated as the written word," Miller's prophecy continues. "It was during this time that the word *simpleton* came to mean *honest, upright, virtuous citizen,* a concept once denoted by the term *common man.*" The only sanctuary to which the surviving scientists were able to flee—and the only institution to survive our civilization's collapse—was the Catholic Church, which "received them, vested them in monks' robes, tried to conceal them from the mobs." At monasteries dotted across a thinly settled New Dark Age North America, devoted if uncomprehending monks lovingly copy and illuminate the manuscripts the refugee savants left behind: blueprints, mathematical calculations, wiring diagrams. In the course of the story one martyred scientist (said to have been alive in 1956), the Blessed Isaac Leibowitz, receives final canonization as a saint from Pope Leo XXII, who, gazing at an authentic Leibowitz relic which little Brother Francis Gerard of Utah has found and given him, declares: "Whatever it means, this bit of learning, though dead, will live again and we shall guard it till that day." Despite the "bitter history of atomic devastation" that lurks in the story's background, editor Anthony Boucher contended, this latter-day Canticle "glows with the light that must lie at the heart of the Darkest Age."

VI

The new maturity evident in the science fiction of the fifties did not often survive translation from the printed page to the tube or the screen. "There are virtually no good films that are good science fiction," says science fiction writer and teacher James Gunn, some of whose own work has done well on TV. Science fiction in the movies, Susan Sontag asserted in 1965, was as hackneyed as it ever had been in the old pulp magazines one pulled off the rack at the corner drug store: "The typical science fiction film has a form as predictable as a Western, and is made up of elements which, to a practiced eye, are as classic as the saloon brawl, the blonde school-teacher from the East, and the gun duel on the deserted main street."

A Western film devotee could properly have retorted that those very elements, in the hands of a master director, transcend themselves; perhaps science fiction was similarly capable of developing its own equivalent of a *Stagecoach*, an *Oxbow Incident*, a *High Noon*. Here and there across the film landscape of the fifties came some encouraging signs such as *Destination Moon*, "the only real science fiction film, in the strictest sense, to be made between *Things to Come* and *2001*," David Hartwell writes. The film took its science seriously, without fudging; there were no loud explosions in airless space, and no spaceships that made banking turns like the Red Baron and Snoopy. According to Robert Heinlein it very nearly did not come off that way. At the last minute "the powers-that-be decided that the story was too cold," and for a time the film-makers were stuck with a script that put dude ranches, guitars, and a female vocal trio on the Moon. The powerful combination of Heinlein, astronomical artist Chesley Bonestell, producer George Pal, and director Irving Pichel somehow purged the show of all such distractions; to us it is dated, but authentic, like a classic antique automobile.

Pal went on to produce two of the H.G. Wells classic novels, *The War of the Worlds* (1953) and *The Time Machine* (1960); these made more concessions to conventional "sci-fi" hokum (e.g., the monster taps the heroine on the shoulder, and she screams), but were still miles in advance of most of what had gone on screen before as sf. Unhappily, the experience taught movie-makers at large absolutely nothing. The new look in film science fiction did not last; we were not yet ready for *2001*, or even *Star Wars*. Repenting of its excursion into scientific believability in *Destination Moon*, Hollywood quickly turned out *Rocketship X-M* which, in order to avoid the expenses of building a moon set on a sound stage, had astronauts who were supposedly heading for the moon to go off course and land on Mars (whose landscape could be faked anywhere in the American Southwest)—a plot line "about as scientifically practical," David Hartwell sarcastically comments, "as driving to the local grocery, getting lost and continuing on to Hong Kong." Moreover, the best of the 1950s films that were labeled "science fiction," Hartwell correctly notes, were not science fiction at all, in the "hard," plausible sense of a *Mission of Gravity* or the convincing almost-here-and-now mood of a *Space Merchants*. Rather they were "science fantasy, unrationalized and powerful . . . but far away from the concerns of written science fiction and antithetical to many tenets of the literature."

The shadow of the old Frankenstein pictures still loomed over Hollywood. If science fiction did not mean zap-guns, it meant horror; either a hobgoblin unleashed by a recklessly experimenting scientist or a detestable intruder from outer space. To be sure a first-rate director (with an adequate special-effects budget) can make a good movie out of the most unpromising material: the original *Invasion of the Body Snatchers* (1956) still has its admirers, as does the first version of *The Thing* (1952). But then came *Them!*, and *The Creature from the Black Lagoon*, and *The Blob;* as usual after any box-office victory, Hollywood then repeated itself—at a lower level each time—to the point of absurdity. For an amusing change of pace from her standard repertoire, Judy Garland sometimes in the fifties would recite a litany of all those monster movie titles and then light-heartedly swing into a song about the "Purple People Eater," the worst of them all.

"Shriek movies," Cyril Kornbluth contemptuously called such pictures in his University of Chicago presentation; and if the day ever came when that kind of film would be "a really major type, right up there with, say, the pretentious Western, the implications for the future of democracy will be bad." Some film critics felt that those dangerous implications were already present. The pod-creatures from space who pass themselves off as ordinary American citizens in order to infiltrate and eventually displace our civilization in the 1956 version of *Invasion of the Body Snatchers* are metaphors for pro-Communist subversion and mental corruption, writes Robert C. Cumbow; if the story line be taken at face value "we must see the film as inescapably pro-McCarthy." Another critic, Ernest G. Laura, concurs: "It is natural to see the pods as standing for the idea of communism which gradually takes possession of a normal person, leaving him outwardly unchanged but transformed within."

Were this in fact the message—latent or manifest—in such a movie, it would be more than enough to cancel the quite contrary message in a book like *Eye in the Sky*. It is hard not to bristle, however, when a critic falls into the peremptory locution "We must." Certainly that film's own makers spiritedly denied this interpretation of their handiwork as McCarthyite. *Invasion of the Body Snatchers* they saw not as a parable about subversives and patriots, nor even as a straight sf story of aliens and earth people, but rather as a statement about the alienness *within* mid-twentieth-century humanity: "All of us who worked on the film," director Donald Siegel told one interviewer, "believed in what it said—that the majority of people in the world unfortunately are pods, existing without any intellectual aspirations and incapable of love."

With her characteristic relentlessness, and going even Cyril Kornbluth one better, Susan Sontag swept all such argumentation aside. Neither McCarthyism, nor anti-McCarthyism, nor the pathology of Organization Man is the real subject of such movies, she insisted: "There is absolutely no social criticism, of even the most implicit kind, in science fiction films." Nor can we get their real message by translating them back into the rational terms of the stories from which many of them derive. "The movies are, naturally, weak just where the science fiction novels (some of them) are strong—on science"; however, fundamentally, "science fiction films are not about science. They are about disaster." The point is not the acting (which in sf films often might as well have been done by pods!), nor the plot, nor the possible political allegory; it is, quite simply, the disaster itself—the flood waters swirling around the New York skyscrapers in *When Worlds Collide,* or the giant winged reptiles flapping up the storm that blows down Tokyo in *Rodan,* or the destruction of London in *The Time Machine.* In one sense this kind of movie calamity was old stuff, going clear back to the silent screen. Long before the science fiction vogue, Sontag pointed out, Sodom and Gomorrah or Gaza or Rome had gone down in flood and flame and plunging stonework in any number of Biblical spectaculars. To the Bible's fire and brimstone we could now add the nuclear scourge: "The accidental awakening of the super-destructive monster who has slept in the earth since prehistory is, often, an obvious metaphor for the Bomb," Sontag argued, and it is no accident that *Gojiru*— Englished as *Godzilla*—should have come forth from the film industry of the one country in the world where that Bomb had actually been used.

Yet we must not take an apocalyptic cry from the sixties (when Sontag's essay first appeared), or from the eighties, as the last word on what was seen and felt and thought in the era of Eisenhower. Contrary to Sontag there *is* social criticism, both explicit and implicit, about Russia and the U.S. and the Cold-potentially-Hot War in at least a few science fiction films that were released in the fifties. Such criticism could be adroit and witty, as in Gore Vidal's *Visit to a Small Planet,* which worked well in three media—on stage, on film, and as a teleplay; or it could be straight-out preachment, most notably in Stanley Kramer's *On the Beach,* which many theatregoers found one of their most emotionally moving experiences of the fifties. Some of them, at intermission time, really did cry .

Think of but three moments from that film: the scene near the beginning, in which some of the surviving Australians speculate as to how the war started (nobody really knows) and comfort themselves that, after all, "we"—who are about to die—"won"; the great power plant near San Diego which roars on, untenanted, so that electricity can flow to the telegraph key which is sending out a hopeful but misleading radio "message," pressed randomly

by a Coke bottle entangled in a window shade; and at the end
the shots of deserted streets, stopped tram cars, and a tattered
Salvation Army banner that reads THERE IS STILL TIME BROTHER.
Truly, as Sontag says, in such a film "one can participate in the
fantasy of living through one's own death and more, the death
of cities, the destruction of humanity itself." But a director as
activist as Stanley Kramer was not content that his audiences
experience mere katharsis. His whole point in making such a
film, and releasing it simultaneously in a dozen of the world's
great and vulnerable cities—including Moscow!—was to state
that, yes, brother, there *is* still time. Do something with it. Now.

EPILOGUE:
A WORLD IN SEARCH OF
A FUTURE

CHAPTER TEN
There Is Still Time, Brother

I

THERE was still time; but perhaps not much. What was
most dangerous about the Cold War was, precisely, its *cold-ness;* it froze the process of thought. Having once lumbered into
position against each other its protagonists stood fixed like gla-
ciated mammoths, their brains too benumbed to generate new,
life-changing ideas. "The unleashed power of the atom," said
Albert Einstein, "has changed everything except our thinking."

Here and there a warm corpuscle stirred in protest. On December 3, 1946—still rather early in the Cold War—Mike Mansfield, on a fact-finding mission for a House Naval Affairs subcommittee, circled in an airplane over Hiroshima and brooded
about the Bomb. "I think it was a mistake to use it on people,"
he confided to his diary. "What did the ordinary person have
to do with bringing on a war? Why should they have to always
suffer for some individual's or small group's mistakes?" Mansfield
would return to the United States from that mission and (as
noted in chapter 3) do his own political bit as a Cold Warrior;
but on his diary's pages the entry remained: "War is responsible
for bringing about all the bad things we fear and few of the
good things we want."

Other statesmen of the Cold War era admitted to equally
disquieting misgivings. When the U.S. and the Soviet Union
detonated their first hydrogen bombs, Sir Winston Churchill

"The unleashed power of the atom has changed everything except our thinking."—Albert Einstein.

told the House of Commons on March 1, 1955, "the entire
foundation of human affairs was revolutionised." The original
atomic bomb, for all its terror, had not carried matters "outside
the scope of human control"; but the new H-bomb placed humanity "in a situation both measureless and laden with doom . . .
What ought we to do?" the 82-year-old Prime Minister asked:

Which way shall we turn to save our lives and the future of the
world? It does not matter so much to old people. They are going
soon anyway. But I find it poignant to look at youth with all its
activities and ardor, and most of all to watch little children playing

their merry games and wonder what would lie before them if God wearied of mankind.

Yet when he went on to spell out *specifically* "what we ought to do," even so experienced and canny a politician as Churchill could only say, in effect, "more of the same." No, we could not press for universal disarmament at this time; it could not be trustworthily inspected and monitored. Yes, the nuclear buildup would have to continue; and Britain would have to possess a strategic deterrent force of its own. The only hope the old war leader could hold out was that since the H-bomb had rendered everybody equally vulnerable, the potential aggressor along with the potential victim, it might bleakly preserve the peace through a "balance of terror." One day, perhaps, the nuclear nightmare would end through disarmament and international control, but not now. "Meanwhile," the Prime Minister concluded in a farewell echo of his World War II style, "never flinch, never weary, never despair."

American Cold War thinking was caught in the same trap. This was especially true for the Republican Administration that came to power in 1952, whose advocates in the campaign had condemned their Democratic predecessors for what Republicans perceived as a static, negative foreign policy. They had triumphantly installed a Secretary of State who talked, frighteningly, of "massive retaliation," "going to the brink," and "liberation." Yet the leader of the new government, like his wartime comrade Winston Churchill, was fully aware of the doom-laden situation into which the contending superpowers had stumbled. On April 16, 1953, about a month after Stalin's death—an event which in itself seemed to promise some mitigation of the Cold War— Eisenhower addressed the American Society of Newspaper Editors and laid before them "the worst to be feared and the best to be expected" in the grim world that had been created by the unleashing of atomic energy in 1945, if nothing changed. "The worst is atomic war," he told them. "The best would be this: a life of perpetual fear and tension; a burden of arms draining the wealth and the labor of all peoples; a wasting of strength that defies the American system or the Soviet system or any system to achieve true abundance and happiness." In addition to the terror carried by the Bomb itself was the galling realization that the astronomical sums of money it and other armaments drained away might have been spent on something far better:

> Every gun that is made, every warship launched, every rocket fired signifies, in the final sense, a theft from those who hunger and are not fed, those who are cold and are not clothed . . .
> The cost of one modern heavy bomber is this: a modern brick school in more than thirty cities.
> It is two electric power plants, each serving a town of sixty thousand population.
> It is two fine, fully equipped hospitals.
> It is some fifty miles of concrete highway.
> We pay for a single fighter plane with a half-million bushels of wheat.
> We pay for a single destroyer with new homes that could have housed more than eight thousand people . . .
> *Is there no other way the world may live?*

Marriage counselors, diplomats, labor-management negotiators, and others whose job it is to reconcile the irreconcilable have long known that one sometimes effective approach when there is massive disagreement on major issues is to search creatively for matters—small matters at first, perhaps—on which the disputants *can* agree. For much of 1953, its first year in office, the Eisenhower Administration groped for just such small incremental steps toward peace. Its first task, however, was to bring the American people to a realization of just how real and comprehensive the nuclear danger was. Too many of them, ill-trained in the post-Newtonian scientific understanding of the universe, believed that the nuclear weapon was just another great big bomb. Too many of them, including too many in government, *still* believe it, and blithely claim that the citizen's best defense against radioactive fallout is a few shovelfuls of dirt! Accordingly, scores of drafts of a public declaration on the atom circulated through the Atomic Energy Commission and the Pentagon between April and June of 1953. They were grisly and realistic, and they came to be characterized by the single word "Bang!" All that this could accomplish, said Eisenhower, turning away with a shudder, would be "to scare the country to death."

A second batch began circulating in July. These in turn became known as the "Bang! BANG!" papers, because they linked the horrors nuclear bombs could wreak upon the U.S. with the vengeance the U.S. could work in return; this was, presumably, reassuring. Eisenhower was not reassured. At the end of the month, reports John Lear, "the President read the finished paper, shook his head, and said, 'This leaves everybody dead on both sides, with no hope anywhere. Can't we find some hope?' "

And then, early in August, the Russians exploded what was reported at the time as their first H-bomb. (It wasn't, exactly, but they made up for it with an atmosphere-fouling super-explosion only two years later.)

This was a moment ripe for manifestation of Toynbee's "challenge-and-response," and in a modest, indirect way Ike responded. "I have been thinking about this atom business," he told James Hagerty, his able and respected press secretary.

> and it seems to me there ought to be some way for us to give a certain amount of uranium to some kind of international agency that might be set up for the purpose. We couldn't give much at first without scaring our own people. But it should be enough to show the have-not peoples of the world that we sincerely want to develop the atom in a peaceful, friendly way.

Such, after the normal quota of ponderous paper-shuffling and bureaucratic infighting which accompanies any change of policy along the Potomac, was the proposal Eisenhower, on December 8, 1953, laid before the General Assembly of the United Nations. "To the extent permitted by elementary prudence," he proposed, "the governments principally involved"— of which "the Soviet Union must, of course, be one"—should "begin now and continue to make joint contributions from their stockpiles of normal uranium and fissionable materials to an international atomic energy agency . . . set up under the aegis of the United Nations." Such a mutually beneficial activity could be undertaken "without the irritations and mutual suspicions incident to any attempt to set up a completely acceptable system of world-wide inspection and control." And it was something the United Nations could do immediately; "peaceful power from atomic energy is no dream for the future [but] is here—now—today." Such a world Atomic Energy Agency could mobilize experts "to apply atomic energy to the needs of agriculture, medicine, and other activities"; "to provide abundant electrical energy in the power-starved areas of the world"; "to serve the needs rather than the fears of mankind." Concluding what may have been the greatest speech of his Presidency, Ike pledged that the United States would "devote its entire heart and mind to find the way by which the miraculous inventiveness of man shall not be dedicated to his death, but consecrated to his life."

II

"There were tears in the President's eyes when he sat down," an observer reported. "Even the Russian delegates so far forgot themselves as to join in the thunder of applause." UN delegate Henry Cabot Lodge drove Eisenhower to the airport afterward, and returned home to receive—to his astonishment—a phone call from V.K. Krishna Menon of India, who was known most recently at the UN (and at international student gatherings in New York) for his brilliantly critical attacks on Western colonialism and on the foreign policy of the U.S. Menon came over to Lodge's apartment and talked enthusiastically about the Eisenhower proposal for several hours, leaving his already-tired host "not only completely exhausted but somewhat confused" (a reaction Lodge shared with others who had had dialectical encounters with Mr. Menon). Such high enthusiasm was the reaction, multiplied many times in other parts of the world, to the slender ray of light the American President had sent up against the encroaching nuclear darkness.

American public life, however, had known many other such moments of fervent evangelism. Typically, a major U.S. political statement—Bryan's "cross of gold" oration; McGovern's acceptance speech; even, in a quieter way, Lincoln's Gettysburg Address—takes the rhetorical form of a revival sermon, ending with a call to the faithful to come forward and be saved. The trouble with any such mountain-top experience is that it is always necessary afterwards to come back down into the hot and noisy valley. Time passed, and the glow faded. The administration's proposal to amend the Atomic Energy Act of 1946, which would be necesary before anything else could be done since the act flatly forbade the AEC to "distribute any fissionable material to any foreign government," met at once the predictable opposition of isolationist Senators, renewing their suspicious stance against sharing any of "our" secrets with those unwashed foreigners, and—more disconcertingly—the cautious, shrewd *support* of American business forces who foresaw in the opening up of those secrets an opportunity not so much for public statecraft as for private gain. (Rather than "Atoms for Peace," Thomas R. Phillips argued, the program should have been called "Atoms for Industry"; nuclear-generated electricity would in due course not only power defense plants but also turn up in charges on the bill from your local electric company.) Some, quite cynically, concluded that "Eisenhower, tricked by his advisers into making a propaganda speech, had been caught flat-footed by the clamorous response of a hopeful world."

In the opinion of John Lear, so far the most acute student of the proposed program, this was a total misreading of the situation. "Atoms for Peace" had become "the one real crusade of General Dwight D. Eisenhower's period in the presidency," showing "his own strongest personal traits: the fortitude of the soldier and the patience of the man of simple faith . . . At times alone, at best with only the liberals of his party about him, always

with Republican doubters and dissenters dragging out and slowing down the march . . . stopping often for stragglers," Eisenhower
slogged on toward his goal. He got from a reluctant Republican
Congress his rewritten Atomic Energy Act of 1954; he got from
a reluctant, bureaucratically rule-bound Atomic Energy Commission the donation for international research purposes of 100
kilograms of fissionable material—about enough, using the
technology of the day, to make a single bomb. When bureaucrats
dragged their feet he enlisted new ones, such as Nelson Rockefeller and Morehead Patterson, and told them to "get this thing
off dead center and keep it off!" Patterson in turn, acknowledging
that "there is no possible way to prevent peaceful atoms from
being perverted to warlike purposes if someone wants war badly
enough," told his own aides that "if we are going to live in the
atomic age, we have to take the risks that are normal to that
age. Someone who has atoms must give the first atom. If we
don't do it, somebody else will."

In combatting unreasonable suspicion and skepticism, of
course, there was the danger of falling into equally unreasonable
hope. The Russian text of the "Atoms for Peace" posters that
were displayed all over Switzerland in 1955 asserted that "Atoms
Bring Peace"—which was one semantically possible interpretation
of Eisenhower's closing sentences at the U.N. "All scientists
prefer to see science applied to constructive purposes; most of
them favor the broadest possible international cooperation,"
wrote Eugene Rabinowitch, editor of the *Bulletin of the Atomic
Scientists,* early in 1956. But to believe "that emphasizing the
'peaceful atom' can become a serious deterrent to atomic war,"
he cautioned, "would be as irrational as believing that an international convention on the development of commercial avia-
tion will become a guarantee against the use of planes for bom-
bardment in a future war."

What did excite the atomic scientists for whom Rabinowitch
spoke was the re-creation of the international scientific community, long sundered by war and the threat of war. Even
before Eisenhower made his "Atoms for Peace" address to the

U.N., his Atomic Energy Commissioner Lewis Strauss and Churchill's chief scientific adviser, Lord Cherwell, were discussing the possibility of a world conclave of scientists interested in atoms for peace. In 1954 the U.N. General Assembly issued invitations for such a conference. It could not be held in the United States; the Cold War-tightened immigration laws could not allow distinguished Communist scientists, who would have to be among the guests at any truly international gathering, to enter the country! Instead, the U.N. had recourse to the impressive, theretofore little-used buildings which it had inherited from the League of Nations, its extinct predecessor, in Geneva. At the last moment the AEC's iron security bands, which had confined all technical discussion of reactor development, were loosened and literally tons of suddenly declassified information fell into the delighted scientists' laps. "Once on the agenda," Lear sums up, "atomic power took over":

> So much information had been dammed up on that topic for ten years that the resulting flood turned Geneva into the greatest scientific irrigation project of modern times. Before it was finished, both the Russians and the Americans were adding new data to their papers right up to the moment of delivery and even afterward.
> Instead of the hostility [AEC Chairman] Strauss had feared, the competition generated a friendliness that had been unknown between East and West since wartime days. At one point, an American defended the integrity of Soviet research; at another, a Russian chemist pleaded for more recognition for chemists— all chemists in all countries—as opposed to physicists, all physicists everywhere in the world.

On October 1, 1957, the International Atomic Energy Agency opened for business in Vienna. Supported by 58 member nations—and by a generous U.S. pledge of 5,000 kilograms of U-235, plus matching grants equal in amount to all the nuclear material made available by other members—it was empowered by its charter to carry out on a worldwide basis almost any functions it chose, so long as they related to the peaceful use of the atom. As so often happens when an ideal is embodied

in an organization, the performance did not come up to the
promise—in part because of the *success* scientists, business interests, and governments had enjoyed in opening general access
to the atom. Rather than go to a U.N. instrumentality, Madhu
Joshi reported in 1961, "the newly independent nations find it
advantageous and convenient to get whatever atomic assistance
they require from the scientifically advanced members of the
commonwealths, communities, or ideological groups to which
they belong."

For conservative Americans, who had not wanted any of the
AEC's "we've got a secret" rules relaxed lest advantage be given
to the Russians and other socialists, it was an ironic outcome;
the first round in the contest over the peaceful international
use of atomic energy seemed to have ended in an overwhelming
victory for capitalism. "Private industry is simply better equipped
to handle international trade in both reactors and fuel than the
Agency," Joshi pointed out:

> It can, for example, provide capital, accept only part down payment,
> provide for insurance and depreciation of equipment, and other
> advantages that are necessary to attract a client; and it can trade
> with the neutral nations without involving touchy cold war issues.
>   And when industry runs into difficulties—mostly financial—
> the government is right behind, supporting it with economic aid
> to its customers or assuring its credit. The Agency, bound as it
> is by the provisions of its charter, cannot offer these attractive
> sales inducements, and is obliged to include safeguard provisions
> in the package. The IAEA and private atomic industry took off
> almost simultaneously, but industry has left the Agency far behind.

Whether atomic energy went public or private, international
or bilateral, pragmatic or ideological, however, the important
psychological fact—and one of the greatest gains of the fifties—
was that people were learning to distinguish between the de-
structive and constructive potential in nuclear energy:

> They know that the weather man, the medicine man, and others
> who make the world go 'round, as well as those who go 'round
> the world, use the atom to advantage. Of course, they recognize

that there exist among us, too, push-button-happy warriors, . . .
but they have succeeded, so far, in keeping them apart . . . Public
opinion has undergone a steady change, a change toward acceptance of the atomic age, that is once again bringing normality
to life.

III

Yet how could normality be brought to life in the atomic age
when the national political conditions under which scientists
worked on the atom remained so wretchedly abnormal? The
McCarthyists did some of their most effective damage to America
by going after atomic and other scientists' scalps. The files of
the *Bulletin of the Atomic Scientists* for the fifties contain numerous
horror stories of the kind already noted in chapter 7:

Dr. B., told that information had been received "which indicates
that you may have been a member of, affiliated with, or in
sympathetic association with, the Communist Party, U.S.A.," is
removed from a high-grade Civil Service appointment as a
physicist at an Army research installation, despite notarized
personal diary entries showing that he has spoken out strongly
in public against the Soviet Union, against the Progressive Party,
and even against critics of the British Empire. Mr. D., hired by
a Midwestern industrial concern, is denied security clearance
on the ground that "subversive literature; specifically, the *Daily
Worker*," has been seen in his home "on numerous occasions."
He denies it, and backs his denial with affidavits signed by
associates who have visited his home—and by the mailman—
but he loses his job anyway. Dr. F., a physical chemist in a
government laboratory, is removed from his "sensitive" position,
charged with having said that the U.S. should not have entered
the war in Korea. "I have supported our intervention and participation in the Korean War," he replies, having "felt that we
have no other alternative than to support the South Koreans
since checking Russian aggression was our prime objective"—
but he is not reinstated. And Mr. G., accused but finally cleared,

bitterly notes the contrast between the delays and bureaucratic evasions involved in processing a successful appeal against such charges and the swiftness of the same bureaucracy's action when the judgment is negative: "After the final decision to deny clearance is reached, no telephone or wire service seems to be too fast or too expensive to notify the employer quickly that the man is considered a security risk." In such circumstances it is not surprising that a mid-1950s random sample of graduate students in physics stated that they would accept a lower salary—heresy, in the fifties!—if the jobs offered to them required no security clearances.

Popular McCarthyism, when brought to bear upon atomic scientists, had a latent emotional appeal that was in its own way subtly subversive of the Cold War: here was a perfectly safe, patriotic way of expressing protest against the Bomb. If you were a true Cold Warrior you couldn't overtly condemn the Bomb itself, so long as the Russians had it; but you could at least condemn its makers. Had not J. Robert Oppenheimer, director during World War II of the Los Alamos laboratory where the world's first A-bomb was developed and tested, said on behalf of his fellow atomic physicists that "we have known sin"? What could have been more ironically appropriate, therefore—and, at the same time, more outrageously unfair—than for the U.S. government to lift the security clearance of the father of the A-bomb himself?

In December 1953, the very month of Eisenhower's "Atoms-for-Peace" address to the United Nations, the Atomic Energy Commission in a 3400-word letter filed official charges against Oppenheimer. In addition to the usual drab allegations of improper association with left-wingers and of lack of candor in discussing such associations, the document also denounced Oppenheimer for having opposed the development of the hydrogen bomb. There had in fact been a bitter debate in 1949 within the government and among its top scientific advisers over whether to go ahead with the H-bomb, a debate resolved in his usual crisp manner by President Truman. The anti-Bomb faction lost;

there are surviving pro-Bomb advocates who now believe their opponents had the better of the argument.

In a nationwide telecast on April 6, 1954, Joe McCarthy, in one last grandstand play before the meshes of the Army-McCarthy hearings closed around him, momentarily distracted the nation's attention from his own misdoings by loudly proclaiming someone else's. "If there were no Communists in our government," the Senator thundered, "why did we delay for eighteen months, delay our research on the hydrogen bomb, even though our intelligence agencies were reporting day after day that the Russians were feverishly pushing their development of the H-bomb?" President Eisenhower, keeping his usual dignified distance from the Senator, rejected any such interpretation. "Professor Oppenheimer's opposition to the hydrogen-bomb project could well have been a matter of conscience," Ike would later write in his memoirs. "It could have been his belief that, as a practical matter, the world would be better off if this development was stifled before birth."

Indeed, Eisenhower admitted, when FDR's Secretary of War Henry Stimson told him in 1945 that the U.S. was preparing to drop an atomic bomb on Japan, the General himself had "felt that there were a number of reasons to question the wisdom of such an act":

> I was not, of course, called upon, officially, for any advice or counsel concerning the matter, because the European theater, of which I was the commanding general, was not involved . . . But the Secretary, upon giving me the news of the successful bomb test in New Mexico, and of the plan for using it, asked for my reaction, apparently expecting a vigorous assent.
>
> During his recitation of the relevant facts, I had been conscious of a feeling of depression and so I voiced to him my grave misgivings, first on the basis of my belief that Japan was already defeated and that dropping the bomb was completely unnecessary, and secondly because I thought that our country should avoid shocking world opinion . . . The Secretary was deeply perturbed by my attitude, almost angrily refuting the reasons I gave for my quick conclusions.
>
> But in spite of his instant rejection of my opinion, it never

occurred to Secretary Stimson to question my loyalty to America
. . . In the same way I refused to accept any implication that Dr.
Oppenheimer was disloyal to America or was a security risk merely
because he had opposed the development of a weapon many
hundreds of times more terrifying than anything we had then
produced.

However, in this kind of situation it is deeds that count, not
words. The three-person review panel which heard the pro-
and-con testimony on Oppenheimer (it ran to 3300 pages of
typescript) concluded that the Father of the A-bomb "is a loyal
citizen"—but nevertheless found him a security risk! The vote
was 2–1; the single sharp-tongued dissenter, Ward Evans, who
kept asking witnesses whether they thought all scientists were
peculiar, was a professor of chemistry. On May 27, 1954, that
board's report was forwarded to the Atomic Energy Commission,
which concurred in its judgment that Robert Oppenheimer's
long and meritorious service to the U.S. government must come
to an end. The AEC's vote was 4–1; again the lone dissenter
was a scientist, Henry D. Smyth, whose heavily censored but
nonetheless chilling—and straightforwardly readable—mono-
graph titled *Atomic Energy for Military Purposes* had first (in 1945)
brought the facts of nuclear life to the attention of America
and the world.

With the exception of a few partisans on the pro-H-bomb
side, most notably the superbomb's prime creator Edward Teller,
American physicists (and other scientists) were outraged by the
decision. But their support for Oppenheimer, argues science
journalist Robert Jungk, "was only very rarely due to personal
sympathy"; many of them indeed had previously criticized the
accused scientist "for his excessive political pliability and timidity.
Now, to their own astonishment, they found themselves rushing
to his defense." If such a public disgrace could happen to an
Oppenheimer, they reasoned, it could happen to any of them:
Send not to know for whom the bell tolls . . . Nor were scientists the
only kind of citizens whose intellectual liberties were thus endangered. "From start to finish the Oppenheimer case did grave

damage to the principles the United States claims to cherish," John Major concluded his careful, temperate study *The Oppenheimer Hearing* (1971):

> Above all, perhaps, it indicated that the interests of the state could not be reconciled with the freedom of the individual. It may, of course, be that they are irreconcilable, even in a democracy professing full respect for individual rights. If so, then Oppenheimer's experience is an ominous pointer to the future for us all.

Dwight Eisenhower's acceptance of the review board's and the AEC's findings, foreshadowed in his order of December 3 (when the accusations began) that placed a "blank wall" between Oppenheimer and all classified government information, was the final blow. "It was to President Eisenhower that the anti-Oppenheimer camp had most cause to be grateful," John Major charges, a judgment in which I have to concur. Nor was there to be redress under Eisenhower's successors. Late in 1963 Oppenheimer received the Atomic Energy Commission's coveted Fermi Award from the hands of Lyndon Johnson, whom he told "that it has taken some charity and some courage for you to make this award today"; and Edward Teller, his one-time accuser and the previous year's Fermi Award winner, shook Oppenheimer's hand. That award was, however, as the *New York Herald Tribune* pointed out, "an honor, not an indemnity," for the physicist's security clearance was never restored. Such was the hideous mind-lock the nuclear arms race, with its mad logic of extremism, imposed on well-intentioned persons who— an Eisenhower in one fashion, an Oppenheimer in another— sought to follow some course of moderation.

IV

Long before the Bomb poured new flame on old fears, Western civilization had harbored feelings about science and its practitioners that were, to say the least, mixed. The scientist is Albert Einstein, the saintly, absent-minded savant who talks pure mathematics and plays the violin. But he is also Mickey Mouse the Sorcerer's Apprentice, ineptly casting the spell that brings on that horde of menacing brooms. In countless Hollywood-built laboratories he is the *mad* scientist, recklessly bringing destruction by defying the unknown; in other Hollywood-contrived situations he is the dauntless Man in White in an operating room who challenges disease and death. Archetypally he is Prometheus, who defies the gods to bring their guarded secrets' benefits to humankind; but he is also the impious Doctor Frankenstein, who disastrously learns "what man was not meant to know."

If anything, the fifties intensified this paradoxical, contradictory image. The applied scientist, to many in that era, seemed a rootless, emotionally inadequate person, prone to corruption by evil companions and willing for a pittance to sell secrets to the Russians; while the pure scientist seemed an impractical, incomprehensible bungler whose activities were of no benefit to anybody. ("Basic research," said Defense Secretary Charles Wilson, "is when you don't know what you are doing.") On the other hand, by the end of the fifties scientists, "identified not only as the makers of bombs and rockets but as the progenitors of jet planes, computers, and direct dial telephoning, of transistor radios, stereophonic phonographs, and color television," were climbing rapidly in public esteem. Americans in 1947 had ranked nuclear physicists fifteenth in occupational status; by the mid-sixties, before the new anti-science revolt that then was about to erupt, they would rank them third, ahead of everybody except doctors and Supreme Court justices. The community of scientists, wrote Don K. Price in *The Scientific Estate* (1965), had become "something very close to an *establishment,* in the old and proper sense of that word: a set of institutions supported by tax funds, but largely on faith, and without direct responsibility to political control"—and it was in the fifties, Price argued, that the structure of that scientific establishment took its essential form.

James Killian of MIT, whom Eisenhower in 1957 named Special Assistant to the President for Science and Technology, demurs. He and the other members of the President's Science Advisory Committee "did not consider themselves part of an 'establishment,'" Killian has written (in *Sputnik, Scientists, and Eisenhower,* 1977). "They were a 'creative elite' rather than a 'power elite'"—and significantly, "even though they were intellectuals, they achieved a remarkable impedance match with Eisenhower, the alleged nonintellectual." Establishment or not, in a rather freewheeling way such advisers brought scientific expertise closer in to the policy-making process. Only in the Republic's early years "when Jefferson was his own science adviser," and in World War II when Vannevar Bush was advising President Roosevelt, Killian sums up, had science been "so influential in top government councils as it became in Eisenhower's second term." And that influence, he believes, was healthy; in their factual fashion these government scientists countered some of the "wilder fantasies and scare talk" then being propagated by the aerospace industry and voiced in high government circles by romantic, star-struck Air Force officers.

Despite the Oppenheimer case, Killian believes, Ike's act of bringing scientists into his own immediate orbit did much to increase the confidence of the scientific community in the administration. The beneficiary of that increased confidence and heightened morale was John F. Kennedy. Science, we must not forget, was an important ingredient in the mystique of Camelot; but NASA, which put human beings on the moon, began life under Eisenhower. It is unfortunate that Lyndon Johnson, who mistrusted scientists as part of the academic community that was resisting his foreign policy, and Richard Nixon, who mistrusted everyone, packed and put away the useful scientific advisory machinery that had been created under Eisenhower and continued under Kennedy. Problems we became aware of in the seventies, and which still press upon us today, that involve scientific and technical judgment could have been faced—political biases permitting—with considerably more intelligence and imagination.

The creation of Killian's White House post was triggered by Sputnik, which (as noted in chapter 7) generated panic among many Americans. "Knowledge," said Emerson, "is the antidote to fear," and a large part of the fear set off by Sputnik stemmed directly from ignorance. It was not exactly that we had not *known* what the Russians were going to do; they had quite specifically, even stridently, announced their intentions. "But there was," Killian regretfully observes, "a curious indifference and lack of technological sensitivity among the American public and political leaders, and even within the scientific community, toward these clear indications of what was to happen."

People who really ought to have known better were as scared as anyone else. The U.S., Edward Teller declared on national television shortly after the first Soviet satellite went up, had lost "a battle more important and greater than Pearl Harbor." "No matter what we do now," gloomed John Rinehart of the Smithsonian Astrophysical Observatory, "the Russians will beat us to the moon." The appointment of a Presidential science adviser was in part a political gesture, to allay the panic and reassure the public that the government was on the job; taking input from science; getting ready to even the Sputnik score. But it meant a good deal more. Indeed in his first speech in his new official capacity, before the Women's National Press Club in January 1958, Killian argued that competition with Russia was not at all the main issue; "the purpose of the United States should be to surpass itself and not some other nation."

In the field of education, for example, "we should not engage in an academic numbers race with the Soviets," nor should we yield to the pressure to neglect other, nonscientific and nontechnical fields. As he later summarized that address:

> Among the efforts we *should* be making were to modernize and invigorate science education, to strive for a higher degree of scientific literacy among the rank and file of Americans, and to correct the erroneous view that science is only vocational, ma-

terialistic, and antihumanistic. Instead, I emphasized, science is
one of the most powerful and noble means for seeking truth, a
domain of excitement and adventure.

The need for scientific literacy, in that complacently "two-cul-
tured" era, was urgent. When Killian's committee two months
later prepared a popularly written "Introduction to Outer Space,"
which President Eisenhower sent out through the news media
with his blessing, they had to start with a simply worded explanation of "Why Satellites Stay Up"—hoping that the next
generation would not be so dense. The basic laws governing
satellites and space flights, known to scientists since Newton,
"may seem a little puzzling and unreal to many of us" adults
in the fifties; "our children, however, will understand them
quite well."

What was completely lost in the Sputnik uproar was the fact
that the Soviet radio satellite, quite apart from its alarming
missile-race implications, was part of the USSR's contribution
to that ambitious cooperative multinational effort to understand
our planet, better known as the IGY, or International Geophysical
Year. The U.S. scientific establishment—or creative elite, if you
prefer Killian's phrase—had its counterparts in all the other
industrial nations. Karl Marx's "workers of the world" had never,
despite all hopeful prophecies on their behalf, united; but the
scientists of the world on more than one occasion had done so,
and in 1957–58 they were doing so again. They were doing so,
moreover, with more self-direction and autonomy than the Cold
War was supposed to allow, and on an absolutely unprecedented
scale.

The IGY began quietly in a conversation one spring evening
in 1950 at a physicist's home in Silver Spring, Maryland. There
had been International Polar Years in 1882–83 and 1932–33;
a third in the fifties, could use the new rocket, electronic, and
computer technology developed in World War II. ("Every scientific discovery is a two-edged sword," comments Ronald Fraser,
"and you can't blame it on God if man insists on honing the

wrong edge.") From that simple beginning, channeled through the International Council of Scientific Unions in association with national science academies (e.g., the Royal Society) and supported by UNESCO, the International Geophysical Year grew until it involved some 60,000 scientists from 66 nations, working at thousands of stations literally from pole to pole. Timed to coincide with a maximum peak of the eleven-year sunspot cycle, because "the physics of our planet cannot be properly studied without reference to its sun," the IGY scientists fanned out across Canada, Greenland, Scandinavia, the northern portions of the USSR, remote equatorial islands, and the fastnesses of Antarctica, for "simultaneous observation of the winds aloft, of the earth's magnetic field, of the aurora borealis and australis, of the dance of the electrified particles in the upper atmosphere, of the impact of the cosmic rays on the earth's canopy of air, and of the face of the sun." Mainland China boycotted for ideological reasons (Taiwan, however, had an IGY Committee), but mainland Chinese scientists nevertheless gathered and contributed data from their part of the planet which furthered the goals of IGY.

Surely here, in the painstaking labors carried out during the International Geophysical Year, was an example of what the philosopher William James meant by a "moral equivalent of war." It was challenging; it was difficult; in some places, notably Antarctica, it was hazardous—and it had no human enemy except the darkness of ignorance. "Despite all of the tensions that we were able to create at a political level we did demonstrate during the IGY that it is possible to engage in rational and reasonable conduct at the scientific level," the distinguished Antarctic scientist and administrator Laurence M. Gould told a Senate committee in 1960. "It was in the coldest of all of the continents that there was the first memorable thaw in the cold war." Science, said George Kistiakowsky, Killian's successor as presidential science adviser, that same year, not only offered "cooperative attack on problems of interest to all"; it could also "contribute in a major way to the reduction of tension." Independent of ideologies and national boundaries, "science is today one of the few common languages of mankind."

V

The International Geophysical Year, by the time it got under way, had stretched to a year and a half. Even before its scant 1½ Earth orbits had come to an end, the scientists were asking themselves "Why stop now?" In Antarctica, especially, the 5000 explorers lodged on the Earth's coldest continent at the peak of IGY—shrinking to 912 during the dark, cruel polar winter— had barely scraped the frozen surface of what was there to be learned, not only about science but about humanly getting along. "The stark, perilous environment of Antarctica had a remarkable effect in submerging political differences," Walter Sullivan points out: "the expeditions there were bound together by the presence of a common enemy—the everlasting cold." The participating nations, even those which elsewhere on the planet were hopelessly secrecy-bound, had freely exchanged meteorological data through Weather Central at Little America; and scientists, including a Russian at Little America and an American at Mirny, the chief Soviet Antarctic station, had wintered over at each others' bases. (Even today, spending such a winter is the ultimate test; the next plane won't be in for six months, and in the meantime if you get mad and stomp out of the room you must do your sulking at seventy below.) Surely this international cooperative effort was worth cherishing and extending; and it was done.

During the first week in February 1958, at the Hague, a Scientific Committee on Antarctic Research came into being. All countries "actively engaged" in Antarctic research—that is, countries some of whose nationals had endured the rigor of the polar night—were eligible. SCAR wrote itself a constitution, elected officers, and assessed a budget from its members; thus post-IGY scientific work in Antarctica was assured. Three months

later, in an act of creative statecraft that is still far too little
known, the Antarctic powers—with the U.S. taking the lead—
tackled the overlapping nationalist claims on the Southern continent that might legally jeopardize the scientific concerns they
had in common. On May 2, 1958, the United States formally
invited the other ten nations that had done Antarctic work
during IGY, including the Soviet Union, to meet in Washington
to negotiate a formal treaty to govern their work at the bottom
of the world. The negotiations were a brilliant success, and on
December 1, 1959, in Washington, the member nations signed
the Antarctic Treaty into reality.

The seven of those nations that had previously staked formal
territorial claims, mostly in the form of pie-shaped wedges con-
verging on the South Pole, agreed for thirty years to put all
further territorial assertions on "hold." Ducking the potentially
very difficult question of the commercial future of Antarctica,
the diplomats agreed that for the next three decades the whole
vast territory (as large, in acreage, as the United States plus
France) would be in essence a scientists' preserve. Accordingly
they wrote in tough provisions to safeguard the Antarctic ocean
margin's fragile ecosystem. The free right to inspect each other's
stations and facilities, so impossible to agree upon in negotiations
anywhere else on Earth, was accepted in Antarctica by all, including the U.S. and the USSR. Military forces in the far South
would function as they had during IGY, as logistical support
only; there would be no polar-climate training exercises,
launching of missiles, or detonation of nuclear bombs.

The last point brought these Antarctic negotiations jarringly
back into the geopolitics of the Cold War. Bomb testing had
been a sore point throughout the post-Hiroshima age; in a sense
it was *the* central issue of the fifties. Locked into their posture
of mutual deterrence the superpowers found themselves unable
to budge, although horrifying evidence now showed that even
to *test* such weapons inevitably and irreversibly contaminated
the whole Earth. The luckless voyage of the *Lucky Dragon,* a
Japanese fishing boat that was overtaken on March 1, 1954 by

a radioactive-fallout "snowstorm" from a U.S. hydrogen bomb, was only the most publicized of these true horror stories. Well-authenticated news reports continue to appear to this day, detailing the disease and death that were spread downwind from the AEC's Nevada testing ground in the fifties. "Up near the Utah border, where the sky is blue and the living is clean," according to one such account published in 1981, "a little Mormon graveyard may be home for victims of a dirtier day when radioactive fallout wafted into Arizona with the winds," and cattle and people began to die. The scourge reached as far as the cleanest, most remote environment of all; scientists in Antarctica, taking core samples from its pristine frozen crust, have found radioactive fallout in the snow.

Weapons testing could be monitored retroactively, by anyone who cared to; even the bombs the U.S. detonated in outer space in August and September of 1958 in its "Argus" and "Jason" series were promptly recorded—and, embarrassingly, announced—by Soviet scientists. The problem was how to work out a mutually acceptable way of finding out beforehand what the other fellow was going to do. Eisenhower, going at this problem in somewhat the same fashion that had yielded the "Atoms for Peace" program—namely by presenting a dramatic, promising, easily grasped idea—laid before the Russians at a four-power summit conference in Geneva in 1955 what became known as the "open skies" proposal: that the two superpowers each throw open its territories to regular and frequent aerial inspection by the other. "I do not know how I could convince you of our sincerity in this matter and that we mean you no harm," Ike told Chairman Khrushchev and Premier Bulganin. "I only wish that God would give me some means of convincing you of our sincerity and loyalty in making this proposal." "As if on cue," comments diplomatic historian Robert A. Divine, "a late afternoon thunderstorm broke with a flash of lightning and the lights suddenly went out in the conference room plunging the gathering into a few seconds of total darkness."

The Soviets did not so much refuse the "open skies" proposal as let it die of neglect. After a moment of high, hopeful drama, a disappointing anticlimax; that had been the rhythm of affairs throughout the Cold War. But the alternative to negotiation, in this case, was espionage. Eisenhower, very likely aware that a technology was in the making which by the end of the seventies would render all skies open whether the governments under those skies liked it or not, in mid-1956 quietly ordered high-altitude intelligence-gathering flights over the Soviet Union— and so, late in the spring of 1960, he got caught in the shabby lie of the U–2.

The Antarctic Treaty, signed not long after Nikita Khrushchev's stormy, colorful visit to the U.S. in 1959 (the first ever by any Russian ruler) and sent to the Senate in February 1960, while plans were in the making for Eisenhower to return that visit, came up for its Senate Foreign Relations Committee hearing on June 14, near the height of the U–2 uproar. The Treaty could hardly have come before the Committee at a less propitious time; after Eisenhower on May 9 had acknowledged responsibility for the U–2 overflight Khrushchev had angrily withdrawn his invitation for Ike to tour the USSR. The first witness to testify on the Antarctic Treaty, Clair Engle (a moderate Democrat from California), therefore opposed ratification, citing the "current Soviet tantrums of bellicosity and bad names."

The mere fact that in this instance the tantrums were somewhat justified—the U.S. President had, after all, approved spying on another sovereign nation and then refused to apologize—completely escaped the Senator. (Eisenhower's stand, Khrushchev would later argue in his memoirs, really left the Soviet leaders no choice; "He had, so to speak, offered us his back end, and we obliged him by kicking it as hard as we could.") In more specific Cold War terms Engle objected to the Antarctic Treaty's ban on nuclear explosions; the empty Southern continent, he thought, would make an ideal locale to test the Bomb. Besides, by comparison with the other Antarctic powers the Russians really had no business being there: "I would feel a lot better about this Treaty if we hadn't invited the Soviets up to the pie counter . . . They haven't done anything in that area" of the world, the California Senator incredibly asserted, dismissing all the splendid achievements of Russian glaciologists and geophysicists in Antarctica, and their heroism in building and maintaining a base at the Pole of Inaccessibility where winter temperatures hover near the freezing point of carbon dioxide.

Even more surprising was the opposition of Senator Ernest Gruening, of the new state of Alaska, who had long been concerned in Antarctic affairs and who during the Vietnam War would become an able and eloquent apostle of détente. The hearing drew other unfriendly witnesses; from the House of Representatives came John Pillion of New York, who recommended extending the Truman Doctrine of Communist containment to Antarctica and treating any Soviet occupancy beyond the IGY "as a trespass and an unlawful intrusion." But the Treaty also had its friends. "One of the most constructive documents I have had brought before me, I think in my years in the Senate," said committee member Wayne Morse, while Hubert Humphrey noted the parallels between explorations around the perimeter of Antarctica in the late 1700s and explorations at the perimeter of outer space in the late 1900s. State Department witness Herman Phleger picked up Humphrey's cue; to Senator Engle's proposal that the U.S. assert a claim of sovereignty over all Antarctica, Phleger replied: "Apply that principle to the Moon. Somebody gets up there with eight or nine people, and he is the first fellow and lands on it. We are not going to admit that the nation he represents owns the moon." *That* was the level of magnitude the Antarctic venture represented, and it was high time the American political mind grew up into it.

To the isolationists' and narrow nationalists' especial discomfiture the Department of Defense endorsed the Antarctic Treaty, through its impressive representative, Rear Admiral David Tyree, the Department's Antarctic project officer. "The common struggle for survival has tended to erase national boundaries and diminish ideological differences," Tyree testified, and the document before the Senators was "a treaty formalizing the elements of this spirit." Approved by the Foreign Relations Committee, and ratified with little difficulty by the full Senate, the Antarctic Treaty came into force in 1961. "Unique and historic," Eisenhower called it, with its provision "that a large area of the world . . . will be used for peaceful purposes only." For at least twenty years, until the British–Argentine clash over the Falkland Islands—which had long been the administrative center for British Antarctica—the Treaty regime over the great white South stood as the Eisenhower regime's most brilliant (and least known) diplomatic success.

VI

Once again it was both an Olympic year and an American election year. Again the two perennial Greek ideals of physical excellence and popular democracy, however distorted by counter-values deriving from a mass commercial culture, signaled the turn of a new cycle of years. International Olympic Chairman Avery Brundage proposed that the Olympics, in the interest of the individual amateur competitor, stop using national flags and hymns. The presidential candidates, for the first time in over a century, vied for public approval by engaging in face-to-face debate. Vice-President Nixon opened the Winter Games, at Squaw Valley; Pope John XXIII blessed the Summer Games, in Rome. The Euro-American monopoly over the games eroded, as an Ethiopian won the climactic Marathon. The U.S. won the Winter games; the USSR won the Summer Games. Richard Nixon lost the election, and the era of Eisenhower came to a close.

Early in that year the editor of the *Bulletin of Atomic Scientists* engaged in a little symbolism of his own. The *Bulletin's* cover since 1946 had shown, ominously and appropriately, the hands of a clock closing in on midnight. With the January 1960 number, and for each issue in 1960 thereafter, the clock of doom was set back. "In doing so," editor Eugene Rabinowitch wrote,

We are not succumbing to a facile optimism engendered by a
change in the climate of our diplomatic relations with the Soviet
Union, or to the exhilaration engendered by the personal contacts
of the leaders of the great powers and their visits to different
countries of the world. We want to express in this move our
belief that a new cohesive force has entered the interplay of forces
shaping the fate of mankind, and is making the future . . . a little
less foreboding.

As the events of 1960 unfolded, however, a sterner prophetic
vision might have discerned in them a future heavy with foreboding. For example, 1960 saw the birth of the National Front
for the Liberation of South Vietnam, soon to become known
to a new generation of young Americans as the formidable Viet
Cong; the precarious peace that had descended on Asia in the
mid-fifties was about to end. Closer to home, the new government
that had just come to revolutionary power in Cuba—a revolution
the U.S. media had followed throughout 1959 with a mixture
of alarm and romantic admiration—had abolished at a stroke
the common front the Pan-American states had formerly presented toward the rest of the world. Moreover, the new Communist regime in Cuba was a conspicuous improvement over
almost all the other governments that fair island had had to
endure since its liberation from Spain. Some Americans at the
time believed the same would also be true of the Communist
insurgency in South Vietnam. Such thoughts were devastating
to any clean-cut U.S. conception of a "free world."

Domestically, 1960 was the centennial of the Civil War, and
a freshly awakened black America was demanding—with understandable impatience—that the U.S. get on with the century-
old unfinished business left over from that war. The Eisenhower
administration's choice for Chief Justice of the United States,
Earl Warren, had made a creditable start, with his sweeping
school desegregation decision in *Brown* v. *Board of Education*
(347 U.S. 483, 1954), but since then the government had proceeded hesitantly, even half-heartedly, and this was the kind of
historical situation in which half-measures may be worse than
none. In addition to common justice, national self-interest was

at stake; the American political society was in effect on trial before the nonwhite majority of the planet's ever-expanding population.

All such questions led back to the central issue of the fifties, and of all the years since members of Earth's now-dominant species first split—and used—the atom. Dwight Eisenhower, near the end of the time of French hegemony in Vietnam, had already shunted aside one proposal to use the Bomb in that part of the world. The grim temptation would remain, throughout all the frustrating years of the Vietnam War. Similarly, the appearance of a Soviet ally barely hull-down from Miami gave the USSR an alarming impulse to rattle its own Bomb-tipped rockets; and from the failure of the effort Eisenhower's government quietly set in motion to overthrow the Castro regime it was a short step to direct superpower nuclear confrontation, in the Cuban missile crisis of 1962. Finally, the doctrine of nonviolent resistance which Dr. King had learned in India and heroically applied in the American civil rights movement had obvious implications for international affairs as well. In a time "when sputniks dash through outer space and guided ballistic missiles are carving highways of death through the stratosphere," King wrote in the spring of 1960, the Rightist slogan *better dead than Red* had become simply a prescription for suicide: "The choice today is no longer between violence and nonviolence. It is either nonviolence or non-existence."

In the circumstances of 1960 was it legitimate to continue to contend, in the language of the editor of the *Bulletin of the Atomic Scientists,* that "a new cohesive force . . . is making the future of man a little less foreboding"? Yes, editor Rabinowitch insisted. Carefully scanning recent statements before the United Nations by Khrushchev, Eisenhower, and British Prime Minister Harold Macmillan, he found "positive symptoms suggesting a progressive realization on both sides that we are 'in it together,' and that all-out aggressive pursuit of the interests of one side would bear risks too great to allow the abandonment of the alternative possibility of constructive cooperation."

Here again the deeds of international statesmen spoke more loudly than their words. After one last orgy of nuclear detonations in the fall of 1958—nineteen by the AEC, fourteen by the Russians—atmospheric testing of the Bomb had, in fact, ceased. For two blessedly relieved years, no more radioactive Strontium-90 had come sifting down from the skies to be incorporated along with calcium (which it chemically resembles) into babies' milk, and thence into teeth and bones. Neither the U.S. nor the USSR would yet commit itself to making the cessation permanent and formal, but perhaps this was a case of the old Army principle (shrewdly noted by James Gould Cozzens in his 1949 war novel *Guard of Honor*) that "you can do certain things if you just don't say anything about them"; and conversely "you can say certain things if you just don't do anything about them." Keeping their ideologies—their sayings—intact, the nuclear superpowers had tacitly agreed that they would not do certain things.

They would resume doing such things early in the sixties, but that would be a problem to be faced—and solved, in the 1963 Nuclear Test Ban Treaty—by the new generation, "born in war, schooled in a bitter peace," on whose behalf John Kennedy would speak in his inaugural address. Sufficient unto the day are the crises thereof. Meanwhile, for the moment—and for the first time—the Bomb was under some modest degree of world control. One humorist in the fifties defined an optimist as "a guy who still thinks the future is uncertain," and it was on that note of optimistic uncertainty that the age of Eisenhower came to a close.

Bibliographical Essay

1. 1952: Election and Olympiad

Avery Brundage's testament to the Olympic ideal appears in his definitive article on the Games in the *Encyclopaedia Britannica* (1957), 16:781–82. *New York Times* coverage of the 1952 Olympics was adequate, but at times preachy: see for example Harrison Salisbury, "Russia Exalts Over U.S. Defeat in Soccer Trial as Happy Omen," *New York Times,* July 18, 1952, p. 13. The account of the solo peace demonstrator at the opening ceremonies in Helsinki is in *ibid.,* July 20, 1952, 5:1. Another significant Olympic story appeared in *Life,* July 28, 1952. Useful for context on the Olympics are Allen Guttman, *From Ritual to Record: The Nature of Modern Sport* (New York: Columbia University Press, 1979) and Richard R. Mandell, *The Nazi Olympics* (New York: Macmillan, 1971).

William Allen White, *Autobiography* (New York: Macmillan, 1946), chaps. 6, 7, gave a participant's vivid account of the Republican National Convention of 1912, with which I have contrasted that of 1952. My own notes made from radio coverage of the 1952 Democratic and Republican conventions have been checked where possible against *New York Times* accounts for accuracy. The pre-primaries maneuvering which led to Eisenhower's formal decision to run is discussed, rather unsympathetically, in Marquis Childs, *Eisenhower: Captive Hero* (New York: Harcourt, Brace, 1958).

The recent scholarly upgrading of Eisenhower's political reputation has been paralleled by a downgrading of Stevenson's. But a thoughtful review reminds us that the historiographer's greatest temptation is overkill; with Adlai Stevenson, as with Dwight Eisenhower, we must not revise a historical judgment so far as to commit new distortions. "Stevenson meant something" for the 1950s, Barry Karl concludes, and he contributed "as much of the leadership we demanded of him as he could bear." Karl, "Deconstructing Stevenson, or Badly for Adlai," *Reviews in American History,* 5 (September 1977).

Perhaps the earliest of these "revisionist" discussions of Stevenson and his supporters appeared in an essay by David Riesman, "Some Observations on Intellectual Freedom," *American Scholar,* 23 (Winter 1953-54) esp. pp. 15-16. More typical of intellectuals' appraisals at that time, however, is Gerald W. Johnson's judgment that Stevenson, who "comprehends and perhaps shares the spirit of George Washington," would "have to be reckoned with by both parties as long as he retains his health and strength." Johnson, "Something Old Has Been Added: Adlai Stevenson of Illinois," *ibid.,* 22 (Winter 1952-53). Johnson's central point, that one of Stevenson's most attractive features was his genuine reluctance to be a presidential candidate, is vigorously disputed by another Stevenson-watcher, Alistair Cooke: "The truth is that Adlai Stevenson was a man in whom ambition never ceased to palpitate." Cooke, *Six Men* (New York: Knopf, 1977), p. 140. An appreciation of the talents and caliber of Stevenson's leading opponent in the presidential primaries, Estes Kefauver, is in a letter from Raymond Chandler to James Sandoe, March 6, 1951, in Frank MacShane, ed., *Selected Letters of Raymond Chandler* (New York: Columbia University Press, 1981), pp. 266-67.

Stevenson's public statements may be found in *Major Campaign Speeches of Adlai E. Stevenson* (New York: Random House, 1953); see especially "First Fireside Speech" (radio and TV studio, Chicago, September 29), and "Safeguards Against Communism" (Masonic Temple, Detroit, October 7). Eisenhower's comment on having spent his life with America's young people occurs in a speech delivered on June 10, 1953 at Minneapolis, text in *Christian Science Monitor,* June 11, 1953. Some of President Truman's anti-Eisenhower remarks were reported in the *Great Falls* (Montana) *Tribune,* October 1, 1952, pp. 1, 13. It should be noted that Truman leavened his Cold War militancy with some New Deal ploys. In dedicating the towering new Hungry Horse Dam, a few campaign-train stops further on, he praised Congressman Mike Mansfield for fighting to keep the dam appropriation alive against the efforts of Republican budget-cutters.

Chet Huntley's epigram about liberals and conservatives was recalled in a letter by Reuven Frank of NBC News, *Commentary,* December, 1976. The essay by Raymond English on "Conservatism: The Forbidden Faith"—which makes curious reading today—appeared in *American Scholar,* 21 (Autumn 1952). Irwin Edman's comments on the term "egghead" were in his regular column "Under Whatever Sky"; *ibid.,*

22 (Spring 1953). A hopeful interpretation of the election as a sign of growing radicalism among the American masses is Hal Draper's essay "Why Eisenhower Won," *Labor Action,* Nov. 17, 1952. My account of the Columbia faculty's involvement in the Stevenson-Eisenhower contest is essentially taken from firsthand sources, but the formal statements and the participants' names may be checked in the *New York Times.*

2. Domestic Politics: Regular and Irregular

Helpful though they are, *The Eisenhower Diaries,* ed. by Robert H. Ferrell (New York: W. W. Norton, 1981) have disappointing gaps for the presidential years. They must be supplemented by Robert J. Donovan, *Eisenhower: The Inside Story* (New York: Harper, 1956), an informative book based on minutes of Cabinet meetings during the first term. A much more critical contemporary account is Marquis Childs, *Eisenhower: Captive Hero* (cited above); see also the thoughtful testament of a sometime White House insider, Emmet John Hughes, *The Ordeal of Power* (New York: Atheneum, 1963). The President's own memoir, *Mandate For Change, 1953–1956* (Garden City: Doubleday, 1963), is indispensable.

Eventually the contemporary observer has to yield the floor to the historian. The fullest narrative and analytical study of the administration to date is Herbert S. Parmet, *Eisenhower and the American Crusades* (New York: Macmillan, 1972). Since its publication a substantial revisionist, i.e., pro-Ike, literature on Eisenhower has appeared. Much of it is ably described—and, at certain points, criticized—in an article by Stephen Ambrose, "The Ike Age," *New Republic,* May 9, 1981. Ambrose wrote with the then-new Reagan administration in mind, and a similar comparison between Ike and Ronald Reagan was the springboard for a *Time* Essay, "Dreaming of the Eisenhower Years," by Lance Morrow— who, however, cautioned against "a nostalgic distortion, an unconsciously artful forgetfulness about what the Eisenhower years were really like" (*Time,* July 28, 1980, p. 33). An important interpretive synthesis by Robert Griffith, "Dwight D. Eisenhower and the Corporate Commonwealth," appeared in the *American Historical Review,* 87 (February 1982).

Some of the best contemporaneous Ike-watching was done in the pages of *The Reporter,* an independent-minded, highly intelligent magazine whose subsequent disappearance can only be regretted. See for example Joseph C. Harsch, "Eisenhower's First Hundred Days," *Reporter,*

May 12, 1953; William Lee Miller, "Can Government be 'Merchandised'?", October 27, 1953 (also reprinted in Max Ascoli, ed., *The Reporter Reader* (Garden City: Doubleday, 1956); Richard H. Rovere, "Eisenhower: A Trial Balance," April 21, 1955; and—a sample of the journal's astute attention to government activity elsewhere than in the White House and Congress—M. J. Rossant, "The Growing Power of William McChesney Martin," October 17, 1957. The *Reporter* for March 10, 1955 also carried an acute, whimsical yet serious piece on McCarthyism by John Steinbeck, "How To Tell Good Guys from Bad Guys."

The liveliest, and still probably the best, study of the Great Investigator is Richard H. Rovere, *Senator Joe McCarthy* (New York: Harcourt, Brace, 1959). Its judgments, however, are corrected at two crucial points in an essay by Les K. Adler and Richard M. Fried, "McCarthy: the Advent and the Decline," *Continuum*, 6 (Autumn 1968), 404–13. The text of Senator Margaret Chase Smith's "Declaration of Conscience," and a discussion of her pioneering attack on McCarthyism, may be found in Frank Graham, Jr., *Margaret Chase Smith: Woman of Courage* (New York: John Day, 1964). A powerful anti-McCarthy testament by Elmer Davis, whose "first and great commandment was 'don't let them scare you,' " is "Through the Perilous Night," Chapter One in his still very readable book *But We Were Born Free* (Indianapolis: Bobbs-Merrill, 1954).

The *New York Times* regularly carried the full text of President Eisenhower's presidential press conferences—at first in an irritating third person "he said" format—and major speeches. Sometimes one has to follow Ike out into the boondocks through other newspapers; an illuminating example is Max K. Gilstrap, "Eisenhower Dedicates Garrison Dam—And Accents Local Control," *Christian Science Monitor*, June 11, 1953. The *Wall Street Journal*, as always, allowing for its honestly acknowledged biases, reported economic news with wit and insight; see in particular its wickedly funny lead story on the 1958 anti-recession campaign, " 'Buy and Be Happy': Operation Optimism Is Launched To Open the Consumer's Pocketbook," April 14, 1958, p. 1, and accompanying editorial in *ibid.*, p. 10. The *Journal*'s story on the recession's end (October 10, 1958, p. 2) and its 1958 election post-mortems (November 6, p. 12; November 26, p. 16) are also worth consulting.

Another stinging comment on the 1958 recession, "The Price of Inaction," appeared in *The Progressive*, June 1958. A satiric fictional parable on consumer economics—reminding us that the fifties, contrary to our usual image of the decade, had not entirely lost a sense of humor—is Frederik Pohl, "The Midas Plague"; it may be found in Pohl's aptly titled *The Case Against Tomorrow* (New York: Ballantine, 1956). Equally irreverent is White House correspondent William Costello's *The Facts About Nixon: An Unauthorized Biography* (New York: Viking, 1960). For a while during the sixties, when its subject wore an air of sober responsibility, the harshness of Costello's book seemed excessive, but the revelations that began with Watergate now make Costello seem, if anything, understated. And he *did* have the facts about Nixon.

3. United States: United Nations

United Nations Security Council sessions were recorded verbatim (in English and French), as were the plenary sessions of the General Assembly (in English); everything cited in the text from Security Council and General Assembly plenary sessions may therefore be found in the Official Records of those bodies, at the appropriate year and day. UN committee debates, however, were paraphrased rather than directly transcribed, often losing much of their immediacy in the process, and I have therefore supplemented the formal record with my personal observations at the Ninth General Assembly as a spectator. See in particular *General Committee: Summary Records of Meetings, 21 September–17 December 1954,* especially its 96th meeting, Tuesday, 9 October 1954, and *Fourth Committee* [Trusteeship], *Summary Record of Meetings, 22 September to 13 December 1954,* especially its 419th meeting, 2 November 1954.

The Eisenhower address in Minneapolis which gave chapter 3 its title was printed in full in the *Christian Science Monitor,* June 11, 1953; it is cited also in previous chapters. The judgment that Eisenhower, not his speechwriters, controlled what went into such addresses comes from a memoir by Arthur Larson, who helped write some of them, *Eisenhower: The President Nobody Knew* (New York: Scribner's, 1968). The *New York Times,* as always, was indispensable for the record of events, especially for the crucial Eisenhower press conference at the height of the Formosa crisis (February 10, 1955, p. 2). Since the *Times* is a morning paper, its news stories of course appear one day later than the date cited in my text. Other useful general media coverage included Marguerite Higgins's account of Chiang Kai-shek's irregulars, "Formosa Guerrillas Beat Crack Red Unit," *Washington Post,* July 18, 1953, and two White House statements on the Suez situation that appeared in *Time,* November 12, 1956. With Chinese proper nouns

I have followed the Romanizations *then* in current use, not those adopted since U.S. recognition of the People's Republic; the reader will find no reference to, e.g., "Mao Zedong."

Dwight D. Eisenhower's *Waging Peace, 1956-1961* (New York: Doubleday, 1965), takes up where *Mandate For Change* left off. All personal memoirs inevitably argue a case from the standpoint of the memoirist. Eisenhower's are valuable nonetheless, because in the midst of pages and pages of long-winded discourse he will artlessly drop in a statement that is devastatingly direct. He also conveniently included copies of important correspondence, most particularly with Eden and Churchill. Robert Donovan's *Eisenhower: The Inside Story*, previously cited, is also helpful, as is Herbert Parmet's *Eisenhower and the American Crusades*. On particular foreign policy episodes Parmet should be read in conjunction with Townsend Hoopes, *The Devil and John Foster Dulles* (Boston: Little, Brown, 1973); but Hoopes sometimes makes a subtle and complex man sound as moralistically simple as some of Dulles's own speeches, which he was not.

William Appleman Williams's discussion of Eisenhower's foreign policy is part of a much broader thesis on American public life, namely that "The Presidency is . . . in crisis because the system is in crisis"; Williams, *Some Presidents From Wilson to Nixon* (New York: Random House, 1972), p. 18. See also the Machiavellian interpretation by Murray Kempton, "The Underestimation of Dwight David Eisenhower," *Esquire*, September, 1967.

The Mike Mansfield Papers at the University of Montana in Missoula were a rich source on Suez (Series XIII, Foreign Relations, Container #1) and on Formosa (Container #5). I am indebted to Dale Johnson, university archivist, for securing for me the necessary permission to use these papers. The *Reporter* throughout the fifties ably monitored the China situation; see for example Harlan Cleveland, "Troubled Waters: The Formosa Strait," January 13, 1955; Thomas R. Phillips, "The Military Worth of Quemoy," October 2, 1958; Max Ascoli, "For a Formosa Settlement" (incorporating previous Ascoli editorials that dated back to 1950), October 16, 1958; and William H. Hessler, "Time Passes on Taiwan," May 11, 1961. The *Reporter*'s stand on Suez, "The Price of Peacemongering," November 29, 1956, generated a spirited response, mostly adverse, from its readers, December 27, 1956; see also Hans J. Morgenthau, "The Decline and Fall of American Foreign Policy," *New Republic*, December 10, 1956, and an editorial in the *Nation*, December 22, 1956, "International Morality and the UN." Offbeat, but highly relevant as a parable of the growing oil crisis, is Fritz Leiber's short story, "The Black Gondolier," in August Derleth, ed., *Over the Edge* (Arkham House, 1964). My comment on the Western films of the fifties as a metaphor for Americans' self-image of their foreign relations derives from an essay on "The Olympian Cowboy," *American Scholar*, 24 (Summer 1955), by the Swedish film critic Harry Schein, who terms the Western movie *High Noon* "artistically the most convincing and . . . certainly the most honest explanation of American foreign policy." Indeed, Schein continued, the gunmen-heroes of U.S. Westerns were "now grappling with moral problems and an ethical melancholy which could be called existentialist if they were not shared by Mr. Dulles."

4. Conformity and Nonconformism

Adlai Stevenson's Godkin Lectures at Harvard were published as *A Call to Greatness* (New York: Harper, 1954). His commencement address at Smith College in 1955 was excerpted in *Saturday Review*, March 10, 1956. A symposium on Simone de Beauvoir, *The Second Sex* (New York: Knopf, 1953) by Phyllis McGinley, Margaret Mead, Ashley Montagu, Karl Menninger, Philip Wylie, and others appeared in *ibid.*, February 21, 1953. Kay Summersby's account of her wartime romance with Dwight Eisenhower, *Past Forgetting* (New York: Simon & Schuster, 1976) is important both for the light it throws on Eisenhower and for its accurate recapture of a consciousness that may be termed "pre-Simone"; don't be put off by its 1950s women's magazine style and tone.

An essay by Lovell Thompson contrasting the young generation of the fifties with that of the twenties, "The Spirit of Our Times," appeared in *Harper's*, September 1957; see also Robert Langbaum, "This Literary Generation," *American Scholar*, 25 (Winter 1955–56), esp. p. 90. An effective blast against the view of women expounded by Stevenson and Thompson is Margaret Mead, "Return of the Cave Woman," *Saturday Evening Post*, March 3, 1962. Another of Mead's cautionary essays is "Marrying in Haste in College," *Columbia University Forum*, 3 (Spring 1960).

David Riesman's analysis of the college class of 1955 appears in his essay "The Found Generation," *American Scholar*, 25 (Autumn 1956). Riesman wrote that essay from the standpoint previously expressed in the book he had written with Nathan Glazer and Reuel Denney, *The Lonely Crowd* (New Haven: Yale, 1950). This highly influential work appeared in paperback abridgement in 1961 with a new preface by Riesman, whose comments on the reception of the book during the fifties, and his own second thoughts about it in response to critics, are illuminating. Another afterthought on *The Lonely Crowd* and on "The Found Generation" is Riesman's essay "Abundance for What?", *Bulletin of the Atomic Scientists,* April 1958. In a footnote to "The Found Generation" Riesman acknowledged a debt to William H. Whyte, Jr., whose book *The Organization Man* was then on the verge of publication (New York: Simon & Schuster, 1956). Another important comment on Whyte's subject is Thomas C. Cochran, "The Organization Man in Historical Perspective," *Pennsylvania History,* 25 (January 1958); from that article comes the brief quotation from the president of Woolworth's.

Eric Hoffer published two trenchant books in the fifties: *The True Believer* (New York: Harper, 1951, and Mentor paperback, 1958), and *The Passionate State of Mind* (Harper, 1955). A perceptive contemporary appraisal of Hoffer, with biographical data, is Eugene Burdick, "Eric Hoffer: Epigrammist on the Waterfront," *Reporter,* February 21, 1957. Jack Mueller, a former student at the University of Montana, kindly sent me his handwritten transcript of an interview that San Francisco's educational-TV station KQED conducted with Hoffer (letter from Mueller, September 3, 1962). Articles and letters in the *Daily Californian,* indicating sympathetic student reaction (April 14, 16, 17; May 1, 7, 1964), followed an appearance by Hoffer on the Berkeley campus on April 6, 1964, for a lecture which he facetiously titled "Becoming a True Believer in My Old Age." My own notes taken at the lecture are the source for the student's question and Hoffer's answer as they appear in the text. More recent comment on "the world's most famous longshoreman" include Al Kuettner, "Eric Hoffer," *Chicago Tribune Sunday Magazine,* January 28, 1968, and Calvin Tomkins, *Eric Hoffer: An American Odyssey* (New York: Dutton, 1968), the preface for which was contributed by Eric Sevareid.

The conversation between two participants in the Montgomery bus boycott was reported in *Time,* January 16, 1956. Dr. King's comment on the larger implications of Montgomery occurs in Martin Luther King, Jr., "Pilgrimage to Nonviolence," *Christian Century,* April 13, 1960. Portions of Paul Goodman's important polemic *Growing Up Absurd* (New York: Random House, 1960) appeared in *Commentary,* February, March, April, 1960, and in *Dissent* (Spring 1960); the emergence of the latter journal was evidence that by the end of the fifties the Left in America was recovering consciousness. Alfred Kazin's review of *Growing Up Absurd* in *The Reporter,* December 22, 1960, at some points assesses American culture even more harshly than Goodman does: "He quite airily overlooks the hideous satisfactions that very many people now find in made-up jobs."

Adlai Stevenson's A Powell Davies Memorial Lecture in Washington, D.C., "America's Broken Mainspring," was reprinted in *The Progressive,* March 1959. A similarly critical article by James A. Wechsler, "Is Everybody Happy?", was published in *ibid.,* April, 1960. A symposium on John Steinbeck's *Long Island Newsday* letter to Stevenson, "Have We Gone Soft?", appeared in *The New Republic,* February 15, 1960. A reprise by Steinbeck, "Are We Morally Flabby?", was picked up in a campus student newspaper, the *Montana Kaimin,* for March 9, 1960; evidence, as Steinbeck observed, that the young were worried also— probably with more reason, "since they are going to inherit this frightening Pandora's box we're handing to them." A way out of that box— simply vote Democratic!—was implicit in an essay (and frequently delivered lecture) by Arthur M. Schlesinger, Jr., "Sources of the New Deal: Reflections on the Temper of a Time," *Columbia University Forum* (Fall 1959).

5. God and Country

The *Washington Post* for February 8, 1954, p. 12, under the title "Put God in Flag Pledge, Pastor Urges," reported the sermon by George M. Docherty which triggered the Congressional action amending the pledge of allegiance to include "Under God." The adjoining column on that same page carried a typical excerpt from a presidential address on a similar theme: "Eisenhower Cites Nation's Need of Faith." Gerard Kaye and Ferenc M. Szasz take the story from there, in a useful, well-founded essay, "Adding 'Under God' to the Pledge of Allegiance," *Encounter,* 34 (Winter 1973). A brief sketch on Docherty and his church's Washington parish appeared in *Time,* January 7, 1952, p. 59.

A lively seminar taught by Noel Dowling of Columbia University's Law School and that stimulating and unconventional cleric James A. Pike, in the spring of 1952, when several of the church-state cases discussed were decided, was the starting point for much of my subsequent thinking about First Amendment constitutional questions. The cases themselves are conveniently compiled in Joseph Tussman, ed., *The Supreme Court on Church and State* (New York: Oxford, 1962), and Mark de Wolfe Howe has thoughtfully discussed several of them in *The Garden and the Wilderness: Religion and Government in American Constitutional History* (University of Chicago Press, 1965). Issues far broader than religious freedom *per se* were involved, Professor Howe

suggests: "A school's segregation of pupils into two categories—one
. . . made up, apparently, of believers, and the other . . . made up of
apparent non-believers—encourages, at least indirectly, the denigration
of the latter"—an argument strikingly similar to that used two years
later to strike down the schools' segregation of pupils by race.

The Eisenhower quotation that ends—"and I don't care what it is,"
picked up from the *New York Times,* December 23, 1952, is discussed
in Will Herberg, *Protestant-Catholic-Jew* (Garden City, N.Y.: Doubleday,
1955), a book that was provocative, and at the time of its publication
widely influential, but is now in important respects outdated. William
Lee Miller wrote three essays on American religion in the fifties which,
similarly, now carry less impact than they seemed to at the time:
"Religion, Politics, and the 'Great Crusade,'" *Reporter,* July 7, 1953;
"The Irony of Reinhold Niebuhr," *ibid.,* January 13, 1955; "Some
Negative Thinking About Normal Vincent Peale," *ibid.,* and also pub-
lished in Max Ascoli, ed., *The Reporter Reader,* previously cited. See
also Sidney E. Mead, *The Nation with the Soul of a Church* (New York:
Harper & Row, 1975), and my essay "The Pastoral Office of the
President," *Theology Today,* 25 (April 1968).

Morton Borden describes evangelicals' perennial efforts to baptize
the Constitution in "The Christian Amendment," *Civil War History,*
25 (1979). Father Richard Ginder's Rightist weekly essays from *Our
Sunday Visitor* were collected in a paperback book, *Right or Wrong*
(Hungtington, Indiana: Our Sunday Visitor Press, 1959). The Church's
position toward Catholics who professed or supported Communism
is authoritatively discussed in Felician A. Foy, O. F. M., ed., *The 1960
National Catholic Almanac* (Paterson, N.J.: St. Anthony's Guild, 1960),
pp. 360-61. I was shown the Carl McIntire poster of the Devil by
Ralph Lord Roy, whose highly useful work *Apostles of Discord* (Boston:
Beacon Press, 1953) describes the activities of the Protestant ultra-
Right; the book is based on Roy's thoroughly documented Master's
essay, "The Protestant Underworld" (Columbia University, 1952). The
Helen Wood Birnie episode is described at first hand. "Sister" Birnie's
right-wing activities were also described in the vigorous and lively, but
unhappily now defunct, liberal weekly *The People's Voice* (Helena, Montana, 1959 and 1960, *passim*).

The judicious study by Donald F. Crosby, S. J., *God, Church, and
Flag: Senator Joseph R. McCarthy and the Catholic Church, 1950–1957*
(Chapel Hill: University of North Carolina Press, 1978), takes issue
with Richard Rovere's book on McCarthy, previously cited, at several
points. For a much more severe assessment than Crosby's, see Vincent
DeSantis, "American Catholics and McCarthyism," *Catholic Historical*

Review, 51 (April 1965), a moving example of Catholic self-criticism. The descriptions of the Fulton Sheen anti-Communist telecast, and of the McCarthy–Al Smith parallel drawn by some working-class Catholics in Boston, are based on eyewitness testimony. Texts of the statements on behalf of the World and National Councils of Churches have conveniently been collected in H. Shelton Smith, et. al., *American Christianity: An Historical Interpretation with Representative Documents, 2, 1820-1960* (New York: Scribner's 1963).

6. History, Culture, Religion

An insightful sketch of Paul Tillich's career by Raymond F. Bulman appears in the *Dictionary of American Biography,* Supplement VII, 1961-1965 (New York: Scribner's, 1981). The comment about the impact of life in America upon this German theologian's thinking appears in the Author's Introduction to Tillich, *The Protestant Era* (University of Chicago Press, 1948; paperback abridgement, 1957); another quotation is taken from chap. XII. The discussion of Pablo Picasso's painting *Guernica* occurs in Paul Tillich, *The Theology of Culture* (New York: Oxford, 1959), chap. VI. Tillich continued to have an impact long after the fifties were over; as recently as the mid-seventies I had a student tell me he had gotten his own personal act together after having read Tillich's *The Courage To Be* (Scribner's, 1952).

Reinhold Niebuhr, a writer far more accessible to the lay person unversed in philosophy or theology than Tillich and a name to conjure with in the fifties, has also continued to find his readers—most notably, Jimmy Carter—but I have found Niebuhr's works (e.g., *Moral Man and Immoral Society,* 1932) far less "teachable" since the fifties came to an end. Books by Niebuhr that were published during the Eisenhower decade include *The Irony of American History* (New York: Scribner's 1952), *The Self and the Dramas of History* (1955), and *The Structure of Nations and Empires* (1959).

Comments on the *angst* which was the underside of the "peace of mind" ideology of the fifties include Louis Kronenberger, "The Spirit of the Age," *American Scholar,* 21 (Winter 1951-52); Irwin Edman, "Blithe Man in a Crisis," *ibid.,* 22 (Summer 1953); and Wallace W. Douglas, "The Solemn Style of Modern Critics," *ibid.,* 23 (Winter 1953-54). A lively discussion of the contemporary decline in rationalist morale may be found in "The Distrust of Reason," a series of papers and critiques originally delivered at an alumni-faculty seminar—papers by faculty; critiques by alumni—during the weekend of Wesleyan

University's 1959 commencement exercises (Middletown, Connecticut: Wesleyan University Press, 1959). A scathing analysis of the intellectuals' failure of nerve as a reflex of "the psychology of the scared employee" may be found in "Brains, Inc.," chap. 7 in C. Wright Mills, *White Collar: The American Middle Classes* (New York: Oxford, 1951). The quotation from Ralph Waldo Emerson concerning the "minority un-convinced," which derives from Emerson's essay "Boston," is quoted—with pertinent application to the twentieth century—in Kenneth Murdock, *Literature and Theology in Colonial New England* (Cambridge: Harvard University Press, 1949).

A contemporary cautionary essay on "American Studies" by one of its leading advocates is "The Study of Our Own Traditions," the concluding chapter in Arthur Bestor, *The Restoration of Learning* (New York: Knopf, 1955). Oliver Larkin, *Art and Life in America* (New York: Rinehart, 1949, rev. ed., 1960), has some pertinent comment on "Cold War Climate" (rev. ed., p. 470). Abram Chasins, "Van Cliburn in the USSR," and Don Hogan, "The Moiseyev Dancers in the U.S.A." *Reporter,* May 29, 1958), are acute and perceptive. Louis Kronenberger, "America and Art," *American Scholar,* 22 (Autumn 1953) was useful for this discussion, as were Sidney Alexander, "The European Image of Americans" (*ibid.* Winter 1951-52) and Joseph E. Baker, "America Seen From France" (Spring 1957); somewhat wide of the mark was the quoted comment by H. F. Peters, "American Culture and the State Department" (Summer 1952), although some of his other remarks were quite pertinent. I report the deplorable episode in the Chicago Institute of Art at first hand.

Very useful for this chapter was an interview with the distinguished intellectual historian Carl E. Schorske published in *Colloquium,* #7 (Fall 1968). Major texts on American intellectual history produced during the fifties included Henry Steele Commager, *The American Mind* (New Haven: Yale, 1950); Ralph H. Gabriel, *The Course of American Democratic Thought,* 2d ed. (New York: Ronald, 1956); and Stow Persons, *American Minds* (New York: Henry Holt, 1958). Perry Miller, *The American Puritans: Their Prose and Poetry* (New York: Doubleday, 1956) and Edmund S. Morgan, *Puritan Dilemma* (Boston: Little, Brown, 1958), are excellent examples of the kinds of paperbacks teachers of intellectual history and "American Studies" assigned their undergraduate students in the fifties. Some pitfalls in this kind of inquiry are noted in passing by Emil Oberholzer, Jr., "Puritanism Revisited," in *Perspectives on Early American History: Essays in Honor of Richard B. Morris,* ed. Alden T. Vaughn and George Athan Billias (New York: Harper, 1973).

Henry F. May, "The Recovery of American Religious History,"

American Historical Review, 70 (October 1964), documents a process of which some students of American history remain distressingly unaware. Albert C. Outler's presidential address to the American Society of Church History, "Theodosius' Horse: Reflections on the Predicament of the Church Historian," *Church History*, 34 (September 1965), manages to be at once commonsensical and profound. It is quite typical of the high-level reflective thinking which the successive annual presidents of that organization, as they delivered such addresses in the fifties (and on into the sixties), directed toward the nature of their subject matter and of their craft. All historians could profit from reading them.

My interest in Arnold Toynbee was initially kindled back in high school by two perceptive and civilized writers of science fiction, Jack Williamson and L. Sprague de Camp. In shaping my own later response to (and judgment of) Toynbee's work I owe much to former academic mentors and colleagues, but most especially to Carl Schorske, formerly of Wesleyan University. J. W. Smurr, formerly of the University of Montana, suggested the Newton-Galileo-Aristotle comparison. Elmer Davis's spirited rebuttal to Toynbee's conclusions regarding the fate of the West, "Are We Worth Saving? And If So, Why?", appears as the closing chapter in Davis, *But We Were Born Free*, previously cited. Initially the 1953 Phi Beta Kappa oration at Harvard, his essay was "somewhat motivated," Davis confessed in a prefatory note, "by annoyance with the doctrines of Dr. Arnold Toynbee."

7. Higher, or at Least Further, Education

The observation by a school principal that not every child need learn to read and write is quoted in Arthur Bestor, *The Restoration of Learning*, previously cited; see also the acid comments on "life-adjustment" education in Richard Hofstadter, *Anti-Intellectualism in American Life* (New York: Knopf, 1963).

Peter Filene, *Him/Her/Self: Sex Roles in Modern America* (New York: Harcourt, Brace, Jovanovich, 1974), is insightful on college students in the fifties. Ralph E. Ellsworth, who in the fifties was director of libraries successively at the Universities of Iowa and Colorado, commented sharply on "College Students and Reading," *American Scholar*, 27 (Autumn 1958). A thoughtful letter on "Class Consciousness" on the campus—or its absence—by Jim Quin, Class of '57, appeared in the *Columbia Daily Spectator*, October 11, 1954. An impressionistic, but in my judgment (after teaching on twelve U.S. campuses) convincing, assessment of the perennial American student, not simply the 1950s variety, is in George Santayana, *Character and Opinion in the United States* (1920; paperback, New York: Anchor Books, 1956), chap. 2.

Two collections of Richard N. Bibler's college-newspaper cartoons appeared in the fifties: *Little Man on Campus* (Stanford University Press, 1952) and *Little Man, What Now?* (Elkhart, Kansas: Bibler Features, 1959). I have quoted from Jeffrey Smith's foreword to the former. In my own copies of these two paperbacks I have filed copies of other cartoons, cut in the fifties from the *Montana Kaimin,* a lively, serious, and truly *student-controlled* campus newspaper—not all such papers were. Bibler gave an interview in 1968 to another campus paper, the *Spartan Daily,* at San Jose State, from which I have drawn (Carol Grinager, " 'Little Man' Cartoonist Says Morals Changing," photocopy included in an advertising flyer for Bibler's cartoons, 1969). Mr. Bibler kindly gave me a telephone interview on February 2, 1982, which was informative for this essay.

A badly titled, sleazily covered paperback murder mystery by Isaac Asimov, *The Death Dealers* (New York: Avon, 1958), unexpectedly turned out to be a shrewd and perceptive comment on Academia; Asimov, as a youngish Ph.D. in biochemistry, had been teaching in a milieu very like the one he fictionally described. For some two dozen years I have been lending my copy of *The Academic Marketplace,* by Theodore Caplow and Reece J. McGee (New York: Basic Books, 1958) to prospective graduate students, to caution them about what they are letting themselves in for. Another, more polemical but keenly insightful book for the same purpose has been George Williams, *Some of My Best Friends Are Professors* (New York: Abelard-Schuman, 1958). Less lively, but well supported by painstaking questionnaire tabulation, is *The Academic Mind,* by Paul Lazarsfeld and Wagner Thielens, Jr. (Glencoe, Ill.: Free Press,1958).

A ringing trumpet-blast by Archibald MacLeish, "Loyalty and Freedom," in the *American Scholar* (Autumn 1953), provoked a reply, "Some Observations on Intellectual Freedom," by David Riesman (Winter 1953-54, previously cited in chap. 1), with surrebuttal by MacLeish. Some interesting comment by Fritz Stern and others followed in a subsequent letter column ("The Reader Replies," Summer 1954). Elmer Davis's anti-McCarthyist speech at Vassar, "Through the Perilous Night," appears as chapter 1 in Davis, *But We Were Born Free,* previously cited.

I am very much indebted to my University of Arizona colleague, Kent Anderson, whose lively, well researched, and at some points brilliant study *Television Fraud: The History and Implications of the Quiz Show Scandals* (Westport, Connecticut: Greenwood Press, 1978) is the source for most of what I say in this chapter about Charles Van Doren. Also useful were two probing contemporary comments on the quiz show scandals, the first by Murray Hausknecht and the second by Jay Bentham and Bernard Rosenberg, published together under the title "The Rigged Society" in *Dissent*, 7 (Winter 1960).

The shock of Sputnik was an American "media event" for several days, if not years. An example of the new muckraking of American education prompted by the Sputnik trauma is Arthur S. Trace, *What Ivan Knows That Johnny Doesn't* (New York: Random House, 1961). John W. Campbell's sardonic comment on the humiliating failure of Vanguard, Sputnik's U.S. counterpart, appeared in an editorial, "Project Me Too," *Astounding Science Fiction*, January, 1958. A more temperate reaction to Sputnik is recorded in Paul Siple, *90° South* (New York: Putnam, 1959).

Sputnik's scientific organizational context is lucidly discussed in Laurence M. Gould, "The International Geophysical Year," *American Scholar* 26 (Summer 1957). A major obstacle to the scientific enlightenment necessary for full appreciation of the significance of efforts like IGY is discussed in Dael Wolfle, "Science in the Liberal Arts," *ibid.*, 28 (Spring, 1959). Wolfle's essay is an American gloss on a subject broached by C. P. Snow in *The Two Cultures and the Scientific Revolution* (New York: Cambridge University Press, 1959).

8. Entertainment Media

A careful, minuted account of the legitimate stage in the fifties is John Gassner, *Theater at the Crossroads* (New York: Holt, Rinehart & Winston, 1960). Far more polemical and opinionated—and also disconcertingly persuasive—is Walter Kerr, *How Not to Write a Play* (New York: Simon & Schuster, 1955). Although I was able to witness some of the plays discussed by Kerr or Gassner in Broadway productions, most shows that they singled out for critical analysis I had to see—like most U.S. playgoers—in intelligently conceived non-New York versions. At a small university summer theater in the early sixties I was privileged to act in a few of them.

The *Wall Street Journal,* one of the most aware of general newspapers about the economics of the lively arts, devoted several front-page feature articles and other news stories to the motion picture industry's struggle to recapture its TV-seduced audience. See, for example, April 21, September 16, and October 10, 1958; February 25, April 22, July 7, October 10, and November 27, 1959; and January 6, 1960. That industry's technologically most effective weapon for counterattack against the videotube—"wide screen" projection in its various forms— is discussed, along with much else of interest, in Arthur Knight, *The Liveliest Art: A Panoramic History of the Movies* (New York: New American Library, 1959 [copyright 1957]). The quotation from Michael Todd, Sr., who introduced one of those wide-screen forms, is from the article on Todd in the *Dictionary of American Biography,* Supplement 6 (New York: Scribner's, 1980). Andrew Dowdy, *The Films of the Fifties: The American State of Mind* (New York: William Morrow, 1973), is a bit superficial and surveyish, filled with easy pop-culture/political generalizations, but it has some soundly anti-academic sentiments regarding, e.g., Hollywood musicals. A handy browser's book is Paul Michael, *The Academy Awards: A Pictorial History,* 2d rev. ed. (New York: Crown Publishers, 1972). Lurking in the background of this discussion is a pioneering essay by the poet Vachel Lindsay, *The Art of the Moving Picture* (New York, 1915; 1922; reprinted, Liveright Publishing Corporation, 1970).

Two of novelist Raymond Chandler's blasts at television, in letters to Gene Levitt (an adapter of many Chandler stories for radio) and to Charles Norton (associate editor of the *Atlantic Monthly*), both dated November 22, 1950, appear in Frank McShane, ed., *Selected Letters of Raymond Chandler,* previously cited in chapter 1. A convincing rebuttal, so far as the "anthology" television dramas of the early fifties are concerned, by the Pulitzer-prizewinning playwright Tad Mosel, is "The Golden Age of Television," *TV Guide,* August 22, 1981. Perceptive comment on TV history may be found in Eric Barnouw, *Tube of Plenty: The Evolution of American Television* (London, Oxford, New York: Oxford University Press, 1975), which is a large abridgement from the same author's three-volume *A History of Broadcasting in the United States;* and—from a more electronically technical viewpoint, carefully and refreshingly explained in laypeople's language—in Stuart M. DeLuca, *Television's Transformation* (San Diego: A. S. Barnes, 1980).

"Poets, Critics, and Readers," by Randall Jarrell, is one of several clear-headed essays included in a symposium on "Contemporary American Poetry" which appeared in *The American Scholar,* 28 (Summer 1959). In the same journal a discussion by Robert Langbaum of "This Literary Generation," also cited in chapter 4, was useful, as was a heavily overstated but nonetheless compelling polemic by Edmund Fuller, "The New Compassion in the American Novel," *ibid.,* 26 (Spring 1957). Real compassion, in contrast to the kind Fuller referred to, appears in Raymond Chandler's regretful, discouraging letter to H. R. Harwood, in the Frank McShane edition of Chandler's letters. The ludicrous episodes from writing classes were reported in a 1954 lecture by Mary McCarthy, published as "Settling the Colonel's Hash," and may be found in McCarthy, *The Humanist in the Bathtub* (New York: New American Library, 1964). The point of this chapter's closing paragraph is made with eloquence and wit by Fernando Savater, professor of philosophy at the University of Madrid, in *Childhood Regained: The Art of the Storyteller* (New York: Columbia University Press, 1982).

9. Social Science Fiction

Paperback publication is capricious. Items disappear and reappear, sometimes with changed titles (and always with an increase in price). The fact that even so standard a work of science fiction dating from the fifties as Philip K. Dick's *Eye in the Sky* (first published by Ace Books, 1957) was listed as current in the *Paperbound Books in Print* when I wrote this bibliographical essay does not guarantee that such an item will be so listed when the essay reaches your hands. Also, most of the shorter stories derive from science fiction magazines, which are becoming hard to find except in specialized or private libraries. Many of the best tales, however, have been anthologized, and can be found in collections that may be more readily available to the reader by consulting William Contento, *Index to Science Fiction Anthologies and Collections* (Boston: G. K. Hall, 1978). The story "Project Hush," for example, by William Tenn, first published in *Galaxy Science Fiction*, February 1954, appears also in Mr. Tenn's first story collection *The Human Angle* (New York: Ballantine, 1956); Robert Sheckley's "Seventh Victim," similarly, originally in *Galaxy*, April 1953, was included in Sheckley's *Untouched by Human Hands* (New York: Ballantine, 1964).

Galaxy's editor, H. L. Gold, thought highly enough of the psychiatric-science fiction story "Beyond Bedlam," by Wyman Guin, to include it in his *Galaxy Reader of Science Fiction* (New York: Crown, 1952). An essay by Gold, "Ask a Foolish Question," in the magazine issue which carried Guin's story (August 1951) is an excellent example of Gold's conceptual approach to sf, and of his taxing editorial method.

Poul Anderson told the anecdote about the genesis of his story "Sam Hall" in response to a question that is asked of science fiction writers over and over again: "Where do you get your ideas?" In this instance, the question came from the audience at a writers' panel held in conjunction with a science fiction and fantasy film festival at the University of Arizona, DesertCon III, in February 1975. The story appeared in *Astounding Science Fiction*, August, 1953, and is also available in Barry

Malzberg, ed., *The Best of Poul Anderson* (New York: Del Rey Books, 1976).

The short story by Ray Bradbury titled "The Pedestrian" first appeared not in a science fiction setting but in *The Reporter,* August 7, 1951. It was reprinted in *Fantasy and Science Fiction,* February 1952, with the comment I have quoted from that magazine's editor. Bradbury's novella "The Fireman" first appeared in *Galaxy* magazine, February 1951; I have by preference quoted from the sharp and pointed language of that early form of the story that became better known as *Fahrenheit 451* (New York: Ballantine, 1953). My own correspondence with Ray Bradbury in previous years has been helpful for understanding his work.

Basil Davenport, ed., *The Science Fiction Novel: Imagination and Social Criticism* (Chicago: Advent, 1959) is a landmark in the "academicizing," if I may put it that way, of science fiction. It is historically significant because of its own proximity in time to the kind of writings its authors described. One of those writings, *The Space Merchants,* by Cyril M. Kornbluth and Federik Pohl (New York: Ballantine, 1953, after serialization with the title "Gravy Planet," *Galaxy,* June, July, August, 1952), is indispensable not only as an example of science fiction in the fifties but also as a manifestation of the mind of the fifties more generally—an insight about the book for which I am indebted to my University of Arizona colleague, Donna J. Guy.

Pastoral, anti-technological science fiction such as "The Climbing Wave," by Marion Zimmer Bradley, (*Fantasy and Science Fiction,* February 1955), is much admired by academic readers who come to science fiction from a background in the humanities. Within the sf community, however, such work is more controversial. Jacques Sadoul, an omnivorous French reader of American science fiction, takes account of "The Climbing Wave" as a story some sf critics have termed "reactionary," in his compendious *Histoire de la science-fiction moderne, 1911-1971* (Paris: A. Michel, 1973)

Another mode of science fiction with which non-science-oriented people often have trouble is "pure" or "hard" science fiction. On this thorny topic see Norman Spinrad, "Rubber Sciences," and Hal Clement, "Hard Sciences and Tough Technologies," both in R. Bretnor, ed., *The Craft of Science Fiction* (New York: Barnes & Noble, 1977). Clement described how he set up the environment for his best-known story in an article he wrote for *Astounding Science Fiction,* June 1953, titled "Whirligig World." The story, *Mission of Gravity,* ran in serial form in *ibid.,* April, May, June, July, 1953 and afterward appeared in hard covers (New York: Doubleday, 1954).

There may be "rolling, rust-red hills" on Mars, but we know from the Mariner probes that there is much, much more—a typical example of how quickly science is able to outdate science fiction. The story from which that quotation is taken, "Ounce of Prevention," is one of two on the post-nuclear-war theme which I wrote for *The Magazine of Fantasy and Science Fiction* (Summer 1950); the other, "Unbalanced Equation," appeared in *ibid.,* January, 1956, and, retitled, "Disproportion Explosive," in that magazine's Paris offshoot, *Fiction: la revue littéraire de l'étrange* (December 1956), translated by Roger Durand. Stylistically, except for a few untranslatable U.S. colloquialisms, it went better in French.

The editorial headnote with Durand's translation repeated John Campbell's quip in response to the journalist who phoned to ask the editor of *Astounding*—"le plus grand magazine de science-fiction américain"—what he was doing now that Hiroshima had seemingly made his science fiction obsolete. Horace Gold's editorial complaint against the downbeat stories his writers were sending him in 1951, "Gloom and Doom," appeared in *Galaxy,* January 1952. The quoted story which illustrates Gold's own willingness at times to break his rule and publish such stories is Fritz Leiber, "Appointment in Tomorrow," *ibid.,* July 1951; it appears also in Poul Anderson, ed., *The Best of Fritz Leiber* (New York: Ballantine 1974), retitled "Poor Superman."

Other examples of post-nuclear-bomb science fiction include "Wildcat," by Poul Anderson (*Fantasy & Science Fiction,* November 1958) and "A Canticle for Leibowitz," by Walter M. Miller, Jr. (*ibid.,* April 1955). The Miller story was expanded into a full-length novel with the same title (Philadelphia: Lippincott, 1959; New York: Bantam, 1961). A perceptive discussion of *Canticle*—and a model of good literary criticism of science fiction—appears in Robert Scholes and Eric Rabkin, *Science Fiction: History, Science, Vision* (New York: Oxford, 1977), pp. 221-26.

The statement by James Gunn occurs in his article, "The Tinsel Screen: Science Fiction and the Movies," a chapter in Jack Williamson, ed., *Teaching SF: Education for Tomorrow* (Philadelphia: Owlswick Press, 1980). Susan Sontag's comments occur in her perceptive essay "The Imagination of Disaster," from *Against Interpretation and Other Essays* (New York: Farrar, Strauss & Giroux, 1965). Robert Heinlein's reminiscence of "Shooting Destination Moon," originally in *Astounding Science Fiction,* July 1950, and David G. Hartwell's editorial comment on that and other sf films, appear in Robert A. Heinlein, *Destination Moon* (Boston: G. K. Hall, 1979). Useful on the Japanese monster-movie vogue is Jun Inouye, "Godzilla in Postwar Japan," *Japanese Fantasy Film Journal*, #12 (1979).

Robert C. Cumbow, "Imitation of Life," *Movietone News*, #3 (March 1974), pp. 1-8, is a persuasive, tightly reasoned essay in film criticism—a model of its kind—with which I happen to disagree. Worthwhile further comment on the film Cumbow discusses, titled simply "A Note on Style," and signed "R. T. J." [Richard T. Jameson], appears in *ibid.*, pp. 8-10.

10. Atomic Fears and Hopes

The comment by Mike Mansfield after flying over Hiroshima on December 3, 1946, is recorded in a diary Mansfield kept while on a fact-finding tour for a subcommittee of the House Committee on Naval Affairs; it is shelved with the China Mission Folders in the Mansfield Papers, University of Montana (previously cited in chapter 3). The Churchill address to the House of Commons on March 1, 1955—one of his last before stepping down as Prime Minister—may be found (marred by annoying typographical errors!) in *Vital Speeches of the Day*, 21 (March 15, 1955). Eisenhower quotes himself, in a speech before the American Society of Newspaper Editors on April 16, 1953, in his *Mandate for Change*, previously cited. In the same work (p. 252) the former President affirmed his own definite personal authorship of the proposal which became the "Atoms-for-Peace" program: "One day I hit upon the idea. . ."

James Hagerty's memorandum of one early version of that proposal appears in an important article by John Lear, "Ike and the Peaceful Atom," *Reporter*, January 12, 1956, a pioneering account whose cue surprisingly few historians have taken up and followed. Marred though it is by Cold War presuppositions and by a controvertible judgment concerning the role of AEC Chairman Lewis Strauss, it is still the starting point for all historical discussion of the "Atoms for Peace" program. Lear's narrative is enlivened by reference to protagonists' personal quirks and foibles; his comment about the verbal style of India's UN Delegate V. K. Krishna Menon, to take one example, can be verified by anyone who has ever seen Menon in action.

Thomas R. Phillips's skeptical comment that "Atoms for Peace" should have been called "Atoms for Industry" is quoted in Eugene Rabinowitch, "Ten Years That Changed the World," *Bulletin of the Atomic Scientists*, 12 (January 1956). The *Bulletin*, by the way, for any comprehensive understanding of the mind of the fifties, is indispensable.

Its concerns ranged far beyond the problem of atomic weaponry and its control; *Bulletin* contributors took up also such question as space exploration, the population explosion, the environment, genetics, the changing American character, and even modern art. On the "Atoms-for-Peace" program I have quoted Bernard C. Bechhoefer, "The International Atomic Energy Agency," *ibid.*, 14 (April 1958), and from Madhu Joshi, "Dead or Alive? International Atomic Energy Agency," *ibid.*, 17 (March 1961). On related topics see Etienne Hirsch, "A Guide to Euratom," *ibid.*, 14 (June 1959), and C. J. Bakker, "CERN as an Institute for International Cooperation," *ibid.*, 16 (February 1960).

The entire contents of the April, 1955 issue of the *Bulletin* were devoted to the topic "Secrecy, Security, and Loyalty." I have quoted from an article in that issue by the Scientists' Committee on Loyalty and Security, titled "Some Individual Cases." The survey which found that physics graduate students in the mid-fifties would rather take a lower salary than put up with security screening is mentioned in an excellent history, *The Physicists,* by Daniel J. Kevles (New York: Knopf, 1978), citing *Physics Today,* 8 (March 1955). The internal debate over the decision to build the H-bomb is authoritatively described in *The Advisers: Oppenheimer, Teller, and the Superbomb,* by Herbert York, a junior participant in that debate who has since changed his mind (San Francisco: W. H. Freeman, 1976). The controversy over J. Robert Oppenheimer's security clearance is discussed judiciously in John Major, *The Oppenheimer Hearing* (New York: Stein and Day, 1971). Eisenhower's *Mandate for Change,* pp. 312-313, describes his own objections in 1945 to the use of the A-bomb on Japan. *Brighter Than a Thousand Suns: A Personal History of the Atomic Scientists,* by Robert Jungk (New York: Harcourt, Brace, 1958), a gossipy and opinionated but nonetheless useful book, contains some penetrating comments on the implications of the Oppenheimer episode.

The statement by Don K. Price on the rise of science into a formal, traditional-style establishment is quoted in Kevles. James Killian dissents from that assessment in his indispensable account *Sputnik, Scientists, and Eisenhower* (Cambridge: MIT Press, 1977), which contains also as an Appendix the widely disseminated report by the President's Science Advisory committee titled "Introduction to Outer Space." A telephone conversation with Dr. Killian on May 25, 1982 was very helpful, and I look forward to his own forthcoming memoir.

A brief preliminary report on the IGY and its objectives by Ronald Fraser, *Once Around the Sun: The Story of the International Geophysical Year* (New York: Macmillan, 1957), was followed by *New York Times* Science Editor Walter Sullivan's careful, thorough, and at certain points first-hand history of the IGY, *Assault on the Unknown* (New York: McGraw-Hill, 1961). A further comment on the constructive political implications of international scientific activities is George B. Kistiakowsky, "Science and Foreign Affairs," *Bulletin of the Atomic Scientists,* 16 (April 1960).

Surprisingly little has been published on the Antarctic Treaty, and James Lyerzapf of the Eisenhower Library in Abilene has informed me (telephone conversation of June 2, 1982) that very few researchers have been working on the Treaty using the abundant papers there. The news media, similarly, seem unaware of the Treaty's existence; their coverage of the British-Argentine Falklands crisis of 1982 rarely, if ever, took note of that quarrel's very important Antarctic dimension. See, however, Laurence M. Gould, "The History of the Scientific Committee on Antarctic Research (SCAR)," and T. O. Jones, "The Antarctic Treaty," in Louis D. Quam and Horace D. Porter, eds., *Research in the Antarctic* (Washington: American Association for the Advancement of Science, 1971); also Paul C. Daniels, "The Antarctic Treaty," and Finn Sollie, "The Political Experiment in Antarctica," in Richard S. Lewis and Philip M. Smith, eds., *Frozen Future: A Prophetic Report from Antarctica* (New York: Quadrangle, 1973). The quotations from the Senate hearing on the Treaty are taken from *Hearings before the Committee on Foreign Relations, United States Senate, on Ex.B., 86th Congress, Second Session, June 14, 1960.* Laurence M. Gould, the star scientific witness before that Committee, has given me his recollections of the hearing and also of meetings he and other scientists had with Eisenhower concerning "Operation Deep Freeze" and IGY.

Robert A. Divine ably discusses the negotiations on banning the testing of nuclear weapons in the atmosphere, briefly in *Eisenhower and the Cold War* (New York: Oxford, 1981), and at greater length in *Blowing on the Wind: The Nuclear Test Ban Debate, 1954–1960* (New York: Oxford, 1978). A few of the continuing human consequences of U.S. atmospheric bomb testing in the fifties are graphically depicted in Jane Kay, "Mushroom clouds gone, but death lingers," (Tucson) *Arizona Daily Star,* November 15, 1981. Thomas F. Soapes argues, in "A Cold Warrior Seeks Peace: Eisenhower's Strategy for Nuclear Disarmament," *Diplomatic History,* 4 (December 1980), that the President's initiative in the test-ban issue—and in other matters having to do with disarmament—was not only limited by his basic Cold War presuppositions but also inhibited by his unwillingness to take risks, a judgment with which I find myself in partial disagreement, considering that risk-taking characterized several of Eisenhower's other international actions.

A particularly effective and pointed discussion of the U–2 episode by A. J. Liebling, "The Coast Recedes," appeared in *The New Yorker*, May 21, 1960, in that magazine's regular column "The Wayward Press." Continuing optimism despite the new coldness in U.S.-Soviet relations following the U–2 incident was expressed by Eugene Rabinowitch in an editorial "Eppur si muove"—"And still, it moves" (what Galileo is supposed to have said after formally recanting his theory of the Earth's motion), *Bulletin of the Atomic Scientists*, 17 (January 1961). The statement by Dr. Martin Luther King, Jr. first appeared in King's contribution to a series of articles, "How my Mind Has Changed in This Decade," *Christian Century*, April 13, 1960, cited also in chapter 4.

Index